Byrne's Book of Great Pool Stories

Robert Byrne

BYRNE'S BOOK of GREAT POOL STORIES

A Harvest Original

Harcourt Brace & Company

San Diego   New York   London

Library of Congress Cataloging-in-Publication Data
Byrne's book of great pool stories/[compiled by] Robert Byrne.—1st ed.
p.   cm.
"A Harvest original."
Includes bibliographical references.
ISBN 0-15-600223-X
1. Pool (Game)—Literary collections.   2. Billiards—Literary collections.
I. Byrne, Robert, 1930–
PN6071.P575B97   1995
808.83'9355—dc20   95-12589

Text set in Galliard
Designed by Camilla Filancia
Printed in the United States of America
First edition   A B C D E

In memory of
my mother and father,
with thanks
for putting a pool table in the basement

Contents

*Look at that guy—can't run six balls
and he's president of the United States.*

—Pool hustler JOHNNY IRISH

on RICHARD NIXON,

as quoted by DANNY McGOORTY circa 1969

Nice shot, you bastard.

—Remark overheard by ROBERT BYRNE

in a pool hall, 1994

Introduction

In play there are two pleasures for your choosing—
The one is winning and the other is losing.
                                                —LORD BYRON

IT CAN BE argued that people's hobbies are more their measure than are their jobs. Never mind what they are forced to do, like
fight wars or make a living or embrace the king's religion. What do
they *choose* to do in their spare time, if they have any? The answers
can be very revealing.

One thing people have been doing for thousands of years in their
spare time is knocking around balls with sticks. Balls and people hitting them with sticks can be seen in the hieroglyphics of ancient
Egypt as well as in the tapestries and paintings of medieval Europe.
Exactly what games those ancients were playing is not clear.

What *is* clear is that in the 1400s, in both France and England,
some form of ground ball game was brought indoors and put on a
table. Green is the color of billiard table cloth, more than likely because it is the color of grass. Various wickets, posts, and cones were
common accessories in the beginning, gradually giving way to the
uncluttered playing surface we know today.

By the late 1500s, the game was well established in Europe among all social classes, from highwaymen to royal highnesses. Mary, Queen of Scots, complained about the loss of her billiard table during her imprisonment in the Tower of London. Louis XIII and Louis XIV of France were avid players; the royal game room had two tables lit by twenty-six crystal chandeliers and sixteen silver candlesticks. Marie Antoinette was beating Louis XVI at billiards right up to the French Revolution, while Mozart was shooting a few games with the boys in the coffeehouses of Vienna. George Washington played, as did Napoleon, Queen Victoria, Abraham Lincoln, and Mark Twain, who said that "the billiard table is better than the doctors."

In the early centuries, table beds, rails, and even balls were made of wood, and blunt rods called maces were used to push the balls around like so many shuffleboard pucks. Ivory balls appeared in the early 1600s; cues in the late 1700s; and leather tips, chalk, slate beds, and rubber cushions in the early 1800s. By the time François Minguad was exciting the sovereigns of Europe with his 1827 book, *The Noble Game of Billiards*—and certainly by the time Michael Phelan was winning the first United States Championship in 1859—the equipment was essentially the same as it is today. Ivory balls gradually yielded to clay, clay to plastic, and finally plastic to cast phenolic resin, after World War II. The plastic industry itself, in fact, began with the search for an inexpensive substitute for ivory billiard balls, which were costing the lives of twelve thousand elephants a year. The race was won by John and Wesley Hyatt, who in 1870 patented a combustible substance they called celluloid. The formula soon had to modified. Players found to their dismay that the balls would, if driven together with too much enthusiasm, explode. (A case can be made for bringing back celluloid billiard balls as a means of attracting a larger audience to the game. Certainly a sporting event punctuated by unpredictable explosions would play well on TV.)

Few games or sports have been played continuously for five hundred years. If billiards is a game rather than a sport, it takes second place in age to chess—a game called "solitary and selfish" by Phelan—which goes back an additional five hundred years. If billiards is a sport rather than a game, then it bows to boxing and wrestling, which probably date back to the first family. Billiards falls somewhere between a game and a sport, which is part of the reason it doesn't get the publicity it deserves. Newspaper editors don't think it belongs in the sports section, and they don't feel it goes well with the bridge and chess columns, either. Since there is no logical place to put it, it rarely gets into the paper at all.

Is billiards a sport or a game? The difference between the two was sharply defined in 1993 during the telecast of a professional tennis tournament. The announcer asked his expert commentator, John McEnroe, what he thought of a survey showing that golf had overtaken tennis as a popular sport. McEnroe replied, "I thought [for it] to be a sport, you had to run at some point."

As far as popularity is concerned, billiards is second only to bowling in the United States among participant "sports." Between thirty-five and forty-five million people play pool at least once a year, researchers estimate, more than play golf or tennis. Surveys have shown repeatedly that Americans are much more likely to pick up pool cues than they are golf clubs, tennis rackets, jogging shoes, or baseball bats. They play in private homes, clubs, taverns, colleges, retirement communities, boys' and girls' clubs, and in the upscale billiard centers that have been opening across the country at a record pace. The current boom in the game can be pinned to a specific event: the 1986 release of the Paul Newman–Tom Cruise film *The Color of Money,* which was based on a novel by Walter Tevis. A quieter boom had followed *The Hustler* twenty-five years earlier, a movie also based on a Tevis novel. Two Tevis short stories are included in *Great Pool Stories.*

With the game's colorful characters, the incredible skill of the great players, the mystique and technique of sharks and gamblers, the addictive nature of the game, and its visual appeal, it's not surprising that writers have been attracted to what billiard historian William Hendricks has called "the green island of high seriousness." References to billiards can be found in Shakespeare's *Antony and Cleopatra,* Jane Austen's *Mansfield Park,* Pushkin's *The Captain's Daughter,* Dickens's *Dombey and Son,* Thackeray's *Vanity Fair,* Flaubert's *Madame Bovary,* George (Mary Ann Evans) Eliot's *Felix Holt, the Radical,* Dostoyevsky's *Crime and Punishment,* and Conrad's *Lord Jim,* to name some works written before 1900. Later works are too numerous to list. Extracts from novels are not included in the present work, with the exception of a scene from *The Captain's Daughter,* an absorbing glimpse at pool hustling in Russia 160 years ago.

Short story writers have made especially good use of the game and approached it from every direction imaginable, maybe because every game of pool, snooker, and billiards is *like* a short story. In these pages, gambling is a common theme, together with the ego clashes and macho posturing that sometimes lead to violence. There is adolescent angst, the desperate scams of hustlers, the joy of a player who is "hot," a science fiction selection, and some superb humor. Two of my favorite stories in this collection are by A. A. Milne and Jonathan Baumbach, both of which concern the growing exasperation of a man trying to teach the game to an incredibly lucky woman.

George Plimpton once suggested that when it comes to writing about sports, the smaller the ball the better the writing. That's why there's so much good writing about golf and baseball and so little about football and basketball. Snooker, pool, and billiard balls, sizewise, fall between golf balls and baseballs. So the writing about cue games, as you are about to see, is indeed wonderful.

Byrne's Book of Great Pool Stories

THE BILLIARD TABLE

BY *James Hall*

This is very likely the first short story on a billiard theme ever published anywhere in the world. It appeared in an anthology of cautionary and uplifting yarns titled The Western Souvenir, A Christmas and New Year's Gift for 1829. *The setting is Pittsburgh, Pennsylvania, in the days when it was still considered "western." James Hall (1793–1868) was a pioneer judge and author; now almost totally forgotten, he was in fact one of the fathers of the short story form. His style ranged from the impossibly stilted (stars are "silent orbs that glowed so beauteously in the firmament") to the acceptably stilted (a billiard table is "a gay altar of dissipation"). If Judge Hall were suddenly to appear among us, he would no doubt be perplexed at how difficult we find it today to read his sugared sentiments without alternately cringing and laughing.*

A technical note: The game in the story is probably a then-popular version of English billiards played with three or four balls on a pocket table.

ON ONE OF those clear nights in December, when the cloudless, blue sky is studded with millions of brilliant luminaries, shining with more than ordinary luster, a young gentleman was seen rapidly pacing one of the principal streets of Pittsburgh. Had he been a lover

1

of nature, the beauty of the heavens must have attracted his observation; but he was too much wrapt up in his thoughts—or in his cloak—to throw a single glance toward the silent orbs that glowed so beauteously in the firmament. A piercing wind swept through the streets, moaning and sighing, as if it felt the pain that it inflicted. The intense coldness of the weather had driven the usual loiterers of the night from their accustomed lounging places. Every door and shutter was closed against the common enemy save where the

> *Blue spirits and red,*
> *Black spirits and grey,*

which adorn the shelves of the druggist, mingled their hues with the shadows of the night; or where the window of the confectioner, redolent of light, and fruit, and sugar plums, shed its refulgence upon the half-petrified wanderer. The streets were forsaken, except by a fearless, or necessitous, few, who glided rapidly and silently along, as the specters of the night. Aught else than love or murder would scarcely have ventured to stalk abroad on such a night; and yet it would be hardly fair to set down the few unfortunate stragglers, who faced the blast on this eventful evening, as lovers or assassins. Pleasure sends forth her thousands, and necessity her millions, into all the dangers and troubles of this boisterous world.

On reaching the outlet of an obscure alley, the young gentleman paused, cast a suspicious glance around, as if fearful of observation, and then darted into the gloomy passage. A few rapid steps brought him to the front of a wretched frame building, apparently untenanted, or occupied only as a warehouse, through whose broken panes the wind whistled, while the locked doors seemed to bid defiance to any ingress by that of the piercing element. It was in truth a lonely back building, in the heart of the town; but so concealed by the surrounding houses, that it might as well have been in the silent bosom of the forest. A narrow flight of stairs, ascending the outside of the edifice, led to an upper story. Ascending there, the youth, opening the door with the familiarity of an accustomed visitor, emerged from the gloom of the night into the light and life of the billiard room.

It was a large apartment, indifferently lighted, and meanly furnished. In the center stood the billiard table, whose allurements had enticed so many on this evening to forsake the quiet and virtuous comforts of social life, and to brave the bighting blast and, not less, "pitiless peltings" of parental or conjugal admonition. Its polished mahogany frame and neatly brushed cover of green cloth, its silken pockets and party-colored ivory balls, presenting a striking contrast to the rude negligence of the rest of the furniture; while a large canopy suspended over the table, and intended to collect and refract the rays of a number of well-trimmed lamps, which hung within its circumference, shed an intense brilliance over that little spot, and threw a corresponding gloom upon the surrounding scene. Indeed if that gay altar of dissipation had been withdrawn, the temple of pleasure would have presented rather the desolate appearance of the house of mourning.

The stained and dirty floor was strewed with fragments of segars, playbills, and nutshells; the walls, blackened with smoke, seemed to have witnessed the orgies of many a midnight revel. A few candles, destined to illumine the distant recesses of the room, hung neglected against the walls—bowing their long wicks, and marking their stations by streams of tallow, which had been suffered to accumulate through many a long winter night. The ceiling was hung with cobwebs, curiously intermingled with dense clouds of tobacco smoke, and tinged by the straggling rays of light, which occasionally shot from the sickly tapers. A set of benches, attached to the walls, and raised sufficiently high to overlook the table, accommodated the loungers, who were not engaged at play, and who sat or reclined—solemnly puffing their segars, idly sipping their brandy and water—or industriously counting the chances of the game; but all observed a profound silence, which would have done honor to a turbaned divan, and was well suited to the important subjects of their contemplation. Little coteries of gayer spirits laughed and chatted aside or made their criticisms on the players in subdued accents—any remarks on that subject being forbidden to all but the parties engaged; while the marker announced the state of the game, trimmed the lamps, and supplied refreshments to the guests.

Mr. St. Clair, the gentleman whom we have taken the liberty of tracing to this varied scene, was cordially greeted on his entrance by the party at the table, who had been denouncing the adverse elements which had caused the absence of several of their choicest spirits. The game at which they were then playing being one which admitted of an indefinite number of players, St. Clair was readily permitted to take a ball; and, engaging with ardor in the fascinating amusement, was soon lost to all that occurred beyond the little circle of its witchery.

The intense coldness of the night was so severely felt in the badly warmed apartment which we have attempted to describe, that the party broke up earlier than usual. One by one they dropped off until St. Clair and another of the players were left alone. These, being both skillful, engaged each other single-handed, and became so deeply interested as scarcely to observe the defection of their companions, until they found the room entirely deserted. The night was far spent. The marker, whose services were no longer required, was nodding over the grate; the candles were wasting in their sockets, and although a steady brilliance still fell upon the table, the background was as dark as it was solitary.

The most careless observer might have remarked the great disparity of character exhibited in the two players, who now matched their skill in this graceful and fascinating game. St. Clair was a genteel young man of about five and twenty. His manners had all the ease of one accustomed to the best society; his countenance was open and prepossessing; his whole demeanor frank and manly. There was a careless gaiety in his air, happily blended with an habitual politeness and dignity of carriage, which added much to the ordinary graces of youth and amiability. His features displayed no trace of thought or genius; for Mr. St. Clair was one of that large class who please without design and without talent, and who, by dint of light hearts and graceful exteriors, thrive better in this world than those who think and feel more acutely. Feeling he had, but it was rather amiable than deep; and his understanding, though solid, was of that plain and practical kind, which, though adapted to the ordinary business of life, seldom expands itself to grasp at any object beyond that narrow sphere. It was very evident that he had known neither guile nor sorrow. In his brief journey through life, he had as yet trod only in flowery paths; and having passed joyously along, was not aware that the snares which catch the feet of the unwary lie ambushed in the sunniest spots of our existence. He was a man of small fortune and was happily married to a lovely young woman to whom he was devotedly attached; and who, when she bestowed her hand, had given him the entire possession of a warm and spotless heart. They had arrived lately in Pittsburgh, and being about to settle in some part of the western country, had determined to spend the ensuing spring and summer in this city, where Mrs. St. Clair might enjoy the comforts of good society until her husband prepared their future residence for her reception.

His opponent was some ten years older than himself—a short, thin, straight man—with a keen eye and shallow complexion. He was one of those persons who may be seen in shoals at the taverns and gambling houses of a large town, and who mingle with better people in stagecoaches and steamboats. He had knocked about the world, as his own expression was, until, like an old coin whose original impression has been worn off, he had but few marks left by which his birth or country could be traced. But, like that same coin, the surface only was altered, the base metal was unchanged. He aped the gentility which he did not possess, and was ambitious of shining both in dress and manners—but nature, when she placed him in a low condition, had never intended he should rise above it.

It is unfortunate for such people that, like hypocrites in religion, demagogues in politics, and empirics of all sorts, they always overact their parts, and by an excessive zeal betray their ignorance or knavery. Thus the person in question, by misapplying the language of his superiors in education, betrayed his ignorance, and by going to the extreme of every fashion, was always too well dressed for a gentleman. In short, he was a gambler—who roamed from town to town, preying upon young libertines and old debauchees; and employing as much ingenuity in his vocation as would set up half a dozen lawyers and as much industry as would make the fortunes of half a dozen mechanics.

Such were the players who were left together, like the last champions at a tournament—who, after vanquishing all their competitors, now turned their arms against each other. For a while they displayed a courtesy which seemed to be the effect of a respect for each other's skill. It was natural to St. Clair; in the gambler it was assumed. The latter having found the opportunity he had long eagerly sought, soon began to practice the arts of his profession. The game of billiards, requiring great precision of eye and steadiness of hand, can only be played well by one who is completely master of his temper; and the experienced opponent of St. Clair essayed to touch a string, on which he had often worked with success.

"You are a married man, I believe?" said he.

"Yes, sir—"

"That was bad play—you had nearly missed the ball."

"You spoke to me just as I was striking," said St. Clair good-humoredly.

"Oh! I beg pardon. Where did you learn to play billiards?"

"In Philadelphia."

"Do they understand the game?"

"I have seen some fine players there."

"Very likely. But I doubt whether they play the scientific game. New Orleans is the only place. There they go it in style. See there now! That was a very bad play of yours. You played on the wrong ball."

"No, sir, I was right."

"Pardon me, sir. I profess to understand this game. There was an easy cannon on the table, when you aimed to pocket the white ball."

"You are mistaken," said St. Clair.

"Oh, very well! I meant no offense. Now mark how I shall count off these balls. Do you see that? There's play for you! You say you are a married man?"

"I said so. What then?"

"I thought as much by your play."

"What has that to do with it?"

"Why, you married men are accustomed to early hours, and get sleepy earlier than we do."

"I did not think I had shown any symptoms of drowsiness."

"Oh, no! I meant no allusion. There's another bad play of yours."

"You will find I play sufficiently well before we are done."

"Oh! No doubt. I meant nothing. You play an elegant game. But then, you married men get scared when it grows late. No man can play billiards when he is in a hurry to go home: A married gentleman can't help thinking of the sour looks and cross answers he is apt to get when he goes home after midnight."

"I will thank you to make no such allusions to me," said St. Clair. "I am neither scared nor sleepy, but able to beat you as long as you please."

"Oh, very well! I don't value myself on my playing. Shall we double the bet and have another bottle of wine?"

"If you please."

"Agreed. Now do your best—or I shall beat you."

Pestered by this impertinence, St. Clair lost several games. His want of success added to his impatience; and his tormentor continued to vex him with taunting remarks until his agitation became uncontrollable. He drank to steady his nerves; but drink only inflamed his passion. He doubled, trebled, quadrupled the bet to change his luck;

but in vain. Every desperate attempt urged him toward his ruin; and it was happy for him that his natural good sense enabled him to stop before his fate was consummated—though not until he had lost a large sum.

Vexed with his bad fortune, St. Clair left the house of dissipation and turned his reluctant steps toward his own dwelling. His slow and thoughtful pace was now far different from the usual lightness of his graceful carriage. It was not that he feared the frown of his lovely wife; for to him her brow had always been unclouded, and her lips had only breathed affection. She was one of those gentle beings whose sweetness withers not with the hour or the season but endured through all the vicissitudes.

It was the recollection of that fervent and forbearing love that now pressed like a leaden weight upon the conscience of the gambler when he reflected upon the many little luxuries, and innocent enjoyments, of which that lovely woman had deprived herself, while he had squandered vast sums in selfish dissipation. Having never before lost so much at play, this view of the case had not occurred to him; and it now came home to his bosom with full force—bringing pangs of the keenest self-reproach. He recalled the many projects of domestic comfort they had planned together, some of which must now be delayed by his imprudence. That very evening they had spoken of the rural dwelling they intended to inhabit; and Louisa's taste had suggested a variety of improvements with which it should be embellished. When he left her, he promised to return soon; and now, after a long absence, he came, the messenger—if not of ruin—at least of disappointment. The influence of wine, and the agitation of his mind, had wrought up the usually placid feelings of St. Clair into a state of high excitement. His imagination wandered to the past and to the future; and every picture that he contemplated added to his pain.

"I will go to Louisa," said he. "I will confess all. Late as it is, she is still watching for me. Poor girl! She little thinks that while she has been counting the heavy hours of my absence, I have been madly courting wretchedness for myself, and preparing the bitter cup of affliction for her."

In this frame of mind, he reached his own door, and tapped gently for admittance. He was surprised that his summons was not immediately answered; for the watchful solicitude of his wife had always kept her from retiring in his absence. He knocked again and again—and at last, when his patience was nearly exhausted, a slipshod housemaid came shivering to the door. He snatched the candle from her hand, and ascended to his chamber. It was deserted!

"Where is Mrs. St. Clair?" said he to the maid who had followed him.

"Gone."

"Gone! Where?"

"Why, sir, she went away with a gentleman."

"Away with a gentleman! Impossible!"

"Yes, sir, indeed she went off with a gentleman in a carriage."

"When?— Where did she go?"

"I don't know where she went, sir. She never intimated a word to me. She started just after you left home."

"Did she leave no message?"

"No, sir, not any. She was in a great hurry."

St. Clair motioned the girl to retire, and sank into a chair.

"She has left me," he exclaimed, "cruel, faithless Louise! Never did I believe you would have forsaken me! No, no—it cannot be. Louisa eloped! The best, the kindest, the sincerest of human beings? Impossible!"

He rose, and paced the room—tortured with pangs of unutterable anguish. He gazed round the apartment, and his dwelling, once so happy, seemed desolate as a tomb. He murmured the name of Louisa, and a thousand joys rose to his recollection. All—all were blasted! For she, in whose love he had confided, that pure, angelic being, whose very existence seemed to be entwined with his own, had never loved him! She preferred another! He endeavored to calm his passions, and to reason deliberately—but in vain. Who could have reasoned at such a moment? He mechanically drew out his watch—it was past two o'clock. Where could Louisa be at such an hour? She had no intimates and few acquaintances in the city. Could anyone have carried her away by force? No, no—the truth was too plain! Louisa was a faithless woman—and he a forsaken, wretched, broken-hearted man!

In an agony of grief, he left his house, and wandered distractedly through the streets, until, chance directed, he reached the confluence of the rivers. To this spot he had strolled with his Louisa in their last walk. There they had stood, gazing at the Monongahela and the Allegheny uniting their streams and losing their own names in that of the Ohio; and Louisa had compared this "meeting of the waters" to the mingling of two kindred souls, joining to part no more—until both shall be plunged in the vast ocean of eternity. To the lover—and St. Clair was still a fervent lover—there is no remembrance so dear as the recollection of a tender and poetic sentiment, breathed from the eloquent lips of affection; and the afflicted husband, when he recalled the deep and animated tone of feeling with which this natural image was uttered by his wife, could not doubt but that it was the language of her heart. All his tenderness and confidence revived; and he turned mournfully, with a full but softened heart, determined to seek his dwelling, and wait, as patiently as he could, until the return of day should bring some explanation of Louisa's conduct.

At this moment, a light appeared, passing rapidly from the bank of the Allegheny toward the town. In an instant it was lost—and again it glimmered among the ancient ramparts of Fort Duquesne—and then disappeared. He advanced cautiously toward the ruined fort, and clambering over the remains of the breastwork, entered the area—carefully examining the whole ground by the clear moonlight. But no animate object was to be seen. A confused mass of misshappen ridges and broken rocks were alone to be discovered—the vestiges of a powerful bulwark which had once breasted the storm of war.

"It is deserted," said the bereaved husband, "like my once happy dwelling. The flag is gone—the music is silent—the strong towers have fallen, and all is desolate!"

Perplexed by the sudden disappearance of the light, and indulging a vague suspicion that it was in some way connected with his own misfortune, he continued to explore the ruins. A faint ray of light now caught his eye, and he silently approached it. He soon reached the entrance of an arched vault, formerly a powder magazine, from which the light emanated. The doorway was closed by a few loose boards leaned carefully against it, and evidently intended only to afford a brief concealment; but a crevice, which had been inadvertently left, permitted the escape of that straggling beam of light, which had attracted his attention, and which proceeded from a small taper placed in a dark lantern. Two persons sat before it, in one of whom, the astonished St. Clair recognized his late companion, the gambler! The other was a coarse, ill-dressed ruffian, with a ferocious and sinister expression of countenance which at once bespoke his character. They were busily handling a number of large keys, which seemed newly made.

"Bad, awkward, clumsy work!" said the gambler, "but no odds about that, if they do but fit."

"It's ill working in the night, and with bad tools," rejoined the other. "Me and Dick has been at 'em for a week, steady—and if them keys don't do, I'll be hanged if I can make any better."

"Haven't I been working in the night too, my boy?" said the gambler. "I have made more money for us since dark than a clumsy rascal like you could earn in a month."

"Clumsy or no, you put us into danger always, and play gentleman yourself."

"Well, that's right. Don't I always plan everything? And don't I always give you a full share? Come, don't get out of heart. That key will do—and so will that—"

St. Clair could listen no longer. Under any other circumstances, the scene before him would have excited his curiosity; but the discovery that he had been duped by a sharper—a mere groveling felon—added to the sorrows that already filled his bosom, stung him so keenly that he had not patience nor spirits to push his discoveries any further.

"It was for the company of such a wretch," said he, as he again mournfully bent his steps homeward, "that I left my Louisa! Perhaps she may have guessed the truth. Some eavesdroppers may have whispered to her that I was the associate of gamblers and housebreakers! Shocked at my duplicity and guilt, she has fled from contamination!— No, no! She would not have believed it. She would have told me. She would have heard my explanation. Her kind heart would have pitied and forgiven me. Perhaps my neglect has alienated her affection. I have left her too often alone, and in doubt. She has suffered what I have felt tonight, the pangs of suspense and jealousy. She could bear it no longer; my cruelty has driven her forever from me!"

He again entered his habitation. How changed! No hand was extended to receive him, no smile to welcome him. All was cheerless, cold, and silent. A candle, nearly exhausted to the socket, was burning in the parlor, shedding a pale light over the gloom of the apartment; but that bright, particular orb, which had given warmth and luster to his little world, was extinguished! St. Clair shuddered as he looked around. Every object reminded him of the happiness he had destroyed; and he felt himself a moral suicide. Half dead with cold, fatigue, and distress, he approached the fire—when a note, which had fallen from the card rack to the floor, caught his eye. The address was to himself and in Louisa's handwriting. He tore it open and read as follows:

That agreeable woman, Mrs. B., who has paid us so many kind attentions, has just sent for me. She is very ill, and fancies that no one can nurse her so well as myself. Of course I cannot refuse, and only regret that I must part with my dear Charles for a few hours. Good night.

Your devoted,
Louisa

The feelings of St. Clair can be better imagined than described, as he thus suddenly passed from a state of doubt and despair to the full tide of joy. He kissed the charming billet and enacted several other extravagances, which our readers will excuse us from relating. He retired, at length, to his couch—where his exhausted frame soon sank to repose.

He rose early the next morning. Louisa was already in the parlor to welcome him with smiles. He frankly related to her all that had happened on the preceding night. Louisa's affectionate heart sympathized in the pain he had suffered, and tears stole down her cheek, which was pale with watching.

"Do not tell me," said St. Clair, "that I have only suffered that which you have often endured. No—you will not reproach me—but I know it, I feel it; and I here renounce gaming forever! Never again shall you have cause to complain of my dissipation or neglect."

He kept his word, and acknowledged that the peace and joy of his after days were cheaply purchased with the miseries of that eventful night.

THE CAPTAIN'S DAUGHTER

BY *Alexander Pushkin*

Alexander Pushkin (1799–1837) is Russia's greatest poet and is revered the way Shakespeare is in English-speaking countries. Unfortunately, Pushkin's poetry is so deeply based on the subtleties of his native tongue that it is untranslatable. He didn't turn to prose until 1830, when he was in his early thirties. In 1837, an anonymous letter alleged that a certain French nobleman was having an affair with Pushkin's wife. Pushkin demanded a duel and was killed defending his honor.

One of his prose works, a novella titled The Captain's Daughter, *is based on a peasant uprising of 1773–75. An excerpt is presented here.*

We join the story when Pyotr Andreyitch, called Petrusha by his parents, is about to turn seventeen. To his mother's dismay, his father suddenly announces that he is sending the lad off to the army, not to officer training school in glamorous St. Petersburg but to infantry boot camp in decidedly unglamorous Orenburg. He will be accompanied on the journey by an old family servant, Savelyitch. Their first taste of the dangers of military life comes at the hands of a pool hustler.

MY MOTHER WAS so overwhelmed at the thought of parting from me that she dropped the spoon into the saucepan and tears flowed down her cheeks. My delight, however, could hardly be described. The idea of military service was connected in my mind with thoughts of freedom and of the pleasures of Petersburg life. I imagined myself as an officer of the Guards, which, to my mind, was the height of human bliss.

My father did not like to change his plans or to put them off. The day for my departure was fixed. On the eve of it my father said that he intended sending with me a letter to my future chief and asked for paper and a pen.

"Don't forget, Andrey Petrovitch, to send my greetings to Prince B.," said my mother, "and to tell him that I hope he will be kind to Petrusha."

"What nonsense!" my father answered, with a frown. "Why should I write to Prince B.?"

"Why, you said you were going to write to Petrusha's chief?"

"Well, what of it?"

"But Petrusha's chief is Prince B., to be sure. Petrusha is registered in the Semyonovsky regiment."

"Registered! What do I care about it? Petrusha is not going to Petersburg. What would he learn if he did his service there? To be a spendthrift and a rake? No, let him serve in the army and learn the routine of it and know the smell of powder and be a soldier and not a fop in the Guards! Where is his passport? Give it to me."

My mother found my passport, which she kept put away in a chest together with my christening robe, and, with a trembling hand, gave it to my father. My father read it attentively, put it before him on the table, and began his letter.

I was consumed by curiosity. Where was I being sent if not to Petersburg? I did not take my eyes off my father's pen, which moved rather slowly. At last he finished, sealed the letter in the same envelope with the passport, took off his spectacles, called me, and said:

"Here is a letter for you to Andrey Karlovitch R., my old friend and comrade. You are going to Orenburg to serve under him."

And so all my brilliant hopes were dashed to the ground! Instead of the gay Petersburg life, boredom in a distant and wild part of the country awaited me. Going into the army, of which I had thought with such delight only a moment before, now seemed to me a dreadful misfortune. But it was no use protesting! Next morning a traveling chaise drove up to the house; my bag, a box with tea things, and bundles of pies and rolls, the last tokens of family affection, were packed into it. My parents blessed me. My father said to me:

"Good-bye, Pyotr. Carry out faithfully your oath of allegiance; obey your superiors; don't seek their favor; don't put yourself forward and do not shirk your duty; remember the saying: 'Watch over your clothes while they are new, and over your honor while you are young.' "

My mother admonished me with tears to take care of myself and bade Savelyitch look after "the child." They dressed me in a hare-skin jacket and a fox-fur coat over it. I stepped into the chaise with Savelyitch and set off on my journey weeping bitterly.

In the evening I arrived at Simbirsk, where I was to spend the next day in order to buy the things I needed; Savelyitch was entrusted with the purchase of them. I put up at an inn. Savelyitch went out shopping early in the morning. Bored with looking out of the window into the dirty street, I wandered about the inn. Coming into the billiard room I saw a tall man of about thirty-five, with a long black mustache, in a dressing gown, a billiard cue in his hand, and a pipe in his mouth. He was playing with the marker, who drank a glass of vodka upon winning and crawled under the billiard table on all fours when he lost. I watched their game. The longer it continued, the oftener the marker had to go on all fours, till at last he remained under the table altogether. The gentleman pronounced some expressive sentences by the way of a funeral oration and asked me to have a game. I refused, saying I could not play. This seemed to strike him as strange. He looked at me with something like pity; nevertheless, we entered into conversation. I learned that his name was Ivan Ivanovitch Zurin, that he was captain of a Hussar regiment, that he had come to Simbirsk to receive recruits and was staying at the inn. Zurin invited me to share his dinner, such as it was, like a fellow soldier. I readily agreed. We sat down to dinner. Zurin drank a great deal and treated me, saying that I must get used to army ways; he told me military anecdotes, which made me rock with laughter, and we got up from the table on the best of terms. Then he offered to teach me to play billiards.

"It is quite essential to us soldiers," he said. "On a march, for instance, one comes to some wretched little place by the western frontier; what is one to do? One can't be always beating Jews, you know. So there is nothing for it but to go to the inn and play billiards; and to do that, one must be able to play!"

He convinced me completely and I set to work very diligently. Zurin encouraged me loudly, marveled at the rapid progress I was making, and after several lessons suggested we should play for money, with three-farthings stakes, not for the sake of gain, but simply so as not to play for nothing, which, he said, was a most objectionable habit. I agreed to this, too, and Zurin ordered some punch and persuaded me to try it, repeating that I must get used to army life; what would the army be without punch! I did as he told me. We went on playing. The oftener I sipped from my glass, the more reckless I grew. My balls flew beyond the boundary every minute; I grew excited, abused the marker who did not know how to count, kept raising the stakes—in short, behaved like a silly boy who was having his first taste of freedom. I did not notice how the time passed. Zurin looked at the clock, put down his cue, and told me that I had lost a hundred rubles. I was somewhat taken aback. My money was with Savelyitch; I began to apologize; Zurin interrupted me:

"Please do not trouble; it does not matter at all. I can wait; and meanwhile let us go and see Arinushka."

What can I say? I finished the day as recklessly as I had begun it. We had supper at Arinushka's. Zurin kept filling my glass and repeating that I ought to get used to army ways. I could hardly stand when we got up from the table; at midnight Zurin drove me back to the inn.

Savelyitch met us on the steps. He cried out when he saw the unmistakable signs of my zeal for the Service.

"What has come over you, sir?" he said in a shaking voice. "Wherever did you get yourself into such a state? Good Lord! Such a dreadful thing has never happened to you before!"

"Be quiet, you old dodderer!" I mumbled. "You must be drunk; go and lie down . . . and put me to bed."

Next day I woke up with a headache, vaguely recalling the events of the day before. My reflections were interrupted by Savelyitch, who came in to me with a cup of tea.

"It's early you have taken to drinking, Pyotr Andreyitch," he said to me, shaking his head, "much too early. And whom do you get it from? Neither your father nor your grandfather were drunkards; and your mother, it goes without saying, never tastes anything stronger than kvass."

I was ashamed. I turned away and said to him: "Leave me,

Savelyitch. I don't want any tea." But it was not easy to stop Savelyitch once he began sermonizing.

"You see now what it is to take too much, Pyotr Andreyitch. Your
head is heavy, and you have no appetite. A man who drinks is no
good for anything. . . . Have some cucumber-water with honey or,
better still, half a glass of homemade brandy. Shall I bring you some?"

At that moment a servant boy came in and gave me a note from
Zurin.

> Dear Pyotr Andreyitch,
> Please send me by the boy the hundred rubles you lost to me
> at billiards yesterday. I am in urgent need of money.
>
> > Always at your service,
> > Ivan Zurin.

There was nothing for it. Assuming an air of indifference, I turned
to Savelyitch, who had charge of my money, my clothes, and all my
affairs, and told him to give the boy a hundred rubles.

"What! Why should I give it to him?"

"I owe it to him," I answered, as coolly as possible.

"Owe it!" repeated Savelyitch, growing more and more amazed.
"But when did you have time to contract a debt, sir? There's something wrong about this. You may say what you like, but I won't give
the money."

I thought that if at that decisive moment I did not get the better
of the obstinate old man, it would be difficult for me in the future
to free myself from his tutelage, and so I said, looking at him
haughtily:

"I am your master, and you are my servant. The money is mine.
I lost it at billiards because it was my pleasure to do so; and I advise
you not to argue, but to do as you are told."

Savelyitch was so struck by my words that he clasped his hands
and remained motionless.

"Well, why don't you go?" I cried angrily.

Savelyitch began to weep.

"My dear Pyotr Andreyitch," he said in a shaking voice, "do not
make me die of grief. My friend, do as I tell you, old man that I am;
write to that brigand that it was all a joke and that we have no such
sum. A hundred rubles! Good Lord! Tell him that your parents have
strictly forbidden you to play unless it be for nuts—"

"That will do," I interrupted him sternly. "Give me the money or I will turn you out."

Savelyitch looked at me with profound grief and went to fetch the money. I was sorry for the poor old man, but I wanted to assert my independence and to prove that I was no longer a child.

The money was sent to Zurin. Savelyitch hastened to get me out of the accursed inn. He came to tell me that the horses were ready. I left Simbirsk with an uneasy conscience and silent remorse, not saying good-bye to my teacher and not expecting ever to meet him again.

MY REFLECTIONS on the journey were not particularly pleasant. The sum I had lost was considerable according to the standards of that time. I could not help confessing to myself that I had behaved stupidly at the Simbirsk inn, and I felt that I had been in the wrong with Savelyitch. It all made me wretched. The old man sat gloomily on the coach box, his head turned away from me; occasionally he cleared his throat but said nothing. I was determined to make peace with him but did not know how to begin. At last I said to him:

"There, there, Savelyitch, let us make it up! I am sorry; I see myself I was to blame. I got into mischief yesterday and offended you for nothing. I promise you I will be more sensible now and do as you tell me. There, don't be cross; let us make peace."

"Ah, my dear Pyotr Andreyitch," he answered, with a deep sigh. "I am cross with myself—it was all my fault. How could I have left you alone at the inn! There it is—I yielded to temptation: I thought I would call on the deacon's wife, an old friend of mine. It's just as the proverb says—you go and see your friends and in jail your visit ends. It is simply dreadful! How shall I show myself before my master and mistress? What will they say when they hear that the child gambles and drinks?"

To comfort poor Savelyitch I gave him my word not to dispose of a single farthing without his consent in the future. He calmed down after a time, though now and again he still muttered to himself, shaking his head, "A hundred rubles! It's no joke!"

RECOLLECTIONS OF A BILLIARD SCORER

BY *Leo Tolstoy*

When Count Leo Tolstoy (1828–1910) was in his early twenties and in the Russian army, he wrote "Recollections of a Billiard Scorer," sometimes translated as "Recollections of a Billiard Marker." (A marker is a billiard room handyman, one of whose jobs is to keep score for the players.) The story is thought to be based on an incident that Tolstoy either witnessed or heard about during his military service. An entry in his diary at the time reads: "All the officers did nothing but gamble, and the stakes were high. . . . I played with a marker and lost . . . indeed, I might have lost my all."

While the story dramatizes what can happen to a compulsive gambler who doubles the bet again and again in an effort to recoup his losses, it isn't written with the mastery that characterizes War and Peace *and* Anna Karenina. *As a result, it is seldom anthologized and is among his lesser-known works.*

What game the characters are playing isn't clear; it probably is English billiards or a version of it. Pan *and* bárin *are old Russian-Polish words for "lord" or "gentleman."*

Tolstoy loved gambling, even in his later years when he had become a tiresome moralist. Maxim Gorky described playing cards with a seventy-four-year-old Tolstoy in 1902: "He plays passionately! His hands become nervous when he picks up the cards, exactly as if he were holding live birds instead of inanimate pieces of cardboard."

WELL, IT HAPPENED about three o'clock. The gentlemen were playing. There was the big stranger, as our men called him. The prince was there—the two are always together. The whiskered bárin was there; also the little hussar, Oliver, who was an actor; and there was the pan. It was a pretty good crowd.

The big stranger and the prince were playing together. Now, here I was walking up and down around the billiard table with my stick, keeping tally—ten and forty-seven, twelve and forty-seven.

Everybody knows it's our business to score. You don't get a chance to get a bite of anything, and you don't get to bed till two o'clock at night, but you're always being screamed at to bring the balls.

I was keeping tally; and I look and see a new bárin come in at the door. He gazed and gazed and then sat down on the sofa. Very well!

"Now, who can that be?" thinks I to myself. "He must be somebody."

His dress was neat—neat as a pin—checkered tricot pants, stylish little short coat, plush vest, and gold chain with all sorts of trinkets dangling from it.

He was dressed neat; but there was something about the man neater still: slim, tall, his hair brushed forward in style, and his face fair and ruddy—well, in a word, a fine young fellow.

You must know our business brings us into contact with all sorts of people. And there's many that ain't of much consequence, and there's a good deal of poor trash. So, though you're only a scorer, you get used to telling folks; that is, in a certain way you learn a thing or two.

I looked at the bárin. I see him sit down, modest and quiet, not knowing anybody; and the clothes on him are so brand-new, that, thinks I, "Either he's a foreigner—an Englishman maybe—or some count just come. And though he's so young, he has an air of some distinction." Oliver sat down next him, so he moved along a little.

They began a game. The big man lost. He shouts to me. Says he, "You're always cheating. You don't count straight. Why don't you pay attention?"

He scolded away, then threw down his cue, and went out. Now, just look here! Evenings, he and the prince play for fifty silver rubles a game; and here he only lost a bottle of Makon wine and got mad. That's the kind of a character he is.

Another time he and the prince play till two o'clock. They don't bank down any cash; and so I know neither of them's got any cash, but they are simply playing a bluff game.

"I'll go you twenty-five rubles," says he.

"All right."

Just yawning and not even stopping to place the ball—you see, he was not made of stone—now just notice what he said. "We are playing for money," says he, "and not for chips."

But this man puzzled me worse than all the rest. Well, then, when the big man left, the prince says to the new bárin, "Wouldn't you like," says he, "to play a game with me?"

"With pleasure," says he.

He sat there and looked rather foolish, indeed he did. He may have been courageous in reality; but, at all events, he got up, went over to the billiard table, and did not seem flustered as yet. He was not exactly flustered, but you couldn't help seeing that he was not quite at his ease.

Either his clothes were a little too new, or he was embarrassed because everybody was looking at him; at any rate, he seemed to have no energy. He sort of sidled up to the table, caught his pocket on the edge, began to chalk his cue, dropped his chalk.

Whenever he hit the ball, he always glanced around and reddened. Not so the prince. He was used to it; he chalked and chalked his hand, tucked up his sleeve; he goes and sits down when he pockets the ball, even though he is such a little man.

They played two or three games; then I notice the prince puts up the cue and says, "Would you mind telling me your name?"

"Nekhliudof," says he.

Says the prince, "Was your father commander in the corps of cadets?"

"Yes," says the other.

Then they began to talk in French, and I could not understand them. I suppose they were talking about family affairs.

"*Au revoir,*" says the prince. "I am very glad to have made your acquaintance." He washed his hands and went to get a lunch; but the other stood by the billiard table with his cue and was knocking the balls about.

It's our business, you know, when a new man comes along, to be rather sharp: it's the best way. I took the balls and went to put them up. He reddened and said, "Can't I play any longer?"

"Certainly you can," says I. "That's what billiards is for." But I don't pay any attention to him. I straighten the cues.

"Will you play with me?"

"Certainly, sir," says I.

I place the balls. "Shall we play for odds?"

"What do you mean, 'play for odds'?"

"Well," says I, "you give me a half-ruble, and I crawl under the table."

Of course, as he had never seen that sort of thing, it seemed strange to him; he laughs.

"Go ahead," says he.

"Very well," says I, "only you must give me odds."

"What!" says he. "Are you a worse player than I am?"

"Most likely," says I. "We have few players who can be compared with you."

We began to play. He certainly had the idea that he was a crack shot. It was a caution to see him shoot; but the Pole sat there and kept shouting out every time, "Ah, what a chance! Ah, what a shot!"

But what a man he was! His ideas were good enough, but he didn't know how to carry them out. Well, as usual I lost the first game, crawled under the table, and grunted.

Thereupon Oliver and the Pole jumped down from their seats and applauded, thumping with their cues.

"Splendid! Do it again," they cried. "Once more."

Well enough to cry "Once more," especially for the Pole. That fellow would have been glad enough to crawl under the billiard table, or even under the Blue bridge, for a half-ruble! Yet he was the first to cry, "Splendid! But you haven't wiped off all the dust yet."

I, Petrushka the marker, was pretty well known to everybody.

Only, of course, I did not care to show my hand yet. I lost my second game.

"It does not become me at all to play with you, sir," says I.

He laughs. Then, as I was playing the third game, he stood forty-nine and I nothing. I laid the cue on the billiard table and said, "Bárin, shall we play off?"

"What do you mean by playing off?" says he. "How would you have it?"

"You make it three rubles or nothing," says I.

"Why," says he, "have I been playing with you for money?" The fool!

He turned rather red.

Very good. He lost the game. He took out his pocketbook—quite a new one, evidently just from the English shop—opened it: I see he wanted to make a little splurge. It is stuffed full of bills—nothing but hundred-ruble notes.

"No," says he, "there's no small stuff here."

He took three rubles from his purse. "There," says he, "there's your two rubles; the other pays for the games, and you keep the rest for vodka."

"Thank you, sir, most kindly." I see that he is a splendid fellow. For such a one I would crawl under anything. For one thing, it's a pity that he won't play for money. "For then," thinks I, "I should know how to work him for twenty rubles, and maybe I could stretch it out to forty."

As soon as the Pole saw the young man's money, he says, "Wouldn't you like to try a little game with me? You play so admirably." Such sharpers prowl around.

"No," says the young man, "excuse me. I have not the time." And he went out.

I don't know who that man was, that Pole. Some one called him Pan or the Pole, and so it stuck to him. Every day he used to sit in the billiard room and always look on. He was no longer allowed to take a hand in any game whatsoever; but he always sat by himself and got out his pipe and smoked. But then he could play well.

Very good. Nekhliudof came a second time, a third time; he began to come frequently. He would come morning and evening. He learned to play French carom and pyramid pool—everything in fact. He became less bashful, got acquainted with everybody, and played tolerably well. Of course, being a young man of a good family, with money, everybody liked him. The only exception was the "big guest": he quarreled with him.

And the whole thing grew out of a trifle.

They were playing pool—the prince, the big guest, Nekhliudof, Oliver, and someone else. Nekhliudof was standing near the stove, talking with someone. When it came the big man's turn to play, it happened that his ball was just opposite the stove. There was very little space there, and he liked to have elbowroom.

Now, either he didn't see Nekhliudof, or he did it on purpose;

but, as he was flourishing his cue, he hit Nekhliudof in the chest, a tremendous rap. It actually made him groan. What then? He did not think of apologizing, he was so boorish. He even went further: he didn't look at him; he walks off grumbling, "Who's jostling me there? It made me miss my shot. Why can't we have some room?"

Then the other went up to him, pale as a sheet, but quite self-possessed, and says so politely, "You ought first, sir, to apologize: you struck me."

"Catch me apologizing now! I should have won the game," says he, "but now you have spoiled it for me."

Then the other one says, "You ought to apologize."

"Get out of my way! I insist upon it, I won't."

And he turned away to look after his ball.

Nekhliudof went up to him and took him by the arm.

"You're a boor," says he, "my dear sir."

Though he was a slender young fellow, almost like a girl, still he was all ready for a quarrel. His eyes flash fire; he looks as if he could eat him alive. The big guest was a strong, tremendous fellow, no match for Nekhliudof.

"Wha-at!" says he. "You call me a boor?" Yelling out these words, he raises his hand to strike him.

Then everybody there rushed up and seized them both by the arms and separated them.

After much talk, Nekhliudof says, "Let him give me satisfaction: he has insulted me."

"Not at all," says the other. "I don't care a whit about any satisfaction. He's nothing but a boy, a mere nothing. I'll pull his ears for him."

"If you aren't willing to give me satisfaction, then you are no gentleman."

And, saying this, he almost cried.

"Well, and you, you are a little boy: nothing you say or do can offend me."

Well, we separated them—led them off, as the custom is, to different rooms. Nekhliudof and the prince were friends.

"Go," says the former. "For God's sake make him listen to reason."

The prince went. The big man says, "I ain't afraid of anyone. I am not going to have any explanation with such a baby. I won't do it, and that's the end of it."

Well, they talked and talked, and then the matter died out, only the big guest ceased to come to us anymore.

As a result of this—this row, I might call it—he was regarded as quite the cock of the walk. He was quick to take offense—I mean Nekhliudof—to so many other things, however, he was as unsophisticated as a newborn babe.

I remember once, the prince says to Nekhliudof, "Whom do you keep here?"

"No one," says he.

"What do you mean, 'no one'!"

"Why should I?" says Nekhliudof.

"How so—why should you?"

"I have always lived thus. Why shouldn't I continue to live the same way?"

"You don't say so? Did you ever!"

And saying this, the prince burst into a peal of laughter, and the whiskered bárin also roared. They couldn't get over it.

"What, never?" they ask.

"Never!"

They were dying with laughter. Of course I understood well enough what they were laughing at him for. I keep my eyes open. "What," thinks I, "will come of it?"

"Come," says the prince, "come right off."

"No, not for anything," was his answer.

"Now, that is absurd," says the prince. "Come along!"

They went out.

They came back at one o'clock. They sat down to supper; quite a crowd of them were assembled. Some of our very best customers—Atánof, Prince Razin, Count Shustakh, Mirtsof. And all congratulate Nekhliudof, laughing as they do so. They call me in. I see that they are pretty jolly.

"Congratulate the bárin," they shout.

"What on?" I ask.

How did he call it? His initiation or his enlightenment; I can't remember exactly.

"I have the honor," says I, "to congratulate you."

And he sits there very red in the face, yet he smiles. Didn't they have fun with him though!

Well and good. They went afterward to the billiard room, all very gay; and Nekhliudof went up to the billiard table, leaned on his elbow, and said, "It's amusing to you, gentlemen, but it's sad for me. Why," says he, "did I do it? Prince," says he, "I shall never forgive you or myself as long as I live."

And he actually burst into tears. Evidently, he did not know himself what he was saying. The prince went up to him with a smile.

"Don't talk nonsense," says he. "Let's go home, Anatoli."

"I won't go anywhere," says the other. "Why did I do that?"

And the tears poured down his cheeks. He would not leave the billiard table, and that was the end of it. That's what it means for a young and inexperienced man to . . .

In this way he often used to come to us. Once he came with the prince and the whiskered man who was the prince's crony—the gentlemen always called him Fedotka. He had prominent cheekbones and was homely enough, to be sure; but he used to dress neatly and ride in a carriage. What was the reason that the gentlemen were so fond of him? I really could not tell.

"Fedotka! Fedotka!" they'd call, and ask him to eat and to drink, and they'd spend their money paying up for him; but he was a thoroughgoing deadbeat. If ever he lost, he would be sure not to pay; but if he won, you bet he wouldn't fail to collect his money. Often, too, he came to grief. Yet there he was, walking arm in arm with the prince.

"You are lost without me," he would say to the prince.

And what jokes he used to crack, to be sure! Well, as I said, they had already arrived that time, and one of them says, "Let's have the balls for three-handed pool."

"All right," says the other.

They began to play at three rubles a stake. Nekhliudof and the prince play and chat about all sorts of things meantime.

"Ah!" says one of them, "you mind only what a neat little foot she has."

"Oh," says the other, "her foot is nothing; her beauty is her wealth of hair."

Of course they paid no attention to the game, only kept on talking to one another.

As to Fedotka, that fellow was alive to his work; he played his very best, but they didn't do themselves justice at all.

And so he won six rubles from each of them. God knows how many games he had won from the prince, yet I never knew them to pay each other any money; but Nekhliudof took out two greenbacks and handed them over to him.

"No," says he, "I don't want to take your money. Let's square it: play 'quits or double'—either double or nothing."

I set the balls. Fedotka began to play the first hand. Nekhliudof seemed to play only for fun: sometimes he would come very near winning a game, yet just fail of it. Says he, "It would be too easy a move. I won't have it so." But Fedotka did not forget what he was up to. Carelessly he proceeded with the game and thus, as if it were unexpected, won.

"Let us play double stakes once more," says he.

"All right," says Nekhliudof.

Once more Fedotka won the game.

"Well," says he, "it began with a mere trifle. I don't wish to win much from you. Shall we make it once more or nothing?"

"Yes."

Say what you may, but fifty rubles is a pretty sum, and Nekhliudof himself began to propose, "Let us make it double or quit." So they played and played.

It kept going worse and worse for Nekhliudof. Two hundred and eighty rubles were written up against him. As to Fedotka, he had his own method: he would lose a simple game, but when the stake was doubled, he would win sure.

As for the prince, he sits by and looks on. He sees that the matter is growing serious.

"Enough!" says he. "Hold on."

My! They keep increasing the stake.

At last it went so far that Nekhliudof was in for more than five hundred rubles. Fedotka laid down his cue and said, "Aren't you satisfied for today? I'm tired."

Yet I knew he was ready to play till dawn of day, provided there was money to be won. Stratagem, of course. And the other was all the more anxious to go on. "Come on! Come on!"

"No—'pon my honor, I'm tired. Come," says Fedotka, "let's go upstairs. There you shall have your *revanche*."

Upstairs with us meant the place where the gentlemen used to play cards. From that very day, Fedotka wound his net round him so that he began to come every day. He would play one or two games of billiards and then proceed upstairs—every day upstairs.

What they used to do there, God only knows; but it is a fact that from that time he began to be an entirely different kind of man and seemed hand in glove with Fedotka. Formerly he used to be stylish, neat in his dress, with his hair slightly curled even; but now it would be only in the morning that he would be anything like himself; but as soon as he had paid his visit upstairs, he would not be at all like himself.

Once he came down from upstairs with the prince, pale, his lips trembling, and talking excitedly.

"I cannot permit such a one as *he* is," says he, "to say that I am not"—How did he express himself? I cannot recollect, something like "not refined enough," or what—"and that he won't play with me anymore. I tell you I have paid him ten thousand, and I should think that he might be a little more considerate, before others, at least."

"Oh, bother!" says the prince. "Is it worthwhile to lose one's temper with Fedotka?"

"No," says the other, "I will not let it go so."

"Why, old fellow, how can you think of such a thing as lowering yourself to have a row with Fedotka?"

"That is all very well; but there were strangers there, mind you."

"Well, what of that?" says the prince. "Strangers? Well, if you wish, I will go and make him ask your pardon."

"No," says the other.

And then they began to chatter in French, and I could not understand what it was they were talking about.

And what would you think of it? That very evening he and Fedotka ate supper together, and they became friends again.

Well and good. At other times again he would come alone.

"Well," he would say, "do I play well?"

It's our business, you know, to try to make everybody contented, and so I would say, "Yes, indeed"; and yet how could it be called good play when he would poke about with his cue without any sense whatsoever?

And from that very evening when he took in with Fedotka, he began to play for money all the time. Formerly, he didn't care to play for stakes, either for a dinner or for champagne. Sometimes the prince would say, "Let's play for a bottle of champagne."

"No," he would say, "let us rather have the wine by itself. Hello there! Bring a bottle!"

And now he began to play for money all the time; he used to spend his entire days in our establishment. He would either play with someone in the billiard room, or he would go "upstairs."

"Well," thinks I to myself, "everyone else gets something from him, why don't I get some advantage out of it?"

"Well, sir," says I one day, "it's a long time since you have had a game with me."

And so we began to play. Well, when I won ten half-rubles of him, I say, "Don't you want to make it double or quit, sir?"

He said nothing. Formerly, if you remember, he would call me a fool for such a boldness. And we went to playing "quit or double."

I won eighty rubles of him.

Well, what would you think? Since that first time, he used to play with me every day. He would wait till there was no one about, for of course he would have been ashamed to play with a mere marker in the presence of others. Once, he had got rather warmed up by the play (he already owed me sixty rubles), and so he says, "Do you want to stake all you have won?"

"All right," says I.

I won. "One hundred and twenty to one hundred and twenty?"

"All right," says I.

Again I won. "Two hundred and forty against two hundred and forty?"

"Isn't that too much?" I ask.

He made no reply. We played the game. Once more it was mine. "Four hundred and eighty against four hundred and eighty?"

I say, "Well, sir, I don't want to wrong you. Let us make it a hundred rubles that you owe me and call it square."

You ought to have heard how he yelled at this, and yet he was not a proud man at all. "Either play or don't play!" says he.

Well, I see there's nothing to be done. "Three hundred and eighty, then, if you please," says I.

I really wanted to lose. I allowed him forty points in advance. He stood fifty-two to my thirty-six. He began to cut the yellow one and missed eighteen points; and I was standing just at the turning point. I made a stroke so as to knock the ball off of the billiard table. No so luck would have it. Do what I might, he even missed the doublet. I had won again.

"Listen," says he. "Peter,"—he did not call me Petrushka then—"I can't pay you the whole right away. In a couple of months I could pay three thousand even, if it were necessary."

And there he stood just as red, and his voice kind of trembled.

"Very good, sir," says I.

With this he laid down the cue. Then he began to walk up and down, up and down, the perspiration running down his face.

"Peter," says he, "let's try it again, double or quit."

And he almost burst into tears.

"What, sir, what! Would you play against such luck?"

"Oh, let us play, I beg of you." And he brings the cue and puts it in my hand.

I took the cue, and I threw the balls on the table so that they bounced over onto the floor; I could not help showing off a little, naturally. I say, "All right, sir."

But he was in such a hurry that he went and picked up the balls himself, and I think to myself, "Anyway, I'll never be able to get the seven hundred rubles from him, so I can lose them to him all the same." I began to play carelessly on purpose. But no—he won't have it so. "Why," says he, "you are playing badly on purpose."

But his hands trembled, and when the ball went toward a pocket, his fingers would spread out and his mouth would screw up to one side, as if he could by any means force the ball into the pocket. Even I couldn't stand it, and I say, "That won't do any good, sir."

Very well. As he won this game, I say, "This will make it one hundred and eighty rubles you owe me and fifty games; and now I must go and get my supper." So I laid down my cue and went off.

I went and sat down all by myself at a small table opposite the door; and I look in and see and wonder what he will do. Well, what would you think? He began to walk up and down, up and down, probably thinking that no one's looking at him; and then he would give a pull at his hair and then walk up and down again and keep muttering to himself; and then he would pull his hair again.

After that he wasn't seen for a week. Once he came into the dining room as gloomy as could be, but he didn't enter the billiard room. The prince caught sight of him.

"Come," says he, "let's have a game."

"No," says the other, "I am not going to play anymore."

"Nonsense! Come along."

"No," says he, "I won't come, I tell you. For you it's all one whether I go or not, yet for me it's no good to come here."

And so he did not come for ten days more. And then, it being the holidays, he came dressed up in a dress suit: he'd evidently been into company. And he was here all day long; he kept playing, and he came the next day and the third . . .

And it began to go in the old style, and I thought it would be fine to have another trial with him.

"No," says he, "I'm not going to play with you; and as to the one hundred and eighty rubles that I owe you, if you'll come at the end of a month, you shall have it."

Very good. So I went to him at the end of a month.

"By God," says he, "I can't give it to you; but come back on Thursday."

Well, I went on Thursday. I found that he had a splendid suite of apartments.

"Well," says I, "is he at home?"

"He hasn't got up yet," I was told.

"Very good. I will wait."

For a body servant he had one of his own serfs, such a gray-haired old man! That servant was perfectly single-minded—he didn't know anything about beating about the bush. So we got into conversation.

"Well," says he, "what is the use of our living here, master and I? He's squandered all his property, and it's mighty little honor or good that we get out of this Petersburg of yours. As we started from the country, I thought it would be as it was with the last bárin (may his soul rest in peace!) and we would go about with princes and counts and generals; he thought to himself, 'I'll find a countess for a sweetheart, and she'll have a big dowry, and we'll live on a big scale.' But it's quite a different thing from what he expected; here we are, running about from one tavern to another as bad off as we could be! The Princess Rtishcheva, you know, is his own aunt, and Prince Borotintsef is his godfather. What do you think? He went to see them only once—that was at Christmastime; he never shows his nose there. Yes, and even their people laugh about it to me. 'Why,' they say, 'your bárin is not a bit like his father!' And once I take it upon myself to say to him, 'Why wouldn't you go, sir, and visit your aunt? They are feeling bad because you haven't been for so long.'

" 'It's stupid there, Demyánitch,' says he. Just to think, he found his only amusement here in the saloon! If he only would enter the service! Yet, no. He has got entangled with cards and all the rest of it. When men get going that way, there's no good in anything; nothing comes to any good. . . . *E-ekh!* We are going to the dogs, and, no mistake, the late mistress (may her soul rest in peace!) left us a rich inheritance: no less than a thousand souls and about three hundred thousand rubles worth of timberlands. He has mortgaged it all, sold the timber, let the estate go to rack and ruin, and still no money on hand. When the master is away, of course, the overseer is more than the master. What does he care? He only cares to stuff his own pockets.

"A few days ago, a couple of peasants brought complaints from the whole estate. 'He has wasted the last of the property,' they say. What do you think? He pondered over the complaints and gave the peasants ten rubles apiece. Says he, 'I'll be there very soon. I shall have some money, and I will settle all accounts when I come.'

"But how can he settle accounts when we are getting into debt all the time? Money or no money, yet the winter here has cost eighty thousand rubles, and now there isn't a silver ruble in the house. And all owing to his kindheartedness. You see, he's such a simple bárin that it would be hard to find his equal: that's the very reason that he's going to ruin—going to ruin, all for nothing." And the old man almost wept.

Nekhliudof woke up about eleven and called me in.

"They haven't sent me any money yet," says he. "But it isn't my fault. Shut the door."

I shut the door.

"Here," says he, "take my watch or this diamond pin and pawn it. They will give you more than one hundred and eighty rubles for it, and when I get my money I will redeem it."

"No matter, sir," says I. "If you don't happen to have any money, it's no consequence; let me have the watch if you don't mind. I can wait for your convenience."

I can see that the watch is worth more than three hundred.

Very good. I pawned the watch for a hundred rubles and carried him the ticket. "You will owe me eighty rubles," says I, "and you had better redeem the watch."

And so it happened that he still owed me eighty rubles.

After that he began to come to us again every day. I don't know how matters stood between him and the prince, but at all events he kept coming with him all the time, or else they would go and play cards upstairs with Fedotka. And what queer accounts those three men kept between them! This one would lend money to the other, the other to the third, yet who it was that owed the money you never could find out.

And in this way he kept on coming our way for well-nigh two years; only it was to be plainly seen that he was a changed man, such a devil-may-care manner he assumed at times. He even went so far at times as to borrow a ruble of me to pay a hack driver; and yet he would still play with the prince for a hundred-rubles stake.

He grew gloomy, thin, sallow. As soon as he came, he used to order a little glass of absinthe, take a bite of something, and drink some port wine, and then he would grow more lively.

He came one time before dinner; it happened to be carnival time, and he began to play with a hussar.

Says he, "Do you want to play for a stake?"

"Very well," says he. "What shall it be?"

"A bottle of Claude Vougeaux? What do you say?"

"All right."

Very good. The hussar won, and they went off for their dinner. They sat down at a table, and then Nekhliudof says, "Simon, a bottle of Claude Vougeaux, and see that you warm it to the proper point."

Simon went out, brought in the dinner, but no wine.

"Well," says he, "where's the wine?"

Simon hurried out, brought in the roast.

"Let us have the wine," says he.

Simon makes no reply.

"What's got into you? Here we've almost finished dinner, and no wine. Who wants to drink with dessert?"

Simon hurried out. "The landlord," says he, "wants to speak to you."

Nekhliudof turned scarlet. He sprang up from the table.

"What's the need of calling me?"

The landlord is standing at the door.

Says he, "I can't trust you anymore, unless you settle my little bill."

"Well, didn't I tell you that I would pay the first of the month?"

"That will be all very well," says the landlord, "but I can't be all the time giving credit and having no settlement. There are more than ten thousand rubles of debts outstanding now."

"Well, that'll do, *monshoor*, you know that you can trust me! Send the bottle, and I assure you that I will pay you very soon."

And he hurried back.

"What was it? Why did they call you out?" asked the hussar.

"Oh, someone wanted to ask me a question."

"Now it would be a good time," says the hussar, "to have a little warm wine to drink."

"Simon, hurry up!"

Simon came back, but still no wine, nothing. Too bad! Nekhliudof left the table and came to me.

"For God's sake," says he, "Petrushka, let me have six rubles!"

He was pale as a sheet. "No, sir," says I. "By God, you owe me quite too much now."

"I will give forty rubles for six, in a week's time."

"If only I had it," says I, "I should not think of refusing you, but I haven't."

What do you think! He rushed away, his teeth set, his fist doubled up, and ran down the corridor like one mad, and all at once he gave himself a knock on the forehead.

"Oh my God!" says he. "What has it come to?"

But he did not return to the dining room; he jumped into a carriage and drove away. Didn't we have our laugh over it! The hussar asks, "Where is the gentleman who was dining with me?"

"He has gone," says someone.

"Where has he gone? What message did he leave?"

"He didn't leave any; he just took to his carriage and went off."

"That's a fine way of entertaining a man!" says he.

"Now," thinks I to myself, "it'll be a long time before he comes again after this; that is, on account of this scandal." But no. On the next day he came about evening. He came into the billiard room. He had a sort of a box in his hand. Took off his overcoat.

"Now let us have a game," says he.

He looked out from under his eyebrows, rather fiercelike.

We played a game. "That's enough now," says he. "Go and bring me a pen and paper. I must write a letter."

Not thinking anything, not suspecting anything, I bring some paper and put it on the table in the little room.

"It's all ready, sir," says I.

"Very good." He sat down at the table. He kept on writing and writing and muttering to himself all the time. Then he jumps up and, frowning, says, "Look and see if my carriage has come yet."

It was on a Friday, during carnival time, and so there weren't any of the customers on hand; they were all at some ball. I went to see about the carriage, and just as I was going out of the door, he shouts, "Petrushka! Petrushka!" as if something suddenly frightened him.

I turn around. I see he's pale as a sheet, standing here and looking at me.

"Did you call me, sir?" says I.

He makes no reply.

"What do you want?" says I.

He says nothing. "Oh, yes!" says he. "Let's have another game."

Then says he, "Haven't I learned to play pretty well?"

He had just won the game. "Yes," says I.

"All right," says he. "Go now and see about my carriage." He himself walked up and down the room.

Without thinking anything, I went down to the door. I didn't see any carriage at all. I started to go up again.

Just as I am going up, I hear what sounds like the thud of a billiard cue. I go into the billiard room. I notice a peculiar smell.

I look around; and there he is lying on the floor in a pool of blood, with a pistol beside him. I was so scared that I could not speak a word.

He keeps twitching, twitching his leg, and stretched himself a little. Then he sort of snored and stretched out his full length in such a strange way. And God knows why such a sin came about—how it was that it occurred to him to ruin his own soul—but as to what he left written on this paper, I don't understand it at all. Truly, you can never account for what is going on in the world.

God gave me all that a man can desire—wealth, name, intellect, noble aspirations. I wanted to enjoy myself, and I trod in the mire all that was best in me. I have done nothing dishonorable, I am not unfortunate, I have not committed any crime; but I have done worse: I have destroyed my feelings, my intellect, my youth. I became entangled in a filthy net, from which I could not escape and to which I could not accustom myself. I feel that I am falling lower and lower every moment, and I cannot stop my fall.

And what ruined me? Was there in me some strange passion which I might plead as an excuse? No!

My recollections are pleasant. One fearful moment of forgetfulness, which can never be erased from my mind, led me to come to my senses. I shuddered when I saw what a measureless abyss separated me from what I desired to be and might have been. In my imagination arose the hopes, the dreams, and the thoughts of my youth.

Where are those lofty thoughts of life, of eternity, of God, which at times filled my soul with light and strength? Where that aimless power of love, which kindled my heart with its comforting warmth? . . .

But how good and happy I might have been, had I trodden that path which, at the very entrance of life, was pointed out to me by my fresh mind and true feelings! More than once did I try to go from the ruts in which my life ran, into that sacred path.

I said to myself, "Now I will use my whole strength of will"; and yet I could not do it. When I happened to be alone, I felt awkward and timid. When I was with others, I no longer heard the inward voice; and I fell all the time lower and lower.

At last I came to a terrible conviction that it was impossible for me to lift myself from this low plane. I ceased to think about it, and I wished to forget all; but hopeless repentance worried me still more and more. Then, for the first time, the thought of suicide occurred to me. . . .

I once thought that the nearness of death would rouse my soul. I was mistaken. In a quarter of an hour I shall be no more, yet my view has not in the least changed. I see with the same eyes, I hear with the same ears, I think the same thoughts; there is the same strange incoherence, unsteadiness, and lightness in my thoughts.

1869

A GAME OF BILLIARDS

BY *Alphonse Daudet*

In the stories by Hall, Pushkin, and Tolstoy, we saw foolish men risking wives, rubles, and their own lives in pursuit of victory on the green cloth. In "A Game of Billiards" by Alphonse Daudet (1840–1897), an entire war is at stake.

Daudet is one of France's most cherished authors. A poet, novelist, and short story writer who often worked fifteen hours a day, his work is characterized by naturalism and humor. In 1954, three of his stories were made into a very funny film titled Letters from My Windmill, *which is available in some video rental stores.*

EVEN SOLDIERS are exhausted after two days' fighting, especially if they have passed the night, knapsacks upon their backs, torrents of rain descending upon them. And yet for three mortal hours they had been left to wait in the puddles along the highway, in the mire of fields soaked with rain.

Heavy with fatigue, weakened by the effects of previous nights, their uniforms drenched, they pressed closer together for warmth and support. Here and there, leaning upon a neighbor's knapsack, a man had fallen asleep standing; and upon the relaxed faces of these men, overcome by sleep, might be read more plainly than before the traces which weariness and privations had made. In the mud and rain, without fire, without food, overhead a sky heavy and lowering—around them, on every side, the enemy! Dismal indeed!

What are they doing yonder? What is going on?

The guns, their mouths turned toward the woods, seem to be lying in wait. From their hiding places the machine guns stare fixedly at the horizon. All is ready for an attack. Why is none made? For what are they waiting?

They await orders from headquarters, but none come.

And yet it is only a short distance to headquarters, to that beautiful Louis XIII château whose red-brick walls, washed by the rain, are seen halfway up the hill, glistening through the thickets. Truly a princely dwelling, well worthy of bearing the banner of a marshal of France. Separated from the main road by a big trench and a ramp of stone are green, smooth-shaven lawns extending even to the stone steps of the château and bordered with vases of flowers. On the side of the house farthest away from the road, the daylight darts through the leafage of the arbors, making bright openings in them. Upon an artificial pond which sparkles like a mirror, swans are swimming, and under the pagoda-shaped roof of a large aviary, peacocks and golden pheasants strut about, spreading their wings and sending their shrill cries through the foliage. Though the owners of the house have departed, there is nowhere a perceptible sign of that ruin and utter desolation which war brings in its train. Under the oriflamme of the chief of the army, not the smallest flower dotting the lawn has been destroyed, and it is indescribably charming to discover, so near the field of battle, that calm and opulence that result from systematic care and to observe such evenly trimmed shrubberies, such silent avenues of shade. The rain, which in its descent elsewhere has rutted the roads and heaped them with mire, in this quarter has been nothing more than an aristocratic shower. Nothing vulgar about it. It has revived the red tints of the bricks, the verdure of the lawns; it has added fresh luster to the leaves of the orange trees, to the swans' white plumage. Everything glistens. The scene is peaceful. In fact, were it not for the flag floating from the top of the roof and the sight of two sentinels before the gate, one would never believe headquarters were here.

The horses are resting in the stables; here and there officers' servants are seen, and orderlies in undress, lounging about the kitchens of the château, and now and then a gardener tranquilly dragging his rake through the sand of the grounds.

In the dining room, whose windows front the entrance of the

château, is seen a table partly cleared, bottles uncorked, glasses tarnished, empty, and dimmed, resting upon the wrinkled cloth—in short, every indication that the repast is ended. The guests have departed, but in a side room loud voices are heard, peals of laughter, the rolling of billiard balls, and the clinking of glasses. The Marshal has just started upon his game, and that is why the army is waiting for orders. Once the Marshal has begun, the heavens might fall, but nothing on earth would hinder him from finishing his game.

For if the mighty soldier has a single weakness, it is his fondness for billiards. There he stands, as grave as though a battle had begun; he is in full uniform, his breast covered with decorations; his repast, the grog he has drunken, and the excitement of the game animate him. His eyes sparkle, and his cheekbones are flushed. About him gather his aides-de-camp, most assiduous in their attentions, deferential, and overcome with admiration at each of his shots. When the Marshal makes a point, they rush toward the mark. Is the Marshal thirsty? Each one desires to prepare his grog! Such a rustling of epaulets and panaches, such a rattling of crosses and aiguillettes! How they bow and smile, these courtiers! What elegance and charm of manner! And then to see such embroideries, so many new uniforms, in this lofty chamber carved in oak, opening upon parks and courts of honor! It reminds one of those autumns of Compiègne and makes him forget for a moment those figures in muddied cloaks, gathered yonder in the roads, making such somber groups, as they wait in the rain.

The Marshal's adversary is an officer of his staff, a little captain who curls and laces and wears light gloves; he is an excellent shot at billiards and could beat all the marshals on earth, but he understands how to keep at a respectful distance from his chief and exercises all his skill in playing so that he shall neither win, nor seem to lose, too readily. Evidently an officer with an eye for the future.

Attention, young man, look out! The Marshal is five points ahead. If you can end the game as you have begun it, your promotion is surer than it would be were you standing outside with the others, beneath those torrents of water that darken the horizon. It would be a pity, too, to soil that fine uniform and tarnish the gold of its aiguillettes, waiting for orders that never come.

The game is extremely interesting. The balls roll, graze each other, and pass; they rebound. Every moment the play grows more exciting. But suddenly a flash of light is seen in the sky and the report of a cannon is heard. A heavy, rumbling sound shakes the windows. Everyone starts and casts an uneasy glance about him. The Marshal alone remains unmoved. He sees nothing, hears nothing, for, leaning over the table, he is about to make a magnificent draw shot. Draw shots are his forte!

But again that flash, and again! From the cannon fresh reports, and nearer together now. The aides-de-camp run to the window. Can it be that the Prussians are attacking?

"Let them!" says the Marshal, chalking his cue. "Your turn, captain!"

The staff thrills with admiration. Turenne asleep upon a gun-carriage was nothing compared to this marshal, so calmly absorbed in his game at the moment of action! But all this time the tumult increases. With the shock of the cannon mingles the rattling of the machine guns and the rumbling of volley upon volley; a reddish cloud dark at the edges rises from the further end of the lawn. All the rear of the park is on fire. Frightened peacocks and pheasants clamor in the aviary, Arabian horses, away in the stables, scent the powder and rear in their stalls. At headquarters a general commotion begins. Dispatch follows dispatch. Messengers arrive at a gallop. Everywhere they are asking for the Marshal.

But the Marshal is unapproachable. Have I not told you that nothing in the world could hinder him from finishing a game once begun?

"Your play, captain—"

But the captain is distracted. Ah! Youth is youth. He loses his head, forgets what he is about, and makes two successive runs which almost win the game for him. And now the Marshal is furious. Surprise and indignation are visible upon his manly features. At this very moment a horse rushes into the courtyard at full speed and drops exhausted. An aide-de-camp, covered with mud, forces the sentry, makes one bound over the stone steps, crying, "Marshal, Marshal!" And this is his reception: the Marshal, red as a cock and swelling with anger, appears at the window, cue in hand.

"Who is there? What is it? Is there no sentry here?"

"But, Marshal—"

"Oh, yes, yes—later—let them wait for my orders—in God's name!"

And the window closes with a bang.

Let them wait for his orders! And that is exactly what they are doing, these poor fellows. The wind drives rain and grapeshot in their faces. Whole battalions are slaughtered, whilst others, perfectly useless, stand bearing arms, unable to understand why they remain inactive. Nothing else to do. They wait for orders. But men may die without word of command, and these men die in hundreds, falling behind bushes, dropping in trenches in front of that great silent château. And even after death, the grapeshot continues to lacerate their bodies, and from those gaping wounds flows a silent stream—the generous blood of France. And above, yonder, in the billiard room, all is as excited as upon the battlefield, for the Marshal has regained his advantage, and the little captain is playing like a lion.

Seventeen! Eighteen! Nineteen! Scarcely time to mark the points. The sound of battle grows nearer and nearer. The Marshal has but one more point to play for. Already shells are falling in the park. One has burst in the pond. Its glassy sheet reddens, and a terrified swan is seen swimming amid a whirl of bloody plumage. And now the last shot.

And then—deep silence. Only the sound of rain falling upon the leafage of the arbors, only an indistinct rumbling noise at the foot of the hill, and along the muddy roads a sound like the tramping of hurrying herds. The army is in full retreat. The Marshal has won his game.

···

FATE

BY *H. H. Munro (Saki)*

Political correctness aside, would you set a woman's clothes on fire to get out of a bet? Would you do it if she were threatening to show you her vacation photographs? Those are two of the moral questions not answered in "Fate," by the English writer H. H. Munro (1870–1916), who for some reason used Saki as a nom de plume.

Munro spent many years as a political satirist for the Westminster Gazette *and as a foreign correspondent for the Tory* Morning Post. *His two novels are nearly forgotten, but his short stories live on, thanks to their wit, whimsy, and surprise endings. "The Window" is an almost perfect model of what a short story should be and has long been a favorite of anthologists. Too bad it's about hunting and not billiards.*

H. H. Munro was born in Burma and was killed in France in World War I at the age of forty-six.

R EX D ILLOT was nearly twenty-four, almost good-looking, and quite penniless. His mother was supposed to make him some sort of an allowance out of what her creditors allowed her, and Rex occasionally strayed into the ranks of those who earn fitful salaries as secretaries or companions to people who are unable to cope unaided with their correspondence or their leisure. For a few months he had been assistant editor and business manager of a paper devoted to fancy mice, but the devotion had been all on one side, and the paper disappeared with a certain abruptness from club reading rooms and other haunts where it had made a gratuitous appearance. Still, Rex lived with some air of comfort and well-being, as one can live if one is born with a genius for that sort of thing, and a kindly Providence usually arranged that his weekend invitations coincided with the dates on which his one white dinner waistcoat was in a laundry-returned condition of dazzling cleanness. He played most games badly, and was shrewd enough to recognize the fact, but he had developed a marvelously accurate judgment in estimating the play and chances of other people, whether in a golf match, billiard handicap, or croquet tournament. By dint of parading his opinion of such and such a player's superiority with a sufficient degree of youthful assertiveness, he usually succeeded in provoking a wager at liberal odds, and he looked to his weekend winnings to carry him through the financial embarrassments of his midweek existence. The trouble was, as he confided to Clovis Sangrail, that he never had enough available or even prospective cash at his command to enable him to fix the wager at a figure really worth winning.

"Someday," he said, "I shall come across a really safe thing, a bet that simply can't go astray, and then I shall put it up for all I'm worth, or rather for a good deal more than I'm worth if you sold me up to the last button."

"It would be awkward if it didn't happen to come off," said Clovis.

"It would be more than awkward," said Rex. "It would be a tragedy. All the same, it would be extremely amusing to bring it off. Fancy awaking in the morning with about three hundred pounds standing to one's credit. I should go and clear out my hostess's pigeon loft before breakfast out of sheer good-temper."

"Your hostess of the moment mightn't have a pigeon loft," said Clovis.

"I always choose hostesses that have," said Rex. "A pigeon loft is indicative of a careless, extravagant, genial disposition, such as I like to see around me. People who strew corn broadcast for a lot of feathered inanities that just sit about cooing and giving each other the glad eye in a Louis Quatorze manner are pretty certain to do you well."

"Young Strinnit is coming down this afternoon," said Clovis reflectively. "I dare say you won't find it difficult to get him to back himself at billiards. He plays a pretty useful game, but he's not quite as good as he fancies he is."

"I know one member of the party who can walk round him," said Rex softly, an alert look coming into his eyes. "That cadaverous-looking Major who arrived last night. I've seen him play at St. Moritz. If I could get Strinnit to lay odds on himself against the Major, the money would be safe in my pocket. This looks like the good thing I've been watching and praying for."

"Don't be rash," counseled Clovis. "Strinnit may play up to his self-imagined form once in a blue moon."

"I intend to be rash," said Rex quietly, and the look on his face corroborated his words.

"Are you all going to flock to the billiard room?" asked Teresa Thundleford after dinner, with an air of some disapproval and a good deal of annoyance. "I can't see what particular amusement you find in watching two men prodding little ivory balls about on a table."

"Oh, well," said her hostess, "it's a way of passing the time, you know."

"A very poor way, to my mind," said Mrs. Thundleford. "Now I was going to have shown all of you the photographs I took in Venice last summer."

"You showed them to us last night," said Mrs. Cuvering hastily.

"Those were the ones I took in Florence. These are quite a different lot."

"Oh, well, some time tomorrow we can look at them. You can leave them down in the drawing room, and then everyone can have a look."

"I should prefer to show them when you are all gathered together, as I have quite a lot of explanatory remarks to make about Venetian art and architecture, on the same lines as my remarks last night on the Florentine galleries. Also, there are some verses of mine that I should like to read you, on the rebuilding of the Campanile. But, of course, if you all prefer to watch Major Latton and Mr. Strinnit knocking balls about on a table—"

"They are both supposed to be first-rate players," said the hostess.

"I have yet to learn that my verses and my art *causerie* are of second-rate quality," said Mrs. Thundleford with acerbity. "However, as you all seem bent on watching a silly game, there's no more to be said. I shall go upstairs and finish some writing. Later on, perhaps, I will come down and join you."

To one, at least, of the onlookers the game was anything but silly. It was absorbing, exciting, exasperating, nerve stretching, and finally it grew to be tragic. The Major with the St. Moritz reputation was playing a long way below his form, young Strinnit was playing slightly above his and had all the luck of the game as well. From the very start the balls seemed possessed by a demon of contrariness; they trundled about complacently for one player, they would go nowhere for the other.

"A hundred and seventy, seventy-four," sang out the youth who was marking. In a game of two hundred and fifty up, it was an enormous lead to hold. Clovis watched the flush of excitement die away from Dillot's face and a hard, white look take its place.

"How much have you got on?" whispered Clovis. The other whispered the sum through dry, shaking lips. It was more than he or anyone connected with him could pay; he had done what he had said he would do. He had been rash.

"Two hundred and six, ninety-eight."

Rex heard a clock strike ten somewhere in the hall, then another somewhere else, and another, and another; the house seemed full of striking clocks. Then in the distance the stable clock chimed in. In another hour they would all be striking eleven, and he would be listening to them as a disgraced outcast, unable to pay, even in part, the wager he had challenged.

"Two hundred and eighteen, a hundred and three." The game was as good as over. Rex was as good as done for. He longed desperately for the ceiling to fall in, for the house to catch fire, for anything to happen that would put an end to that horrible rolling to and fro of red and white ivory that was jostling him nearer and nearer to his doom.

"Two hundred and twenty-eight, a hundred and seven."

Rex opened his cigarette case; it was empty. That at least gave him a pretext to slip away from the room for the purpose of refilling it; he would spare himself the drawn-out torture of watching that hopeless game played out to the bitter end. He backed away from the circle of absorbed watchers and made his way up a short stairway to a long, silent corridor of bedrooms, each with a guest's name written in a little square on the door. In the hush that reigned in this part of the house, he could still hear the hateful click-click of the balls; if he waited for a few minutes longer, he would hear the little outbreak of clapping and buzz of congratulation that would hail Strinnit's victory. On the alert tension of his nerves there broke another sound, the aggressive, wrath-inducing breathing of one who sleeps in heavy after-dinner slumber. The sound came from a room just at his elbow; the card on the door bore the announcement "Mrs. Thundleford." The door was just slightly ajar; Rex pushed it open an inch or two more and looked in. The august Teresa had fallen asleep over an illustrated guide to Florentine art galleries; at her side, somewhat dangerously near the edge of the table, was a reading lamp. If Fate had been decently kind to him, thought Rex, bitterly, that lamp would have been knocked over by the sleeper and would have given them something to think of besides billiard matches.

There are occasions when one must take one's Fate in one's hands. Rex took the lamp in his.

"Two hundred and thirty-seven, one hundred and fifteen." Strinnit was at the table, and the balls lay in good position for him; he had a choice of two fairly easy shots, a choice which he was never to decide. A sudden hurricane of shrieks and a rush of stumbling feet sent everyone flocking to the door. The Dillot boy crashed into the room, carrying in his arms the vociferous and somewhat disheveled Teresa Thundleford; her clothing was certainly not a mass of flames, as the more excitable members of the party afterward declared, but the edge of her skirt and part of the table cover in which she had been hastily wrapped were alight in a flickering, halfhearted manner. Rex flung his struggling burden onto the billiard table, and for one breathless minute the work of beating out the sparks with rugs and cushions and playing on them with soda-water siphons engrossed the energies of the entire company.

"It was lucky I was passing when it happened," panted Rex. "Someone had better see to the room. I think the carpet is alight."

As a matter of fact the promptitude and energy of the rescuer had prevented any great damage being done, either to the victim or her surroundings. The billiard table had suffered most and had to be laid up for repairs; perhaps it was not the best place to have chosen for the scene of salvage operations; but then, as Clovis remarked, when one is rushing about with a blazing woman in one's arms, one can't stop to think out exactly where one is going to put her.

A BILLIARD LESSON

BY *A. A. Milne*

English author Alan Alexander Milne (1882–1956), a journalist, short story writer, poet, and playwright, is best remembered for creating Christopher Robin and his toy animal friends Winnie-the-Pooh, Piglet, and Eeyore. Books recounting their adventures have been enjoyed by both adults and children for almost seventy years.

"A Billiard Lesson" was written for the British literary humor magazine Punch *in 1911. A few technical notes: The game is English billiards, played with a white cue ball, a spotted cue ball, and a red ball. A player scores various numbers of points by caroming his cue ball off the other two balls (called a cannon), pocketing one of the two object balls (a pot), or by sending the cue ball off an object ball into a pocket (an in-off). A half-butt is a cue eight or nine feet long, used with an equally long bridge, sometimes needed when playing on a table measuring six by twelve feet. (An American pool table is only four and a half by nine.) Screw means draw or backspin.*

I WAS SHOWING Celia a few fancy strokes on the billiard table. The other members of the house party were in the library, learning their parts for some approaching theatricals—that is to say, they were sitting round the fire and saying to each other, "This *is* a rotten play." We had been offered the position of auditors to several of the company, but we were going to see *Parsifal* on the next day, and I was afraid that the constant excitement would be bad for Celia.

"Why don't you ask me to play with you?" she asked. "You never teach me anything."

"There's ingratitude. Why, I gave you your first lesson at golf only last Thursday."

"So you did. I know golf. Now show me billiards."

I looked at my watch.

"We've only twenty minutes. I'll play you thirty up."

"Righto. What do you give me—a ball or a bisque or what?"

"I can't spare you a ball, I'm afraid. I shall want all three when I get going. You may have fifteen to start, and I'll tell you what to do."

"Well, what do I do first?"

"Select a cue."

She went over to the rack and inspected them.

"This seems a nice brown one. Now then, you begin."

"Celia, you've got the half-butt. Put it back and take a younger one."

"I thought it seemed taller than the others." She took another. "How's this? Good. Then off you go."

"Will you be spot or plain?" I said, chalking my cue.

"Does it matter?"

"Not very much. They're both the same shape."

"Then what's the difference?"

"Well, one is more spotted than the other."

"Then I'll be less spotted."

I went to the table.

"I think," I said, "I'll try and screw in off the red." (I did this once by accident and I've always wanted to do it again.) "Or perhaps," I corrected myself, as soon as the ball had left me, "I had better give a safety miss."

I did. My ball avoided the red and came swiftly back into the left-hand bottom pocket.

"That's three to you," I said without enthusiasm.

Celia seemed surprised.

"But I haven't begun yet," she said. "Well, I suppose you know the rules, but it seems funny. What would you like me to do?"

"Well, there isn't much on. You'd better just try and hit the red ball."

"Right." She leaned over the table and took long and careful aim. I held my breath. . . . Still she aimed. . . . Then, keeping her chin on the cue, she slowly turned her head and looked up at me with a thoughtful expression.

"Oughtn't there to be three balls on the table?" she said, wrinkling her forehead.

"No," I answered shortly.

"But why not?"

"Because I went down by mistake."

"But you said that when you got going, you wanted— I can't argue bending down like this." She raised herself slowly. "You said— Oh, all right, I expect you know. Anyhow, I *have* scored some already, haven't I?"

"Yes. You're eighteen to my nothing."

"Yes. Well, now I shall have to aim all over again." She bent slowly over her cue. "Does it matter where I hit the red?"

"Not much. As long as you hit it on the red part."

She hit it hard on the side, and both balls came into balk.

"Too good," I said.

"Does either of us get anything for it?"

"No." The red and the white were close together, and I went up the table and down again on the off chance of a cannon. I misjudged it, however.

"That's three to you," I said stiffly, as I took my ball out of the right-hand bottom pocket. "Twenty-one to nothing."

"Funny how I'm doing all the scoring," said Celia meditatively. "And I've practically never played before. I shall hit the red hard now and see what happens to it."

She hit, and the red coursed madly about the table, coming to rest near the top right-hand pocket and close to the cushion. With a forcing shot I could get in.

"This will want a lot of chalk," I said pleasantly to Celia, and gave it plenty. Then I let fly. . . .

"Why did that want a lot of chalk?" said Celia with interest.

I went to the fireplace and picked my ball out of the fender.

"That's three to you," I said coldly. "Twenty-four to nothing."

"Am I winning?"

"You're leading," I explained. "Only, you see, I may make a twenty at any moment."

"Oh!" She thought this over. "Well, I may make my three at any moment."

She chalked her cue and went over to her ball.

"What shall I do?"

"Just touch the red on the right-hand side," I said, "and you'll go into the pocket."

"The *right*-hand side? Do you mean *my* right-hand side, or the ball's?"

"The right-hand side of the ball, of course; that is to say, the side opposite your right hand."

"But its right-hand side is opposite my *left* hand, if the ball is facing this way."

"Take it," I said wearily, "that the ball has its back to you."

"How rude of it," said Celia, and hit it on the left-hand side and sank it. "Was that what you mean?"

"Well . . . it's another way of doing it."

"I thought it was. What do I give you for that?"

"You get three."

"Oh, I thought the other person always got the marks. I know the last three times—"

"Go on," I said freezingly. "You have another turn."

"Oh, is it like rounders?"

"Something. Go on, there's a dear. It's getting late."

She went and left the red over the middle pocket.

"Aha!" I said. I found a nice place in the "D" for my ball. "Now then. This is the Grey stroke, you know."

I suppose I was nervous. Anyhow, I just nicked the red ball gently on the wrong side and left it hanging over the pocket. The white traveled slowly up the table.

"Why is that called the gray stroke?" asked Celia with great interest.

"Because once, when Sir Edward Grey was playing the German ambassador— But it's rather a long story. I'll tell you another time."

"Oh! Well, anyhow, did the German ambassador get anything for it?"

"No."

"Then I suppose I don't. Bother."

"But you've only got to knock the red in for the game."

"Oh! . . . There, what's that?"

"That's a miscue. I get one."

"Oh! . . . Oh well," she added magnanimously, "I'm glad you've started scoring. It will make it more interesting for you."

There was just room to creep in off the red, leaving it still over the pocket. With Celia's ball nicely over the other pocket, there was a chance of my twenty break. "Let's see," I said, "how many do I want?"

"Twenty-nine," replied Celia.

"Ah," I said . . . and I crept in.

"That's three to you," I said icily. "Game."

....

A GAME
OF BILLIARDS

BY *Thornton C. McCune*

*Seventy years ago, Thornton C. McCune was either a student or a
member of the faculty at the University of Illinois. Beyond that, I
know nothing about him. The yarn that follows appeared in* The
Best College Short Stories, 1924–1925, *edited by Henry T.
Schnittkind, Ph.D. It's a good story for a student, not a great story
for a professor. I'll say one thing for it: the ending is a surprise.*

*In his one-sentence preface, Dr. Schnittkind wrote: "The Span-
iard tried to cheat Peter Kroll, the sailor, but Kroll's vengeance
was swift—and satisfying."*

*There is not, by the way, a town on the coast of South America
named Alf Said.*

AT THE CLUB, the members lay sprawled about drowsily
enjoying the siesta. The sun, white hot, cast shadows as black as a bit
of midnight lost by day. A peon trotted by, bound on an urgent
mission. As he passed the Club piazza he squinted at the men who
breathed heavily and sweated as they slept.

From the rear of the building came the gentle clink of silver and
the tinkle of glassware. A dishwasher laughed a high-pitched flare. A
dog, frightened by a nightmare, jumped to his feet and, only half
awake, bounded clumsily into a stand loaded with drinks. As it
toppled to the floor, the siphon bottle which had been resting on it

exploded with a sharp report. Men started from their sleep, grumbled, awoke. One looked at his watch.

"Hey, Joe," he called, "time to mosey along." Joe yawned and stretched with great earnestness and seeming enjoyment. "Right," he mumbled. "Wake Bill and let's go."

The native, who had paused for a tropical instant, passed on.

The Club, let it be said, was the rendezvous of any English-speaking gentlemen in the seaport town of Alf Said, somewhere along the South American coast. The term gentlemen is used advisedly and with the connotation implied in the constitution of the organization. Its insertion had a most charming way of excluding remittance men who lacked their remittance, drifters, and other undesirables.

Juan de Grijalva, with the face of a poker player, watched the cue ball as it ricocheted across the baize cloth to score the point to win. The tense group about the table relaxed—the stakes were high—and looked at the loser. Don Grijalva sucked softly at the split between his two front teeth.

"Perhaps the Señor would like to practice a little more so that someday he may be able to give Don Juan de Grijalva a bit more interesting game, no?" It was the tone as much as the words as he uttered them that rankled.

Don Grijalva, whom no one liked and about whom no one seemed to know anything, except that he was often seen in the company of tough denizens of the waterfront, was the frequent guest of Don Feliz, editor of the daily paper. Many members considered the latter the black sheep of the organization and thought less, if possible, of his friend.

Peter Kroll, hard-bitten but just mate of the Norwegian trader *Ulric Bendel,* out of most any port, half a smile tracing his mouth, was slow to reply. Don Grijalva, misinterpreting the situation and as ever the taunter, continued.

"You"—and his eyes swept briefly the circle of onlookers which had seemingly grown smaller—"you foreigners think always that you are so good." His voice pitched low, and withal insinuating, bit deep. "I think that you are all bluff. As for me, I have a son scarce nine, who is in a good way to being better at the billiard table than any of you. Phah!" Don Grijalva carefully spit. "I will gladly play any of you for any stake you will name." The circle had grown very small. The tobacco-smoke-filled room became conscious of itself. A big blue-bottle fly droned his way through the smoke and settled impudently at rest on a billiard ball.

"No-o-o, now, what do you think o' that?" Big Kroll's voice, seemingly without heat, broke the silence. So he wasn't going to take it lying down after all! Not strange, if you knew the man. The circle quite possibly grew less tense. "That last remark o' yours is the only thing you've said worth mentioning. Up my way," he continued, "if there is anything we hate it's a four-flusher." He paused as though considering. "Just to see if you have any guts, you won the last game remember, I'll play you the best two out of three for stakes unnamed. Are you on?" There had been a steely quality in his voice. Don Feliz, at Grijalva's shoulder, whispered something.

"Bravo!" exclaimed Don Juan after a moment, his face wreathing in an enigmatical smile. "You speak of—intestines—what say you to putting the old adage 'An eye for an eye' to some use. I shall pit my right eye against yours!"

"The bloody pig!" "Be careful!" "Just like 'em!" "You don't have to take *that* up!" broke from the bystanders.

Don Feliz looked at Don Grijalva. The two smiled. "Ah! Don Kroll is not now so ready with his boasts—he is, what you call it, faint of heart, no?" said Don Grijalva to Don Feliz.

Kroll's eyes had taken on a metallic glint, reminiscent of the broken ice sheets of his home waters. His face, thrown into sharp contrast by the brilliant glare above the table, looked strangely craggy. There was no hesitancy on his part. "You're on," he snapped. "Please give us room, gentlemen."

The spectators, momentarily struck speechless by his ready acceptance of the deadly wager, found seats. Someone opened a window, the tobacco smoke whirled out as if eager to be gone. A smallish man fortified himself with a gin rickey from the bar.

KROLL IN THE OPENING GAME seemed more interested in watching Don Grijalva than in his own playing. The latter weighed his chances quickly, made his choice, and played with the assurance of a veteran. Kroll, seemingly deaf to the sallies Don Grijalva made when it was his turn to shoot, hurried not but performed with a machinelike precision. Carefully he chalked his cue, carefully he played. Don Grijalva watched and taunted. "The Señor appears afraid. It is nothing, an eye! Look," as his turn came he shot seemingly indifferent, yet confident of the result, "I play as though the stakes were but a very small coin! Fear, let me warn you, is bad for one's eye— Ha! Ha!" He laughed loudly at his own sally, to be echoed by Don Feliz alone. Kroll played on. The game was close and almost over. Grijalva dubbed an easy point, cursed softly, glanced at the markers above him, and shrugged his shoulders. Kroll powdered his sticky hands, carefully chalked his cue, and ran out the string.

THE SECOND GAME started off in deadly earnest. Don Grijalva discarded his bantering air, weighed his shots, and played consistently to a winning score. Kroll lost with the same seeming indifference that he had won the preceding line. Someone offered him a drink. He refused it with a shake of the head. The strain was by this time telling on the tense audience, if not on the players. Don Grijalva had resumed his nonchalant air; he threw bits of humor at those who watched, ordered cigars all around and a drink of whiskey for himself.

"Remember," he addressed Kroll in a loud voice so that all might hear and none have to ask his neighbor what was said, "remember every shot, every miss—pardon me-e-e, the first miss, will in all probability mean the loss of that eye you seem to hold so dearly!" The spectators looked to Kroll to see what effect Don Grijalva had made by the taunt. Kroll merely chalked his cue and played as before, coolly, carefully, and to good effect. Don Grijalva watched. His smile faded. Surreptitiously he loosened his collar. When his turn came he nursed the balls carefully. Finally he missed but stood two to the good. "That," he threatened, "is as it shall be all through the game. It will delight me—"

Was the fool possessed? Don Grijalva's eyes became fixed on the balls as they rebounded and clicked, rebounded and clicked. Finally, and the Don breathed a sigh of relief, Kroll missed, three short of the game. Don Grijalva collected himself.

"You would frighten me," he blustered. "It was luck, nothing else. Watch," he goaded, "and you will see how easily an eye can be removed." He glanced over the throng, but no friendly look other than Don Feliz's could he find. He seemed about to address Kroll again but, thinking perhaps of the antagonistic eyes, thought better of it and started to play. Between each shot he rested, chalked his cue mechanically, and carefully weighed the possibilities on the table. Closer and closer he crept to the score marked up by Kroll—equaled it, passed it by one—and missed. Kroll played out with the same impassiveness that had marked his entire game.

"I believe that that is all," he remarked as he straightened up and started to put on the blouse that he had removed while playing. "In the future, it might be well to remember that a civil tongue is an almost sure way of keeping out of trouble. As for your eye, I do not want it. If it were a diamond, I wouldn't give it to a whore as a keepsake! Now get the hell out of here." The last said with the only fleck of anger that he had shown.

The spectators were going to have their innings, no doubt about that. They crowded about Peter Kroll. "You don't mean to say you're going to let him off?" "The dirty scum!" "He'd a' taken your eye willing enough!" "It'll serve him right. Get a doctor!" "Get Doc Bennett." The tumult of voices rose. Mob spirit had seized the crowd. What they would have done in a saner mood was forgotten. Don Grijalva was bound and thrown on a table. Ready belts bound his hands and feet, a handkerchief was thrust into his mouth. He made no resistance.

As the crowd waited for Doctor Bennett, an English surgeon with a practice in the foreign quarter, it waxed yet more incensed. Possibly ten minutes passed before the doctor arrived. He was quickly apprised of the facts. "Ah! Gentlemen." He mounted a chair. "I fear that you have been hoaxed. Watch!" He hopped down and withdrew a pair of forceps from his case. "It is so easy, thus—" He opened Don Grijalva's right eyelid with his fingertips, made a quick motion, and held up, between the points of the forceps—a glass eye.

A stunning silence followed this turn of affairs. Don Grijalva's breath came in little wheezy jerks. He wriggled, he squirmed, had the grace to crimson. From the rear of the crowd Kroll plowed his way through to the table. Unknowingly, men gave him room. As he stood there, better than six feet tall and nearly half as wide across the shoulders, the quick, angry blood showing in his face, his strong neck corded with the tenseness of his clamped jaws, he was not a pretty sight to look at, at least so must have thought Don Grijalva as he lay flat on his back, the blinding lights in his . . . eye.

Doctor Bennett broke the silence. "So, shall I put his eye back?"

Kroll nodded and asked in a voice well under an imposed control, "Would he," indicating Don Grijalva with a jerk of his head, "be able to play, say, one more game of billiards?"

Doctor Bennett snapped his case of instruments shut. "I see no reason why not, unless perhaps," he looked at Kroll's face and then into Grijalva's sullen one, "unless he is scared into a blue funk."

Peter Kroll stepped to where Don Juan de Grijalva lay, loosened his hands and feet, jerked him to a sitting posture by the lapel of his coat, and untied the gag. The Don appeared to see nothing ludicrous in his position on the table. In fact he seemed very interested in what Kroll was about to say. Peter Kroll, mate of the trader *Ulric Bendel,* hardest of a hard-bitten crew, possibly in sarcasm, closed his left eye and with his right stared into the one good one Grijalva possessed.

"You," he said, and though his voice was pitched low it carried into the farthest corner of the room, "you, who are but a bag of wind, a liar, and a cheat, I ought to kill. For the sake of the mother that bore you, I'll be easy. The terms—I make them this time, my friend. Tomorrow night we play another game of billiards. One game. That my friend, should steady your nerves. I will tell you the stake before we play." He bowed to the members. "Coming my way, Doctor?" The two left the room in a hubbub.

By the following evening there was not a person in the city unaware of the episode of the night before. Opinion favored Kroll. Conjecture as to what stake he would name was heard on all sides. As for Don Grijalva, he had spent the morning as well as the afternoon sopping up strong drink. Between glasses he took great pains to tell how unafraid he was, what he would do to Kroll under his (Kroll's) own terms, how little the whole matter worried *him*—Don Juan de Grijalva. Toward the evening meal hour he had begun to believe it himself. At seven he retired to his rooms and carefully dressed for the occasion.

Peter Kroll had been aboard all day as his ship lay at the quay, loading for its homeward trip. It seemed to the men that he drove them harder even than usual. At seven, he too, all but the finishing touches done, turned the work over to the second mate and prepared himself for shore.

Captain Apple, Maine coast born and bred, resplendent in a uniform reserved for gala occasions, met Peter as he was about to step over the side. "Any particular friends up there," he asked, with a jerk of his thumb toward shore and the Club. A negative shake of the head. "Guess I'd better go along then." The two set off together in the tender alongside.

IN THE BILLIARD ROOM of the Club, already full to the doors, Don Juan de Grijalva was holding forth. He greeted Kroll's appearance with a heavy brand of humor. "What are the stakes, friend Peter? Name them. We want to hear." In this last statement he was correct. Not a sound broke the stillness. Necks craned, ears strained to catch Kroll's voice, low as usual. "Captain Apple will speak for me." Peter removed his blouse of white, removed his seaman's hat, carefully rolled his sleeves above his bulging forearms, and selected a cue from the racks along the wall as Captain Apple mounted a chair and stated the terms.

"It is the wish of my first mate, Peter Kroll, that the stake for this game be a"—he paused to take advantage of the dramatic situation; he looked at Grijalva, who for once was quiet, to finally continue— "handshake, such as sailors give, strong, stout, and sturdy." He got down amid a flurry of protest. "Too easy!" "Give the ——— what he deserves!" "Make him sweat!"

The game was on. The room grew quiet, except for questioning whisperings.

As the play progressed, it was plain that too much drink had spoiled Grijalva's game. He muffed easy shots. He grew abusive to the balls, found fault with the table, changed cues frequently. Peter Kroll played well. Not a word did he speak but once, and then it was a word of caution. "Better save your wind for the game, Don Grijalva, or you may find yourself becalmed." His words were wasted.

It soon became evident that Captain Apple's first mate would come off with flying colors. Impatience grew, for all were anxious for the climax of the evening, the settlement of the stake. There must be a catch in it somewhere, so they told each other.

The game was done. Kroll had won easily in a few minutes.

He walked over to Don Grijalva and offered his hand. For an instant the loser paused, then he extended his own hand. It was over—men started to get up. Kroll had been too lenient, so they said.

Suddenly a cue dropping to the floor startled all. Eyes pivoted as one to the spot. Peter Kroll held Don Grijalva's hand in his. A set smile was on Kroll's face, the smile of one who saw pain and enjoyed the seeing of it. Don Grijalva's body was contorted with agony. The muscles in Peter's forearm bulged a bit, a very little bit, the tendons in his wrist stood out slightly; the Don's hand seemed to melt away, as the great fist of Kroll, toughened by hard work, crunched it within its grasp.

Don Juan de Grijalva's face lost all shape but that of outline. Where flesh and feature had been writhed seething muscle. A low groan escaped him, he sank to his knees, his eyes wide, staring, the glass one at a grotesque angle.

Kroll released his grip. The bloody and smeared pulp that had once been a hand dropped to the side of Don Juan de Grijalva as he lay slumped on the floor.

Doctor Bennett stepped forward and opened his surgical case.

FORTY YEARS
OF BILLIARDS

BY *Stephen Leacock*

In a 1911 book called Nonsense Novels *is one of the finest sentences in the English language: "Lord Ronald said nothing; he flung himself from the room, flung himself on his horse, and rode madly off in all directions." The author was Stephen Leacock (1869–1944), a prolific producer of humorous stories and essays and a professor of political science at McGill University.*

Leacock was an avid player of English billiards. In 1911, he and a former student began a game to 20,000 points, allowing twenty years for completion. When Leacock died thirty-three years later, he was leading 18,975 to 16,793.

The story presented here, or at least the title, may have been prompted by a book published four years earlier, Willie Hoppe's Thirty Years of Billiards.

WHILE PLAYING English billiards the other night with my friend Captain R., it suddenly occurred to me that that very night was the anniversary of the first game I ever played and that I had now been playing billiards for no less than forty years.

My reflections for the moment were cut short by Captain R. coming to the end of his break—he had made three and a half—so that it was my turn to play.

But in the pauses of our play it kept coming into my mind that I had now been for forty years a billiard player. And I fell into thinking that there must be a good deal that a player of my experience could tell to youngsters at the game.

For the rest, the moment was hardly suited to reflection, inasmuch as our game had reached a point of interest that demanded an absorbed attention. We were playing very close together, our scores both moved up from sixty to seventy in the last half hour by quiet, steady play.

I had reached seventy first, but my adversary, Captain R., by a brilliant rush of two, in which he drove the white ball before him into the corner pocket, had closed in on my heels. As there was still three hours to play before the club closed (at one in the morning), there was every prospect that we should finish our game the same evening.

The game indeed had settled down into a matter of rival tactics. For my own part, alarmed at the rapid advance of my opponent from sixty to seventy within a single half hour, I was trying as far as possible to keep my ball away from Captain R., hiding it well under the cushions, while Captain R. in his turn pursued the opposite policy of attempting such a rush at my balls as to drive it off the cloth, his object being to smash the balls together in a general collision even at the risk of straining the legs of the table.

But perhaps if I wish to convey my reflections at the time and to make them useful even to readers who do not know the game of billiards, I must give a word or two of general explanation.

The game of English billiards is played on a table twelve feet by six, with three balls—one red and two white. Each of the two players has a white ball, which he hits with his cue, his aim being to make it strike or impinge on one of the other balls either red or white.

An outsider would here at once exclaim: "What? Can you so hit a ball as to make it move forward and strike another? Is such a thing possible?" I would answer: "Yes, certainly." I do not claim to be a first-class player—I mean in any absolute sense—yet I suppose I could undertake to make this stroke at least every other time.

That, however, is not all. The ball after hitting the other must first go farther on and strike the third ball; or it must drive one of the balls, either the red or the white (good players don't care which) into one of the pockets, which lie at the corners and in the sides of the tables; or else it must itself roll on from the ball it strikes and fall into a pocket.

Scores from the red ball count three, and the others two, the points adding up to one hundred, which is the game. Good players think nothing of reaching the hundred in a single evening, or at any rate quite early in the evening following.

The outline of the game is simple. But when one turns to the question of advice as to the movement, strategy, speed, etc., one feels bewildered. It is difficult to say anything to the beginner without warning him that only long and arduous practice can lead to ultimate success.

Let me talk first of that which may be described as strategy, by which I mean the ability to seize opportunity and make use of it. The veteran player before making his shot takes a rapid survey of the entire position. His experienced eye tells him at once in which direction lies the best chance of success.

I can illustrate what I mean by describing an exciting episode in the earlier part of the game with Captain R. of which I am speaking.

It was my time to shoot. The balls were so situated that the red was well out in the table within no great distance from the side pocket on the right. I saw at once that the thing to do was to drive it into the pocket. I tried but failed. My own ball, then drifting near to the red ball, offered to Captain R., as, of course, he saw it at once, a direct carom shot. He didn't get it. The red and white, however, coming to rest nearly in a line, offered me a pretty example of what we call a follow shot. I didn't make it.

Captain R., seeing that my ball had stopped close to the cushion, at once seized the opportunity for the very showy but gentle shot called a cushion carom. He didn't do it. But in failing he unfortunately left his own ball in such a position as to offer me a beautiful half-ball shot into the end pocket.

It is a shot regarded by all old hands as the key shot of the game: once get it nicely and the object ball may return to its position and the score continue indefinitely. I failed to get it.

By ill luck I left my own ball sitting on the very edge of the pocket, not more than half an inch from the edge. It was in vain for me to hope that the situation would escape my opponent's eye. Captain R. saw at once the line of play suggested by the position of the ball. But he was too experienced a hand to hurry or bungle the shot. He first walked around the table and with his eye measured the distance from the ball to the edge of the pocket; he then chalked his cue, removed his waistcoat and hung it on the hook, and, with one splendid drive at the white ball, sank it to the very bottom of the pocket.

In spite of my mortification I could not help congratulating my adversary, not merely on the stroke itself, which was perfect, but on the strategic insight into the game that led him at once to a shot that others might have passed by.

I have mentioned, in speaking of this shot, the question of speed. I can imagine a junior player asking me, "What about speed? How can you calculate the speed you put on your ball?" To which I can only give the rather mysterious answer, "I don't." What I mean is that a player of experience regulates speed, as it were, automatically and without calculation. I am afraid that the only advice I can give to the beginner on this point is practice, practice, and practice. If I were to try to lay down a rule, I might do more harm than good.

But perhaps one might without risk suggest a few general hints on speed that will be of use to the beginner. In the first place, each player will tend to have his own style and to shoot at a characteristic speed that comes natural to him. Thus Captain R., being French, plays with the characteristic élan and dash of his race and shoots at about one hundred to one hundred fifty miles an hour. He is thus able to lift or drive his ball clean off the table, and on one occasion, I remember, he even drove it out of the open window of the club.

The beginner might ask, "Why do this? What object is there in driving a ball off the table?" The answer is quite simple. The ball may not go off the table, and suppose that with this high speed by good luck it keeps on the table, then it is bound to make a series of concussions right and left, probably setting all three balls in rapid motion. When the table is quiet again Captain R. need only visit all the pockets in turn to be sure of finding something to his score.

But as against this dashing hazardous type of play, you may set, if you like, the opposite form, the quiet, steady bulldog game to which those of us who are British naturally incline. Here the speed is reduced to almost zero; the ball, however, moves steadily but irresistibly forward. Nearer and nearer it comes to the object ball. The slow speed guarantees the deadly accuracy of the shot. It moves nearer and nearer over the cloth.

Moving the length of the table (twelve feet) in six seconds, it is only traveling at the rate of one kilometer, five-eighths of a mile, per hour. But its approach, if sufficiently sustained, is absolutely certain. It gets nearer to its goal with every fraction of a second. Unfortunately it doesn't always get there. But the bulldog player has at least one consolation that he was only prevented from scoring by the fact that his ball stopped.

I am frequently asked—I suppose that in these random notes, the order of the discussion doesn't matter—what is the proper costume to put on for billiards. To which I reply that it is not a question of what costume to put on, but how much to take off.

All players find that it is convenient to take off the coat; without that the movement of the garment itself against the body disturbs the delicacy of the aim. But when the coat is gone, the waistcoat begins to give a similar sense of awkwardness and spoils many and many a good shot. Again and again I have missed very simple shots when I was sure that the miss was due entirely to my waistcoat. Off with it. Without it the player is lighter, nimbler, easier in hand and eye.

The braces should go next. At any critical period of a good game the player will feel that he must discard of his braces. If he is wise, he will discard also his collar and necktie. Many a good shot, such as those in which the player shoots lying upon the table, is hopelessly disturbed by the movement of his collar against his ears.

It is not customary, in the older clubs, to remove more than this. But players of experience often feel that they could play with greater accuracy and finesse if they were allowed to strip to the waist and have their body well oiled between shots.

I suppose that if I were to keep on yarning like this, some young aspirant to billiard honors would start to ask me about fancy shots and how to do them. For instance, the shot called the massé shot is one that always attracts the beginner, but which only the player of long experience need hope to achieve.

In this shot the ball to be hit with the cue is almost touching another ball. The player then, by holding his cue almost vertically in the air, hits downward with such force as to cut a piece out of the cloth of the table.

It is a neat and effective shot, not really as difficult as it looks, but less suited for performance on a public table than for exhibiting to a group of guests on a private table in the host's house.

But I fear that my very love of the game has protracted my remarks beyond any reasonable limit. They represent about the current of my thoughts during the course of the game on my anniversary evening.

It so happened that just when I had reached the point here indicated in my reflections, Captain R. was called from the billiard room of the club to speak on the telephone. The score stood at ninety-six all.

In an instant I realized my opportunity. Every player knows that it is possible to score better, faster, and with greater certainty when the other man is at the telephone than at any other time. I at once requested that the club attendant who was making the score go and fetch me a cigar.

When he returned along with Captain R. I was fortunate enough to be able to tell them that I had made four and won the game. I have not played billiards for forty years quite for nothing.

1932

....

RED BALL

BY *L. A. G. Strong*

*Suppose a woman loved two men and was loved by them in return.
Suppose further that a choice had to be made. What better way to
make it than by a game of billiards on the village table? With the
blessing of the parson, of course. Read all about it . . . and learn
along the way how the red ball got chipped.*

*The story first appeared in a British magazine in 1932 and was
included in a collection called* Don Juan and the Wheelbarrow,
*by L. A. G. Strong (1896–1958), published by Alfred Knopf in
1933. The author was an English novelist, short story writer, poet,
and critic.*

M R. S P A D D A C O T T gloomily eyed the leave, bent down,
straightened up again, grunted, shifted his position, and finally let
drive with a force which only the very experienced, or the very inexperienced, would dare apply upon the village table. His ball, ca-
reering madly round, missed an impossible cannon by at least two
feet. I got ready to follow.

" 'Old 'ard," he cautioned me, with uplifted hand, still anxiously
watching the balls. "Let 'em develop. Let 'em develop."

And, sure enough, his ball, approaching a corner with the last of
its momentum, fell into the well-worn track and dropped exhausted
into the pocket.

"Aaaah!" exclaimed the veteran, with satisfaction. "A development."

And he proceeded to score seven more points.

I offered no comment. "Developments" were a legitimate part of the game of billiards as played upon the village table. The entire neighborhood would have been not so much indignant as bewildered, had any outsider poured scorn upon such a method of remaining in play. When you could see no direct shot, you hit out, hoping to bring one of the balls near one or other of the two top pockets. If not traveling too fast, it might accede to a slight gradient and roll in. Points thus gained Mr. Spaddacott had always called developments, and the name stuck. There was much to be said for his view, for, after all, the law of gravity worked both ways, and many a promising break was cut short by the premature and unsought disappearance of an opponent's ball. On Mr. Spaddacott's table, as on many golf courses, local knowledge was exceedingly valuable. It was an accepted law, in all intervillage contests, that the home team won.

My knowledge of the table at no time equaled Mr. Spaddacott's. Besides, I had not played upon it for eighteen months, during which time certain characteristics had become accentuated, and the dead cushion (a comparative title) had been renewed. Hence I could make no answer to the sparkling fourteen amassed by my adversary. Recollections of the right-hand top pocket stood me in good stead for three long losers; but it was no good. Mr. Spaddacott, with a series of developments which for once deserved the word sensational, rattled out a winner by no less than thirty-seven points.

"You'm short o' practice," he observed.

"Yes," I replied. "But I haven't had to go and fetch up the ball from below, anyway."

"Ah!" He sucked his teeth. "Very impetuous you used to be. Very 'eadstrong with the cue."

Mr. Spaddacott's table, center and chief ornament of the village club, was situated in a loft above a disused stable. One gained access to the loft by a ladder, and the floor was very uneven. It was easy, for a number of reasons, to knock the ball off the table. Expert players, trying to show off; overzealous youths, in quest of developments; persons failing to notice that one of the cushions suffered in places from a depressed lip; purists who stood the red ball in the hole it had worn over the spot, instead of on the nearest suitable edge of sound cloth: all such were liable to send one of the balls shooting off on the floor, whence, unless smartly retrieved, it headed straight for the opening and fell into the stable below, necessitating an adjournment, lantern in hand, before the game could be resumed. For this reason, there was always a coating of straw laid all about the foot of the ladder to protect the balls from injury.

I picked up the balls and turned them over in my hand.

"Several of these marks must be due to me," I said. "Hullo! That's a good chip out of the red ball. That's since my day?"

Mr. Spaddacott adjusted his glasses, and peered.

"No," he said. "Done years back, that was."

"Was it? I don't remember noticing it before."

" 'Twas so, all same."

"Must have been at the very start, before you had the straw down."

"No. No. 'Twasn't done in the stable at all."

He paused and rubbed his nose.

" 'Twas against the corner of the fireplace over yonder, that was done," he said.

"How on earth! The man must have hit like a bull. It's yards away."

"Come on along in here. I see the missus has left some tea for us: come in along, and I'll tell 'ee the pedigree of it."

He led the way into his little inner room and there, while we took tea, recited the following history:

THERE'S BEEN MANY strange happenings have took place on this here table, from the match against Bittacombe when the last pair in the decidin' game had only one point to go, and each went to table seven times without scorin', till our chap hits the ball off the table and gives away the game, to the evenin' when Harry Tozer made a break of eighty-one and another of seventy-eight same time his wife was home dyin', and he wouldn't leave the table, not for all the messages that came, till he'd runned out a winner, and her'd runned out to a better land, poor soul, and a happy release 'twas from the cold-blidded, callous, limpin' toad—that I should so miscall a fellow creature.

"Get out," he says, to each one that come with a message. "I haven't been in form like this, not for a year and more. Her'll bide till I come," he calls after the last messenger. There's a thing, now. A poor woman lyin' 'pon her deathbed, callin' out for her man, and he playin' billiards. Well. There 'twas. A happy release.

But, as I was sayin', not even that there wasn't the strangest thing us have witnessed 'pon this here table. Matter of eight year ago there was livin' up top the road by the blacksmith's a girl by the name of Gertie Exworthy. Big girl she was, big and well carryin', with a freckledly nose and a lot of fair hair. She wasn't what you might call a beauty, but—there, well, you know what I mean. There was more than one what it come into his head how 'twould feel to put a arm round her waist and so beside her of a nice evenin' in the rise of the year and, of they what thought so much, there was two in whose 'eads the idea sticked for a long time. Harry Munday, a dark, good-lookin' sort of a chap, summat wild, but very generous 'earted, was one. Samuel Toop, a bit more steady-goin' like, a good, decent, sizable young fella, was another. Well, 'twas the old, old story over again, like. Each of 'em was after her: one offered the better promise of matrimony, with his chapel-goin' and his steady ways—not that he was one of these here dull psalm-singin', mingy sort, mind 'ee; and t'other offered more excitement. Well, Gertie Exworthy, her didn't know which to favor: so her favored the both. Her wouldn' commit herself to no promise and her wouldn' say her liked one no better than the other: so there 'twas. Gertie wasn't a calculating one, and her didn' play off Harry against Sam, nor yet Sam against Harry. Her just couldn' rightly decide. A warm, affectionate sort of a girl, and never one to make a move till her was prodded.

Well, before long, the rivalry of these two for Gertie Exworthy become the talk of the neighborhood. First her was out with one, then with t'other. Samuel bein' a baker, and Harry workin' for Mr. Sanders up to the Gables, they was off different times: so 'twas boxin' Cox, like, as the sayin' is, for a while. But soon Gertie Exworthy took a situation with Mrs. Legassick—you remember she? Dead this four year—and didn't have but the one evenin' out a week. That caused so much trouble her couldn't keep the situation but five weeks, and her father up and spoke his mind very bitter on the subjick.

"Well," says Harry, doggedlike, when Mr. Exworthy do bring the matter home to en in here one evenin'. "Let her choose," he says, "and us won't have no more foolishness."

This here was Mr. Exworthy's own private, personal opinion, and

many a blawin' up he'd gived the girl, same purpose: but it didn'
please him none the better to hear it from Harry.

"Why *should* her choose," he said. "Why *should* her? If you two
would only leave the poor maid bide, 'stead of turrifyin' her like this
here, us could have some peace."

"Oh, come, come," says old George Smith. "Come, come," he
says. "That bain't reasonable. 'Tis only in nature for the boys to be
after the maid," he says, "and many a man would be only too pleased
if 'twas his maid they was after."

There was a laugh at this here, and Nick Screech what had got five
daughters, all so plain as potato peelin's, made wise his bootlace had
come undoed.

Mr. Exworthy went to see Sam after that, but Sam didn' fall in
with his views no better. Sam was on the high tide of his righteous
passions, and wouldn' agree to nothin'. Savin' only one thing, that
is—how 'twas ridicklus for Harry to be after the maid so well as
himself.

So affairs dragged on, and Gertie still doed her best to run in
double harness, like. Mind, her wasn't in no way flirty-gibbet. Her
liked the both of 'em and jus' couldn' make up her mind to give up
one of 'em for t'other. When it come to her walkin' down to church
Sunday mornin', with one on each side of her, Harry so black as pitch
and Sam like a stuffed bullick—well, then, folks reckoned 'twas a
open scandal, and somethin' should be done to put a end to it.
"Somethin' should be done," they kep' sayin'. "Somethin' should
be done." But when it come to sayin' what the somethin' was, their
tongues sticked back in their heads.

"I moves," says old George Smith at last, "I moves us consults
Reverend Le Vernon Battishill.

There was a bit of a silence, for Reverend Le Vernon, as you well
know, wasn't our parson but incumbent on Stoke Dendle. Still, he
was famed in all parts as a man of high resource: and no one wouldn't
never have thought of consulting Reverend Pethybridge 'pon so
much as settin' a mousetrap. If he hadn't took notice of the trio, all
three together in the front pew, right under his nose, when he got
up to preach, he wouldn't be like to have noticed 'em elsewhere. All
same, there was some to argy the point, as there always will be when
several be congregated together in one place.

"Get out," says George to 'em. "Disloyalty my—," he says. "You know very well us have been over to consult Reverend Battishill half a dozen times," he says, "and with the full approval of Reverend Pethybridge," he says. "So why not now?" he says.

Wherefore, presently, after a little more tell, 'twas carried unanimous by all to consult Reverend Le Vernon Battishill 'pon how to make a girl decide which of two chaps her didn' want to lose. Next, they had to elect a deppitation, to go over and acquaint Reverend Battishill with the point at issue: and, what with one thing and another, 'twas a fortnight past before the deppitation could all be assembled together to keep the appointment what the Reverend Battishill had been able to make. That's the first and only point about deppitation and suchlike in these parts—to choose chaps what can all get off to do their deppitising same time and 'tis the last what ever occurs to their 'eads. Be as 'twill, deppitation consulted Reverend Le Vernon Battishill in doo form. Spokesman, Joe Frapwell, had made up a fine speech: but before he'd been goin' a minute Reverend Battishill asked en two questions and got in possession of the whole matter.

"Well," he says. "What do you want me to do?"

"Ack," says Joe, very dramatic-like.

"What?" says Reverend.

"Ack. Take action, like," says Joe.

"I see," says Reverend. "Well," he says, "I'll see the girl, and then I'll see the two men. That's all I can promise."

He gave 'em a glass of cider all round, same as he always do, and had 'em outside the house in ten minutes; but, such is the high faith in us—they all had in the Reverend Le Vernon Battishill, they all looked to one another in relief, like, and felt, "Now 'tis sure to be all right."

Well, Reverend Battishill seen Gertie Exworthy and he couldn' get nothing out of she: though her did allow, after 'twas all over, that he'd put the most searchin' questions to her 'bout which of the two her'd prefer. Come to blush, he did, speakin' of it. But he couldn' get no decision out of 'er; so he send for Harry and Sam.

They came all right, but not wi' too good a grace, particular on Harry's part. 'Twasn't none of their choosin' to consult Reverend Battishill.

"Now, you two," he says, "the maid can't choose, and I'm bound to say I don't see why her should: but your neighbors are all worried about it, and I daresay the whole business has put you in a very awkward position."

"That's right," says Sam, lookin' severe at Harry.

"Oh," says Harry, "you needn't pull your face across at me. I know you reckon you're the only one in it," he says, "and I know you reckon your money and your godly ways be goin' to prevail. But—"

"Hush, now," says Reverend Battishill. "There's no call to argue. Do you want the matter settled?" he asks Sam.

"Yes," says Sam.

"And you, Munday?"

"Yes. One way or the other."

"Very well, then. How shall us decide?" He put his hand in his pocket. "Shall us toss for it?"

"Reverend!" exclaims Sam, shockedlike.

"You object?" Reverend seemed to be surprised, and Harry, though he grinned to see Sam, didn't act like he favored it neither.

"I do," says Sam. "Strong. 'Tisn't seemly."

"Might be a bit rough on the maid, if her heard of it," says Harry, with a sort of a shrug, sittin' forward, his elbows on his knees, and lookin' up at Reverend Battishill.

"That's a point, certainly," says Reverend. "Well, what do *you* suggest?"

"I wondered," said Sam, "if you was to ask Guidance, p'raps . . ."

"Get out, man," says Reverend. "Have sense. You've just refused to leave it to Providence," he says.

"What!" says Sam. "You call the spin of a coin—*Providence?*"

"My dear Toop," says Reverend. "If Providence be concerned to see that one of you gets Miss Exworthy, It can speak in the spin of a coin as well as by any other means. It has her to consider, you know, as well as you two. What next, then? Will you fight for her?"

" 'Twouldn't be fair," says Sam. "Harry would beat me easy. He can box."

"I couldn't take advantage of the man," says Harry.

"Hmm!" says Reverend, and he gives a good sharp look at Harry, who was lookin' down at the floor. "Well, if 'tis to be neither chance nor skill," he says, "we're up against a difficult proposition. Very difficult."

He stops for a minute, and then, "I've got it!" he says. "You two chaps play billiards, I know."

"Yes," they both says, lookin' at him blank.

"And you're much of a match, for I seen you down to the Memorial Hall when your chaps played ours."

"Yes, but—"

"And you've got a new table in your village—at least, new to you."

"That's right. Three-quarter size."

"Well, it's not new to me," says Reverend Battishill. "I've played on it often, at George Hatherleigh's," he says, "and I reckon 'tis ideal for the purpose. Half skill, half act of God. That ought to satisfy you, Toop," he says. " 'Twill give Providence plenty of chance to take a hand."

"Yes, but," says Sam, bewildered, "I don't see—"

"Get out!" says Harry. "Reverend here wants us to play a match on our table, the winner to get Gertie. Isn't that right, sir?"

Reverend Le Vernon Battishill nodded, lookin' from one of 'em to t'other.

"Well," says Harry, drawin' breath and sittin' up in his chair, "I be game."

"What do you say, Toop?"

" 'Tisn't hardly seemly," says Sam, slowlike. " 'Tisn't hardly seemly, playin' a sportin' game for so serious a matter."

" 'Tisn't hardly seemly the state of things at present," puts in Harry. "And us can't think of no better way to end the matter."

So, after a little more objectin' on the part o' Sam, 'twas covenanted and ordained that Harry Munday and Samuel Toop do play a level game o' two hundred and fifty up, winner to have Gertie Exworthy in the bands o' holy wedlock.

When the evenin' came for the game to take place, you couldn't hardly get into the yard outside for the crush of people. Word had spread through all the four parishes and beyond, and all sorts had turned up for to witness the proceedin's.

That caused trouble. All here felt 'twas our affair and no one else's. But there—you couldn't keep the news of such a unusual performance secret in the countryside. 'Twould be bound to get about, and chaps would want to see the fun. That's only in human nature, like.

Harry and Sam didn't put in a appearance till near before the game was due to start, and when Harry seen the crowd all waitin' round, he went so black as thunder.

"Hullo!" calls a chap from another parish, catchin' sight of the pair. "Here be the two heroes who be goin' to do battle for the bride. How be feelin', eh?"

Harry scowls at him.

"What brings you here?" he asks, very quiet and black.

"Oh, cooriosity, cooriosity," says the chap. "The marriage customs of other folks is always interestin'," he says.

"How's your cue, Harry?" shouts another chap, before Harry could answer.

"How's his summat else, more like," calls another, and a gert laugh goes up from all around.

Harry took no notice. He was still scowlin' at the chap what'd spoke first.

"I don't know what you reckon you're doing here, Saul Bickford," he says, "but you and your rabble had better clear out. We don't want you."

"Oho!" says Saul. "What—ain't I invited to the party? That's *too* bad," he says, "because I'm stayin', all the same."

"As you please," says Harry. "There won't be no game till you've gone, that's all."

Well, the situation began to look ugly then, but some of us got hold of Harry and persuaded him into the building. Sam went quiet enough: he didn't seem to mind. Then we reasoned it out with the other chaps that, so soon as our chaps was all accommodated, we should admit in all of theirs as there was room for. There was a bit of a rush when the time came, and too many got in.

Us had to send a score or more away, for there was crowdin' round the table, and I was feared for the floor. That roused up bad blid again, and some of they what couldn't get in start heavin' pebbles up at the windows, till George Smith goes out and makes a speech to 'em.

"Look 'ee here," he says. "This is a private meetin' of a private parish club, 'pon private parish business," he says. " 'Tidn' a football match, nor a picture show. Have money been took or posters sticked up in the street?" he says. "Very well, then. How would you fancy it, if strangers was to come pokin' into your private concerns?" he says.

"Get home with 'ee, you ole mumphead," one chap sings out and heave a tetty: but the good sense of what George Smith said tooked hold on 'em, and they dispersed off quiet.

Then the game beginned: and I don't think I need to worry 'ee with all the pedigree of the scorin'. 'Twasn't nothing accountable, in the way of play: besides, I can't call much of it to mind. Harry were a dashin' sort of a player, good 'pon his day, and able to bring off a deal of showy strokes if he were in the lead: but no good at all if a chap had a big start of en. Sam were more steady-goin'; didn't take no risks, but a good, sound scorer, with his sevens and tens and suchlike; didn' vary much in his play and hard to beat. Well, be as 'twill, this evenin', of all others, he couldn' thrive. Harry didn' play very well, but the luck favored en, and the balls developed well: Sam played steadyish, but missed more'n he caught, and the balls wouldn' do nothin' for en.

" 'Ard luck, 'ard luck!" chaps would cry to en at first: but soon they settled down and keeped quiet, for reelly, what with the way the game was runnin', it looked like Harry was the man intended to have Gertie Exworthy, and nobody cares to cry out against what will be, like.

Harry passed the two hunnerd a good forty ahead of Sam, and then, playin' careless, he let Sam come up. The crowd shouts to en not to act so foolish, and with the same he put on a break of twenty-three, good, honest scorin'. Sam's forehead come out in a sweat, and he bited his lips but he got down to it, made seven off a poor leave and layed Harry a double balk. But nothin' could stop Harry: and his score stood at two hunnerd and forty-one while Sam, starin' anxious at the scoreboard, couldn' see nothin' better than two hunnerd and three.

"Now then, Harry," calls someone, "run out to your bride!" And a easy enough shot was offered, but Harry, after lookin' to it, turns off by the way to play for somethin' else and misses his score.

"Gaah!" says the chaps all round the room watchin' with their eyes sticked out.

"He'll lost yet," says one. "He'm overconfident." And, as if to give the chap right, Sam gets right down and makes twenty-four. At the close of it he tries to leave a double balk again but hit too ladylike and leaves the balls sittin': another easy shot for Harry.

"Go on, Harry," Joe Pellow calls out. "Now's your chance. Put down the red, man; put down the red."

Harry straightens up from table and looks across at him.

"Look here," he says, "be I playin' this game, or be you?"

"Oh, you, boy," holleys Joe Pellow back. "I don't want to deprive 'ee. I got enough trouble o' me own, home, wi'out addin' to it."

There was a laugh, hushed off short as Harry stooped down again to the table. 'Twas a good shot offered, a easy cannon: but, to the 'mazement of all, Harry, after a good look at it, walks round cool as you like to the other side.

"No," he says, half aloud, "I fancies this better."

With the same, he try some finickin' far-fetched sort of a shot all round the table and missed.

Sam runs to the table, sort of desperate-like, to try and make the most of Harry's mistake, but he losts the white ball and couldn't do no more than five. Worst of all, he leaves Harry another straight clean shot. When he turned and seen how the balls lied, he gived a sort of a groan.

There wasn't but the one shot to try for, this time: a plain in-off to the right' an' top pocket. Harry, a bit set in the face, stoops down, aims very careful, makes a great show of puttin' side on his ball, plays too fine, and miss by inches. Everybody gives a gasp, for 'tis a shot you can't possibly fail to make 'pon this here table, as well you knows, providin' you plays gentle.

" 'Ere," whispered Lias Clarke to me, "I'll lay he missed that one o' purpose."

I didn't say nothin'. I was watchin' Harry.

"Harry," howls Lias of a sudden. "Looks like you bain't tryin' to win."

Harry gives him a cool sort of a stare.

"Oh!" he says. "It do, do it?"

"Yes," says Lias. "Looks like you don't want the girl."

There was a silence then, if you like. Everyone watched at Harry to see how he'd take it. Samuel what was just stoopin' to his leave, looked up at him too. Nobody moved.

"Well," says Harry, smilin' to himself in a queer sort of way and walkin' over to where the chalk was in the little cup under the table, "I don't know that I do."

"*What?*"

Samuel straightens up upright and stares at him with his mouth hangin' open.

"What, Harry?" he says. And then, as Harry didn't say nothin' but went on to chalk his cue, Sam says, "Repeat they words."

"I don't know that I do want her," says Harry, lookin' nowhere in particular.

"You—don't—know—that—you—do—want—her," repeats Sam, very slow. Then, seein' Harry smile, he says, quite sharp, "Why for?"

"Because I've had 'er," shouts Harry back, very brutal and sudden, like.

"Because you've had 'er! What—d'ee mean you'm *married* to 'er?"

"No," says Harry. "Without."

"Without! Without! Aaaah! you—" Sam's face went all red and puckered up, and he spitted out some very bad words. "You low, loose-livin'—," he says, and, lookin' around for somethin', he picks up the red ball from the table and heaves it at Harry's 'ead.

Harry ducks, and the red ball crashes against the fireplace and trickles along over the floor. The room was so still as death. You could hear the ball rollin', slow at first, then faster and faster, to the trapdoor: but us was all under a spell, like, and no one moved to stop it, till it comed to the door, felled 'pon top one of the steps, and bumped down into the straw below.

Then, in a minute, everyone was speakin' at once. Men runned to hold Sam, but he'd spent hisself. There wasn't no need.

"Well, Sam," says Harry at last, "shall us go on with the game?"

"Game be damned!" says Sam. "If her's that sort, *I* don't want her, neither."

"Oh, Sam," says Harry, anxiouslike, comin' round the table and puttin' his hand on Sam's shoulder, "I don't want you to think that," he says. "I tell 'ee, man—"

"Leave me go!" says Sam, shakin' off his hand.

"'WELL, THEN, so it ended," said Mr. Spaddacott lifting the top of the stove and spitting into its interior. "That's how the chip come on the red ball. Made it up, the two did," he added, "and was good friends ever after, till Harry went away and Sam married another girl."

"And Gertie—what about her?"

"Married Joe Metherell, the butcher, out to Stoke Dendle. Reverend Le Vernon Battishill married 'em. Steady-goin' a married 'ooman as you could wish to see. Three pretty little maids her've got. Runnin' a bit to fat: but a good wife to the man, and a happy marriage. Well, well! There 'tis, you see. Now—have us time for another hunnerd up afore you go?"

. . . .

SPORTSMANSHIP

BY *John O'Hara*

Remember the scene in The Hustler *where Fast Eddie gets his thumbs broken? That type of corporal punishment for pool sins was not unprecedented. We saw it in Thornton McCune's 1925 story "A Game of Billiards," now here it is again nine years later. Makes you wonder if Tevis read O'Hara or O'Hara read McCune.*

John O'Hara (1905–1970) made a literary splash in 1934 with his first novel, Appointment in Sumatra, *and went on to pen a formidable list of popular stories and novels, one of which became the musical comedy* Pal Joey. *Realistic rendering of dialogue was one of O'Hara's strong points, and it shows in "Sportsmanship"; for the first time in this book, the characters sound like people you might meet today in a pool hall of the seedier sort.*

JERRY STRAIGHTENED HIS TIE and brushed the sleeves of his coat and went down the stairway where it said "The Subway Arcade." The sign was misleading only to strangers to that neighborhood; there was no subway anywhere near, and it was no arcade.

It was early in the afternoon and there were not many people in the place. Jerry walked over to where a man with glasses and a cigar in an imitation amber holder was sitting quietly with a thin man, who also had a cigar.

"Hyuh, Frank," said Jerry.

"Hyuh," said the man with glasses.

"Well, how's every little thing?" said Jerry.

Frank looked around the place, a little too carefully and slowly. "Why," he said finally, "it looks like every little thing is fine. How about it, Tom? Would you say every little thing was OK?"

"Me?" said Tom. "Yes, I guess so. I guess every little thing is— No. No. I think I smell sumpn. Do you smell sumpn, Frank? I think I do."

"Aw, you guys. I get it," said Jerry. "Still sore. I don't blame you."

"Who? Me? Me sore?" said Frank. "Why, no. Would you say I was sore, Tom? This stranger here says I'm sore. Oh, no, stranger. That's my usual way of looking. Of course you wouldn't have no way of knowing that, being a stranger. It's funny, though, speaking of looks. You look the dead spit of a guy I used to know, to my sorrow. A rat by the name of Jerry. Jerry—Jerry, uh, Daley. You remember that Jerry Daley rat I told you about one time? Remember him, Tom?"

"Oh, yes. Come to think of it," said Tom, "I recall now I did hear you speak of a heel by that name. I recall it now. I would of forgot all about the rat if you wouldn't of reminded me. What ever did happen to him? I heard he was drowned out City Island."

"Oh, no," said Frank. "They sent him to Riker's Island, the party I mean."

"All right. I get it. Still sore. Well, if that's the way you feel about it," said Jerry. He lit a cigarette and turned away. "I only come back to tell you, Frank, I wanted to tell you I'd be satisfied to work out the dough I owe you if you leave me have a job."

"Hmm," said Frank, taking the cigar out of his mouth. "Hear that, Tom? The stranger is looking for work. Wants a job."

"Well, waddia know about that? Wants a job. What doing, I wonder," said Tom.

"Yeah. What doing? Cashier?" said Frank.

"Aw, what the hell's the use trying to talk to you guys? I came here with the best intention, but if that's your attitude, *so long.*"

"Guess he's not satisfied with the salary you offered, Frank," said Tom.

Jerry was back on the stairway when Frank called him. "Wait a minute." Jerry returned. "What's your proposition?" said Frank. Tom looked surprised.

"Give me the job as houseman. Twenty-five a week. Take out ten a week for what I owe you. I'll come here in the mornings and clean up, and practice up my game, and then when I get my eye back, I'll shoot for the house—"

"Using house money, of course," said Tom.

"Let him talk, Tom," said Frank.

"Using house money. What else? And the house and I split what I make." Jerry finished his proposition and his cigarette.

"How long id take you to get shooting good again?" said Frank.

"That's pretty hard to say. Two weeks at least," said Jerry.

Frank thought a minute while Tom watched him incredulously. Then he said, "Well, I might take a chance on you, Daley. Tell you what I'll do. You're on the nut. All right. Here's my proposition: The next two weeks, you can sleep here and I'll give you money to eat on, but no pay. You practice up, and in two weeks I'll play you, say, a hundred points. If you're any good, I'll give you thirty bucks cash and credit you with twenty bucks against what you're in me for. Then you can use your thirty to play with. That oughta be enough to start on, if you're any good. I seen you go into many a game when you were shooting on your nerve and come out the winner, so thirty bucks oughta be plenty. *But* if you're no good at the end of two weeks, then I'll have to leave you go. I'll charge up twenty bucks against what you owe me, and you can go out in the wide, wide world and look for adventure, the way you did once before. Is that a deal?"

"Sure. What can I lose?" said Jerry.

"Sure, what can you lose? How long since you ate last?"

In two weeks Jerry had lost the tan color of his face, and his hands were almost white again, but he looked healthier. Eating regularly was more important than the sun. The regulars who had known Jerry before he stole the hundred and forty dollars from Frank were glad to see him and made no cracks. They may have figured Frank for a real sucker, some of them, but some of the others said there were a lot of angles in a thing like that; nobody knew the whole story in a thing of that kind, and besides, Frank was no dope. It didn't look like it. Jerry was brushing off the tables, putting the cues in their right bins—the twenty-ounce cues into bins marked 20, the nineteen-ouncers in the 19 bins, and so on—and retipping cues, and cleaning garboons and filling them with water, and dusting everywhere. He caught on soon about the new regulars, who wanted what table and what they usually played. For instance, every afternoon at three o'clock two guys in tuxedos would come in and play two fifty-point games, and the rest of the afternoon, before they had to go and play in an orchestra, they would play rotation. Well, you had to keep an eye on them. They paid by the hour, of course, but if you didn't watch them, they would use the ivory cue ball to break with in the games of rotation, instead of using the composition ball, which did not cost as much as the ivory ball and stood the hard usage better. The ivory ball cost Frank around twenty bucks, and you can't afford to have an ivory ball slammed around on the break in a game of rotation. Things like that, little things—that was where an experienced houseman like Jerry could save Frank money.

Meanwhile he practiced up and his game came back to him, so that at the end of the two weeks he could even do massé shots almost to his own satisfaction. He hardly ever left except to go out to a place, a Coffee Pot on Fordham Road, for his meals. Frank gave him a "sayfitty" razor and a tube of no-brush-needed cream. He slept on the leather couch in front of the cigar counter.

He also observed that Frank was shooting just about the same kind of game he always shot—no better, and no worse. Jerry therefore was confident of beating Frank, and when the day came that ended the two weeks agreed upon, he reminded Frank of the date, and Frank said he would be in at noon the next day to play the hundred points.

Next day, Frank arrived a little after twelve. "I brought my own referee," said Frank. "Shake hands with Jerry Daley," he said, and did not add the name of the burly man, who might have been Italian, or even an octoroon. The man was dressed quietly, except for a fancy plaid cap. Frank addressed him as Doc, Jerry first thought, but then he realized that Frank, who was originally from Worcester, Massachusetts, was calling the man Dark.

Dark sat down on one of the high benches and did not seem much interested in the game. He sat there smoking cigarettes, wetting them almost halfway down their length with his thick lips. He hardly looked at the game, and with two players like Frank and Jerry there wasn't much use for a referee. Jerry had Frank forty-four to twenty before Dark even looked up at the marker. "Geez," he said. "Forty-four to twenty. This kid's good, eh?"

"Oh, yeah," said Frank. "I told you one of us was gonna get a good beating."

"Maybe the both of you, huh?" said Dark, and showed that he could laugh. Then Jerry knew there was something wrong. He missed the next two times up, on purpose. "There they are, Frank," said Dark. Frank ran six or seven. "Got a mistake in the score, there," said Dark. He got up and took a twenty-two-ounce cue out of the bin and reached up and slid the markers over so that the score was even.

"Hey," said Jerry. "What is it?"

"That's the right score, ain't it?" said Dark. "Frank just run twenty-four balls. I seen him, and I'm the referee. Neutral referee."

"What is it, Frank? The works or something?" said Jerry.

"He's the referee," said Frank. "Gotta abide by his decision in all matters. 'Specially the scoring. You have to abide by the referee, 'specially on matters of scoring. You know that."

"So it's the works," said Jerry. "OK. I get it. Pick up the marbles." He laid down his cue. "What a sap I been. I thought this was on the up-and-up."

"I hereby declare this game is forfeited. Frank wins the match. Congratulate the winner, why don't you, kid?"

"This means I'm out, I guess, eh, Frank?" said Jerry.

"Well, you know our agreement," said Frank. "We gotta abide by the decision of the referee, and he says you forfeited, so I guess you don't work here anymore."

"Congratulate the winner," said Dark. "Where's your sportman-ship, huh? Where's your sportmanship?"

"Don't look like he has any," said Frank, very sadly. "Well, that's the way it goes."

"Maybe we better teach him a little sportmanship," said Dark.

"All right by me," said Frank. "One thing I thought about Mr. Daley, I thought he'd be a good loser, but it don't look that way. It don't look that way one bit, so maybe you better teach him a little sportmanship. Only a little, though. Just give him a little bit of a lesson."

Jerry reached for the cue that he had laid on the table, but as he did, Dark brought his own cue down on Jerry's hands. "Shouldn't do that," said Dark. "You oughtn't to scream, either. Cops might hear you, and you don't want any cops. You don't want any part of the cops, wise guy."

"You broke me hands, you broke me hands!" Jerry screamed. The pain was awful, and he was crying.

"Keep them out of other people's pockets," said Frank. "Beat it."

....

A JOLLY GAME

BY *Mikhail Zoshchenko*

In old Russia, apparently, beating a man at billiards and taking his money didn't sufficiently humiliate him. Note that our three Russian authors—Pushkin, Tolstoy, and now Zoshchenko—describe losers who are made to crawl under the table. Were such penalties common in that harsh land, and are they still? Were they imposed in other games and sports as well? Slavologists with answers are invited to come forward.

After being gassed in World War I, Mikhail Zoshchenko (1895–1958) wandered the Soviet Union working as a carpenter, trapper, cobbler, policeman, detective, gambler, clerk, and actor. His many humorous short stories made him one of the most beloved writers in the country.

In recognition of his popularity after the Second World War, the communist government called him a "brainless pornographic scribbler."

A SHORT TIME AGO I had dinner in a restaurant and then looked in at a poolroom. I felt like seeing, as they say, how the balls were rolling.

There's no question that it's an interesting game. It's absorbing and can distract a man from any kind of misfortune. Some even find that the game of billiards develops courage, a sharp and steady eye, and good aim, and doctors assert that this game is extremely beneficial to unbalanced men.

I don't know. I don't think so. Some unbalanced man might fill himself so full of beer while playing billiards that he could hardly crawl home after the game. So I doubt that this would be beneficial to the nervous and distraught. And as for its giving you a sharp eye, that all depends. A fellow from our house got both his eyes blackened with the cue when his partner was taking aim, and even though he wasn't blinded, he did go slightly blind in one eye. There's your development of a sharp eye for you. If someone should give him a workout in the other eye now, the man will be completely deprived of any vision at all, let alone aim.

So that in the sense of usefulness, it's all, as they say, old wives' tales.

But the game is certainly amusing. Especially when they're playing "for keeps"—very absorbing to watch.

Of course, they rarely play for money nowadays. But they think up something original instead. Some of them make the loser crawl under the table. Others make him buy a round of beer. Or have him pay for the game.

When I went to the poolroom this time, I saw a very mirth-provoking scene.

A winner was ordering his bewhiskered partner to crawl under the table carrying all the balls. He stuffed some balls in his pockets, put a ball in each hand, and on top of that tucked one under his chin. And in this state the loser crawled under the table to the accompaniment of general laughter.

After the next game the winner once again loaded down the bewhiskered fellow with balls and on top of that made him carry the cue between his teeth. And the poor fellow crawled again, to the Homeric laughter of the assembled company.

For the next game, they had trouble thinking up anything.

The bewhiskered one says, "Let's make it something easier, you've done me in as it is."

And really, even his mustache was drooping, he was so dragged out.

The winner says, "Don't be a fool—with such penalties I'll give you a marvelous lesson in how to play billiards."

An acquaintance of the winner's was there. He said, "I've thought of something. If he loses, let's do this: have him crawl under the table loaded down with the balls and we'll tie a case of beer to his foot. Let him crawl through like that."

The winner, laughing, says, "Bravo! That'll really be some trick!"

The bewhiskered one said in a hurt way, "If there's going to be beer in the case, I won't play. It'll be hard enough to crawl with an empty case."

In a word, he lost, and amid general laughter they again loaded him down with the balls, put the cue between his teeth, and tied a case to his foot. The winner's friend also started poking him with a cue to hasten his journey under the billiard table.

The winner laughed so hard that he fell into a chair and grunted from exhaustion.

The bewhiskered one emerged from under the table in a state of stupefaction. He gazed dully at the company and did not move for a while. Then he dug the balls out of his pockets and began untying the case of beer from his foot, saying that he wasn't playing anymore.

The winner was laughing so hard he shed tears. He said, "Come on, Egorov, old pal, let's play one more game. I've thought up another funny trick."

The other says, "Well, what else have you thought up?"

The winner, choking with laughter, says, "Let's play for your mustache, Egorov! That fluffy mustache of yours has bothered me for a long time. If I win, I'll cut off your mustache. Okay?"

The bewhiskered one says, "No, for my mustache I won't play, not unless you give me a forty-point handicap."

In a word, he lost again. And before anyone could catch his breath, the winner grabbed a table knife and began sawing off one side of his unlucky partner's fluffy mustache.

Everyone in the room was dying of laughter.

Suddenly one of those present goes over to the winner and says to him, "Your partner must be a fool, agreeing to such forfeits. And you take advantage of this and make fun of a man in a public place."

The winner's friend says, "What damn business is it of yours? After all, he agreed of his own free will."

The winner says to his partner in a tired voice, "Egorov, come here. Tell the assembled multitudes that you agreed to all the forfeits of your own free will."

The partner, supporting his half-severed mustache with his hand, says, "Obviously it was of my own free will, Ivan Borisovich."

The winner says, turning to the company, "Some people make

their chauffeur wait in the freezing cold for three hours. But I treat people humanely. This is the chauffeur from our office, and I always bring him inside where it's warm. I don't patronize him but play a friendly game of billiards with him. I teach him, and I punish him a little. And why they're picking on me now, I just can't understand."

The chauffeur says, "Perhaps there's a barber in the house. I'd like my mustache evened off."

A man comes out of the crowd and says, taking a pair of scissors from his pocket, "I will be sincerely happy to even off your mustache. If you like, I'll make you one like Charlie Chaplin's."

While the barber was fussing with the chauffeur, I went up to the winner and said to him, "I didn't know that was your chauffeur. I thought it was your friend. I wouldn't have let you pull such tricks."

The winner, a bit shaken, says, "And what sort of a bird are you?"

I say, "I'll write an article about you."

The winner, really frightened, says, "But I won't tell you my name."

I say, "I'll just describe the actual event and add that it was a fairly stout, reddish-haired man named Ivan Borisovich. Of course, you may even get away with it, but if you do I hope your rotten soul will tremble before the lines of print."

The winner's friend, hearing something about an article, instantly made himself scarce and disappeared from the premises.

The winner drank beer and talked big for a long time, shouting that he didn't give a damn for anyone.

They trimmed the chauffeur's whiskers, and he became somewhat younger looking and handsomer. So that I even decided to tone down my feuilleton.

After I came home, as you see, I wrote it up. And now you're reading it and probably feeling amazed that such passionate gamblers exist and that you can run into such unattractive reddish-haired men.

1950

··

THE BLUE-WINGED TEAL

BY *Wallace Stegner*

Ever try to get to sleep by running imaginary racks of balls in your head? That's what young Henry does in this story by Wallace Stegner (1909–1993), one of America's most distinguished men of letters. But be warned, the story is more about Henry's relationship with his father, the owner of a pool hall, than it is about duck hunting or pool playing.

Stegner was killed in a car accident in Santa Fe, New Mexico, at the age of eighty-four. Novelist, biographer, historian, literary critic, and essayist, he was especially interested in the people and lands of the western United States, once remarking that he wished they had a civilization to match the scenery.

He won the Pulitzer Prize for Angle of Repose *(1971) and the National Book Award for* The Spectator Bird *(1976). He was respected as a teacher of writing at several universities, especially Stanford, where he spent twenty-six years on the faculty.*

"The Blue-Winged Teal" first appeared in Harper's *(April 1950). It was reprinted in* The City of the Living and Other Stories *(1956) and again in the* Collected Stories of Wallace Stegner *(1990).*

STILL IN WADERS, with the string of ducks across his shoulder, he stood hesitating on the sidewalk in the cold November wind. His knees were stiff from being cramped up all day in the blind, and his feet were cold. Today, all day, he had been alive; now he was back ready to be dead again.

Lights were on all up and down the street, and there was a rush of traffic and a hurrying of people past and around him, yet the town was not his town, the people passing were strangers, the sounds of evening in this place were no sounds that carried warmth or familiarity. Though he had spent most of his twenty years in the town, knew hundreds of its people, could draw maps of its streets from memory, he wanted to admit familiarity with none of it.

Then what was he doing here, in front of this pool hall, loaded down with nine dead ducks? What had possessed him in the first place to borrow gun and waders and car from his father and go hunting? If he had wanted to breathe freely for a change, why hadn't he kept right on going? What was there in this place to draw him back? A hunter had to have a lodge to bring his meat to and people who would be glad of his skill. He had this pool hall and his father, John Lederer, Prop.

He stepped out of a woman's path and leaned against the door. Downstairs, in addition to his father, he would find old Max Schmeckebier, who ran a cheap blackjack game in the room under the sidewalk. He would find Giuseppe Sciutti, the Sicilian barber, closing his shop or tidying up the rack of *Artists and Models* and *The Nudist*. He would probably find Billy Hammond, the night clerk from the Windsor Hotel, having his sandwich and beer and pie or moving alone around a pool table, whistling abstractedly, practicing shots. If the afternoon blackjack game had broken up, there would be Navy Edwards, dealer and bouncer for Schmeckebier. At this time of evening there might be a few counter customers and a cop collecting his tribute of a beer or that other tribute that Schmeckebier paid to keep the card room open.

And he would find, sour contrast with the bright sky and the wind of the tule marshes, the cavelike room with its back corners in darkness, would smell that smell compounded of steam heat and cue-chalk dust, of sodden butts in cuspidors, of coffee and meat and beer smells from the counter, of cigarette smoke so unaired that it darkened the walls. From anywhere back of the middle tables there would be the pervasive reek of toilet disinfectant. Back of the counter his father would be presiding, throwing the pool hall light switch to save a few cents when the place was empty, flipping it on to give an air of brilliant and successful use when feet came down the stairs past Sciutti's shop.

The hunter moved his shoulder under the weight of the ducks, his mind full for a moment with the image of his father's face, darkly pale, fallen in on its bones, and the pouched, restless, suspicious eyes that seemed always looking for someone. Over the image came the face of his mother, dead now and six weeks buried. His teeth clicked at the thought of how she had held the old man up for thirty years, kept him at a respectable job, kept him from slipping back into the poolroom Johnny he had been when she married him. Within ten days of her death he had hunted up this old failure of a pool hall.

In anger the hunter turned, thinking of the hotel room he shared with his father. But he had to eat. Broke as he was, a student yanked from his studies, he had no choice but to eat on the old man. Besides, there were the ducks. He felt somehow that the thing would be incomplete unless he brought his game back for his father to see.

His knees unwilling in the stiff waders, he went down the steps, descending into the light shining through Joe Sciutti's door, and into the momentary layer of clean bay rum smell, talcum smell, hair tonic smell, that rose past the still-revolving barber pole in the angle of the stairs.

Joe Sciutti was sweeping wads of hair from his tile floor, and hunched over the counter beyond, their backs to the door, were Schmeckebier, Navy Edwards, Billy Hammond, and an unknown customer. John Lederer was behind the counter, mopping alertly with a rag. The poolroom lights were up bright, but when Lederer saw who was coming he flipped the switch and dropped the big room back into dusk.

As the hunter came to the end of the counter their heads turned toward him. "Well, I'm a son of a bee," Navy Edwards said, and scrambled off his stool. Next to him Billy Hammond half stood up so that his pale yellow hair took a halo from the back-bar lights. "Say!" Max Schmeckebier said. "Say, dot's goot, dot's pooty goot, Henry!"

But Henry was watching his father so intently he did not turn to them. He slid the string of ducks off his shoulder and swung them up onto the wide walnut bar. They landed solidly—offering or tribute or ransom or whatever they were. For a moment it was as if this little act were private between the two of them. He felt queerly moved, his stomach tightened in suspense or triumph. Then the old man's pouchy eyes slipped from his and the old man came quickly forward along the counter and laid hands on the ducks.

He handled them as if he were petting kittens, his big white hands stringing the heads one by one from the wire.

"Two spoonbill," he said, more to himself than to others crowding around. "Shovel ducks. Don't see many of those anymore. And two, no three, hen mallards and one drake. Those make good eating."

Schmeckebier jutted his enormous lower lip. Knowing him for a stingy, crooked, suspicious little man, Henry almost laughed at the air he could put on, the air of a man of probity about to make an honest judgment in a dispute between neighbors. "I take a budderball," he said thickly. "A liddle budderball, dot is vot eats goot."

An arm fell across Henry's shoulders, and he turned his head to see the hand with red hairs rising from its pores, the wristband of a gray silk shirt with four pearl buttons. Navy Edwards's red face was close to his. "Come clean now," Navy said. "You shot 'em all sitting, didn't you, Henry?"

"I just waited till they stuck their heads out of their holes and let them have it," Henry said.

Navy walloped him on the back and convulsed himself laughing. Then his face got serious again, and he bore down on Henry's shoulder. "By God, you could've fooled me," he said. "If I'd been makin' book on what you'd bring in I'd've lost my shirt."

"Such a pretty shirt, too," Billy Hammond said.

Across the counter John Lederer cradled a little drab duck in his hand. Its neck, stretched from the carrier, hung far down, but its body was neat and plump and its feet were waxy. Watching the sallow face of his father, Henry thought it looked oddly soft.

"Ain't that a beauty, though?" the old man said. "There ain't a prettier duck made than a blue-winged teal. You can have all your wood ducks and redheads, all the flashy ones." He spread a wing until the hidden band of bright blue showed. "Pretty?" he said, and shook his head and laughed suddenly, as if he had not expected to. When he laid the duck down beside the others his eyes were bright with sentimental moisture.

So now, Henry thought, you're right in your element. You always did want to be one of the boys from the poolroom pouring out to see the elk on somebody's running board or leaning on a bar with a schooner of beer talking baseball or telling the boys about the big German brown somebody brought in in a cake of ice. We haven't any elk or German browns right now, but we've got some nice ducks, a fine display along five feet of counter. And who brought them in? The student, the alien son. It must gravel you.

He drew himself a beer. Several other men had come in, and he saw three more stooping to look in the door beyond Sciutti's. Then they too came in. Three tables were going; his father had started to hustle, filling orders. After a few minutes Schmeckebier and Navy went into the card room with four men. The poolroom lights were up bright again, there was an ivory click of balls, a rumble of talk. The smoke-filled air was full of movement.

Still more people dropped in, kids in high school athletic sweaters and bums from the fringes of skid road. They all stopped to look at the ducks, and Henry saw glances at his waders, heard questions and answers. John Lederer's boy. Some of them spoke to him, deriving importance from contact with him. A fellowship was promoted by the ducks strung out along the counter. Henry felt it himself. He was so mellowed by the way they spoke to him that when the players at the first table thumped with their cues, he got off his stool to rack them up and collect their nickels. It occurred to him that he ought to go to the room and get into a bath, but he didn't want to leave yet. Instead he came back to the counter and slid the nickels toward his father and drew himself another beer.

"Pretty good night tonight," he said. The old man nodded and slapped his rag on the counter, his eyes already past Henry and fixed on two youths coming in, his mouth fixing itself for the greeting and the "Well, boys, what'll it be?"

Billy Hammond wandered by, stopped beside Henry a moment. "Well, time for my nightly wrestle with temptation," he said.

"I was just going to challenge you to a game of call shot."

"Maybe tomorrow," Billy said, and let himself out carefully as if afraid a noise would disturb someone—a mild, gentle, golden-haired boy who looked as if he ought to be in some prep school learning to say "Sir" to grown-ups instead of clerking in a girlie hotel. He was the only one of the poolroom crowd that Henry half liked. He thought he understood Billy Hammond a little.

He turned back to the counter to hear his father talking with Max Schmeckebier. "I don't see how we could on this rig. That's the hell of it, we need a regular oven."

"In my room in back," Schmeckebier said. "Dot old electric range."

"Does it work?"

"Sure. Vy not? I t'ink so."

"By God," John Lederer said. "Nine ducks, that ought to give us a real old-fashioned feed." He mopped the counter, refilled a coffee cup, came back to the end and pinched the breast of a duck, pulled out a wing, and looked at the band of blue hidden among the drab feathers. "Just like old times, for a change," he said, and his eyes touched Henry's in a look that might have meant anything from a challenge to an apology.

Henry had no desire to ease the strain that had been between them for months. He did not forgive his father the pool hall or forget the way the old man had sprung back into the old pattern, as if his wife had been a jailer and he was now released. He neither forgot nor forgave the red-haired woman who sometimes came to the pool hall late at night and waited on a bar stool while the old man closed up. Yet now when his father remarked that the ducks ought to be drawn and plucked right away, Henry got to his feet.

"I could do ten while you were doing one," his father said.

The blood spread hotter in Henry's face, but he bit off what he might have said. "All right," he said. "You do them and I'll take over the counter for you."

So here he was, in the pool hall he had passionately sworn he would never do a lick of work in, dispensing Mrs. Morrison's meat pies and tamales smothered in chile, clumping behind the counter in the waders which had been the sign of his temporary freedom. Leaning back between orders, watching the Saturday night activity of the place, he half understood why he had gone hunting and why it had seemed to him essential that he bring his trophies back here.

That somewhat disconcerted understanding was still troubling him when his father came back. The old man had put on a clean apron and brushed his hair. His pouched eyes, brighter and less houndlike than usual, darted along the bar, counting, and darted across the bright tables, counting again. His eyes met Henry's, and both smiled. Both of them, Henry thought, were a little astonished.

LATER, PROPPED IN BED in the hotel room, he put down the magazine he had been reading and stared at the drawn blinds, the sleazy drapes, and asked himself why he was here. The story he had told others, and himself, that his mother's death had interrupted his school term and he was waiting for the new term before going back, he knew to be an evasion. He was staying because he couldn't get away, or wouldn't. He hated his father, hated the pool hall, hated the people he was thrown with. He made no move to hobnob with them, or hadn't until tonight, and yet he deliberately avoided seeing any of the people who had been his friends for years. Why?

He could force his mind to the barrier but not across it. Within a half minute he found himself reading again, diving deep, and when he made himself look up from the page he stared for a long time at his father's bed, his father's shoes under the bed, his father's soiled shirts hanging in the open closet. All the home he had anymore was this little room. He could not pretend that as long as he stayed here the fragments of his home and family were held together. He couldn't fool himself that he had any function in his father's life anymore, or his father in his, unless his own hatred and his father's uneasy suspicion were functions. He ought to get out and get a job until he could go back to school. But he didn't.

Thinking made him sleepy, and he knew what that was, too. Sleep was another evasion, like the torpor and monotony of his life. But he let drowsiness drift over him, and drowsily he thought of his father behind the counter tonight, vigorous and jovial, Mine Host, and he saw that the usual fretful petulance had gone from his face.

He snapped off the bed light and dropped the magazine on the floor. Then he heard the rain, the swish and hiss of traffic in the wet street. He felt sad and alone, and he disliked the coldness of his own isolation. Again he thought of his father, of the failing body that had once been tireless and bull-strong, of the face before it had sagged and grown dewlaps of flesh on the square jaws. He thought of the many failures, the jobs that never quite worked out, the schemes that never quite paid off, and of the eyes that could not quite meet, not quite hold, the eyes of his cold son.

Thinking of this, and remembering when they had been a family and when his mother had been alive to hold them together, he felt pity, and he cried.

His father's entrance awakened him. He heard the fumbling at the door, the creak, the quiet click, the footsteps that groped in darkness, the body that bumped into something and halted, getting its bearings. He heard the sighing weight of his father's body on the bed, his father's sighing breath as he bent to untie his shoes. Feigning sleep, he lay unmoving, breathing deeply and steadily, but an anguish of fury had leaped in him as sharp and sudden as a sudden fear, for he smelled the smells his father brought with him: wet wool, stale tobacco, liquor; and above all, more penetrating than any, spreading through the room and polluting everything there, the echo of cheap musky perfume.

The control Henry imposed upon his body was like an ecstasy. He raged at himself for the weak sympathy that had troubled him all evening. One good night, he said to himself now, staring furiously upward. One lively Saturday night in the joint and he can't contain himself, he has to go top off the evening with his girlfriend. And how? A drink in her room? A walk over to some illegal after-hours bar on Rum Alley? Maybe just a trip to bed, blunt and immediate?

His jaws ached from the tight clamping of his teeth, but his orderly breathing went in and out, in and out, while the old man sighed into bed and creaked a little, rolling over, and lay still. The taint of perfume seemed even stronger now. The sow must slop it on by the cupful. And so cuddly. Such a sugar baby. How's my old sweetie tonight? It's been too long since you came to see your baby. I should be real mad at you. The cheek against the lapel, the unreal hair against the collar, the perfume like some gaseous poison tainting the clothes it touched.

The picture of his mother's bureau drawers came to him, the careless simple collection of handkerchiefs and gloves and lace collars and cuffs, and he saw the dusty blue sachet packets and smelled the faint fragrance. That was all the scent she had ever used.

My God, he said, how can he stand himself?

After a time his father began to breathe heavily, then to snore. In the little prison of the room his breathing was obscene—loose and bubbling, undisciplined, animal. Henry with an effort relaxed his tense arms and legs, let himself sink. He tried to concentrate on his own breathing, but the other dominated him, burst out and died and whiffled and sighed again. By now he had resolution in him like an iron bar. Tomorrow, for sure, for good, he would break out of his self-imposed isolation and see Frank, see Welby. They would lend him enough to get to the coast. Not another day in this hateful relationship. Not another night in this room.

He yawned. It must be late, two or three o'clock. He ought to get to sleep. But he lay uneasily, his mind tainted with hatred as the room was tainted with perfume. He tried cunningly to elude his mind, to get to sleep before it could notice, but no matter how he composed himself for blankness and shut his eyes and breathed deeply, his mind was out again in a half minute, bright-eyed, lively as a weasel, and he was helplessly hunted again from hiding place to hiding place.

Eventually he fell back upon his old device.

He went into a big dark room in his mind, a room shadowy with great half-seen tables. He groped and found a string above him and pulled, and light fell suddenly in a bright cone from the darker cone of the shade. Below the light lay an expanse of dark green cloth, and this was the only lighted thing in all that darkness. Carefully he gathered bright balls into a wooden triangle, pushing them forward until the apex lay over a round spot on the cloth. Quietly and thoroughly he chalked a cue: the inlaid handle and the smooth taper of the shaft were very real to his eyes and hands. He lined up the cue ball, aimed, drew the cue back and forth in smooth motions over the bridge of his left hand. He saw the balls run from the spinning shock of the break, and carom, and come to rest, and he hunted up the yellow 1 ball and got a shot at it between two others. He had to cut it very fine, but he saw the shot go true, the 1 angle off cleanly into the side pocket. He saw the cue ball rebound and kiss and stop, and he shot the 2 in a straight shot for the left corner pocket, putting drawers on the cue ball to get shape for the 3.

Yellow and blue and red, spotted and striped, he shot pool balls into pockets as deep and black and silent as the cellars of his consciousness. He was not now quarry that his mind chased, but an actor, a willer, a doer, a man in command. By an act of will or of flight he focused his whole awareness on the game he played. His mind undertook it with intent concentration. He took pride in little two-cushion banks, little triumphs of accuracy, small successes of foresight. When he had finished one game and the green cloth was bare, he dug the balls from the bin under the end of the table and racked them and began another.

Eventually, he knew, nothing would remain in his mind but the clean green cloth traced with running color and bounded by simple problems, and sometime in the middle of an intricately planned combination shot he would pale off into sleep.

AT NOON, after the rain, the sun seemed very bright. It poured down from a clearing sky, glittered on wet roofs, gleamed in reflection from pavements and sidewalks. On the peaks beyond the city there was a purity of snow.

Coming down the hill, Henry noticed the excessive brightness and could not tell whether it was really as it seemed, or whether his plunge out of the dark and isolated hole of his life had restored a lost capacity to see. A slavery, or a paralysis, was ended; he had been for three hours in the company of a friend; he had been eyed with concern; he had been warmed by solicitude and generosity. In his pocket he had fifty dollars, enough to get him to the coast and let him renew his life. It seemed to him incredible that he had alternated between dismal hotel and dismal poolroom so long. He could not understand why he had not before this moved his legs in the direction of the hill. He perceived that he had been sullen and morbid, and he concluded with some surprise that even Schmeckebier and Edwards and the rest might have found him a difficult companion.

His father too. The fury of the night before had passed, but he knew he would not bend again toward companionship. That antipathy was too deep. He would never think of his father again without getting the whiff of that perfume. Let him have it; it was what he wanted, let him have it. They could part without an open quarrel, maybe, but they would part without love. They could part right now, within an hour.

Two grimy stairways led down into the cellar from the alley he turned into. One went to the furnace room, the other to the pool hall. The iron rail was blockaded with filled ash cans. Descent into Avernus, he said to himself, and went down the left-hand stair.

The door was locked. He knocked, and after some time knocked again. Finally someone pulled on the door from inside. It stuck and was yanked irritably inward. His father stood there in his shirtsleeves, a cigar in his mouth.

"Oh," he said. "I was wondering what had become of you."

The basement air was foul and heavy, dense with the reek from the toilets. Henry saw as he stepped inside that at the far end only the night-light behind the bar was on, but that light was coming from Schmeckebier's door at this end too, the two weak illuminations diffusing in the shadowy poolroom, leaving the middle in almost absolute dark. It was the appropriate time, the appropriate place, the stink of his prison appropriately concentrated. He drew his lungs full of it with a kind of passion, and he said, "I just came down to—"

"Who is dot?" Schmeckebier called out. He came to his door, wrapped to the armpits in a bar apron, with a spoon in his hand, and he bent, peering out into the dusk like a disturbed dwarf in an underhill cave. "John? Who? Oh, Henry. Shust in time, shust in time. It is not long now." His lower lip waggled, and he pulled it up, apparently with an effort.

Henry said, "What's not long?"

"Vot?" Schmeckebier said, and thrust his big head far out. "You forgot about it?"

"I must have," Henry said.

"The duck feed," his father said impatiently.

They stood staring at one another in the dusk. The right moment was gone. With a little twitch of the shoulder Henry let it go. He would wait a while, pick his time. When Schmeckebier went back to his cooking, Henry saw through the doorway the lumpy bed, the big chair with a blanket folded over it, the rolltop desk littered with pots and pans, the green and white enamel of the range. A rich smell of roasting came out and mingled oddly with the chemical stink of toilet disinfectant.

"Are we going to eat in there?" he asked.

His father snorted. "How could we eat in there? Old Maxie lived in the ghetto too damn long. By God, I never saw such a boar's nest."

"Vot's duh matter? Vot's duh matter?" Schmeckebier said. His big lip thrust out, he stooped to look into the oven, and John Lederer went shaking his head up between the tables to the counter. Henry followed him, intending to make the break when he got the old man alone. But he saw the three plates set up on the bar, the three glasses of tomato juice, the platter of olives and celery, and he hesitated. His father reached with a saltshaker and shook a little salt into each glass of tomato juice.

"All the fixings," he said. "Soon as Max gets those birds out of the oven we can take her on."

Now it was easy to say, "As soon as the feed's over I'll be shoving off." Henry opened his mouth to say it but was interrupted this time by a light tapping at the glass door beyond Sciutti's shop. He swung around angrily and saw duskily beyond the glass the smooth blond hair, the even smile.

"It's Billy," he said. "Shall I let him in?"

"Sure," the old man said. "Tell him to come in and have a duck with us."

But Billy Hammond shook his head when Henry asked him. He was shaking his head almost as he came through the door. "No, thanks, I just ate. I'm full of chow mein. This is a family dinner any-way. You go on ahead."

"Got plenty," John Lederer said, and made a motion as if to set a fourth place at the counter.

"Who is dot?" Schmeckebier bawled from the back. "Who come in? Is dot Billy Hammond? Set him up a blate."

"By God, his nose sticks as far into things as his lip," Lederer said. Still holding the plate, he roared back, "Catch up with the parade, for Christ sake, or else tend to your cooking." He looked at Henry and Billy and chuckled.

Schmeckebier had disappeared, but now his squat figure blotted the lighted doorway again. "Vot? Vot you say?"

"Vot?" John Lederer said. "Vot, vot, vot? Vot does it matter vot I said? Get the hell back to your kitchen."

He was, Henry saw, in a high humor. The effect of last night was still with him. He was still playing Mine Host. He looked at the two of them and laughed so naturally that Henry almost joined him. "I think old Maxie's head is full of duck dressing," he said, and leaned on the counter. "I ever tell you about the time we came back from Reno together? We stopped off in the desert to look at a mine, and got lost on a little dirt road so we had to camp. I was trying to figure out where we were and started looking for stars, but it was clouded over, hard to locate anything. So I ask old Maxie if he can see the Big Dipper anywhere. He thinks about that maybe ten minutes with his lip stuck out and then he says, 'I t'ink it's in duh water bucket.' "

He did the grating gutturals of Schmeckebier's speech so accurately that Henry smiled in spite of himself. His old man made another motion with the plate at Billy Hammond. "Better let me set you up a place."

"Thanks," Billy said. His voice was as polite and soft as his face, and his eyes had the ingenuous liquid softness of a girl's. "Thanks, I really just ate. You go on, I'll shoot a little pool if it's all right."

Now came Schmeckebier with a big platter held in both hands. He bore it smoking through the gloom of the pool hall and up the steps to the counter, and John Lederer took it from him there and with a flourish speared one after another three tight-skinned brown ducks and slid them onto the plates set side by side for the feast. The one frugal light from the back bar shone on them as they sat down. Henry looked over his shoulder to see Billy Hammond pull the cord and flood a table with a sharp-edged cone of brilliance. Deliberately, already absorbed, he chalked a cue. His lips pursed, and he whistled and, whistling, bent to take aim.

Lined up in a row, they were not placed for conversation, but John Lederer kept attempting it, leaning forward over his plate to see Schmeckebier or Henry. He filled his mouth with duck and dressing and chewed, shaking his head with pleasure, and snapped off a bite of celery with a crack like a breaking stick. When his mouth was clear he leaned and said to Schmeckebier, "Ah, *das schmeckt gut,* hey, Maxie?"

"*Ja,*" Schmeckebier said, and sucked grease off his lip and only then turned in surprise. "Say, you speak German?"

"Sure, I speak German," Lederer said. "I worked three weeks once with an old square-head brick mason that taught me the whole language. He taught me about *sehr gut* and *nicht wahr* and *besser I bleiben* right *hier,* and he always had his *Frau* make me up a lunch full of *kalter Aufschnitt* and *gemixte pickeln.* I know all about German."

Schmeckebier stared a moment, grunted, and went back to his eating. He had already stripped the meat from the bones and was gnawing the carcass.

"Anyway," John Lederer said, "*es schmeckt* Goddamn good." He got up and went around the counter and drew a mug of coffee from the urn. "Coffee?" he said to Henry.

"Please."

His father drew another mug and set it before him. "Maxie?"

Schmeckebier shook his head, his mouth too full for talk. For a minute, after he had set out two little jugs of cream, Lederer stood as if thinking. He was watching Billy Hammond move quietly around the one lighted table, whistling. "Look at that sucker," Lederer said. "I bet he doesn't even know where he is."

By the time he got around to his stool he was back at the German. "*Schmeckebier,*" he said. "What's that mean?"

"Uh?"

"What's your name mean? Tastes beer? Likes beer?"

Schmeckebier rolled his shoulders. The sounds he made eating were like sounds from a sty. Henry was half sickened, sitting next to him, and he wished the old man would let the conversation drop. But apparently it had to be a feast, and a feast called for chatter.

"That's a hell of a name, you know it?" Lederer said, and already he was up again and around the end of the counter. "You couldn't get into any church with a name like that." His eyes fastened on the big drooping greasy lip, and he grinned.

"Schmeckeduck, that ought to be your name," he said. "What's German for duck? *Vogel?* Old Man Schmeckevogel. How about number two?"

Schmeckebier pushed his plate forward and Lederer forked a duck out of the steam table. Henry did not take a second.

"You ought to have one," his father told him. "You don't get grub like this every day."

"One's my limit," Henry said.

For a while they worked at their plates. Back of him Henry heard the clack of balls hitting, and a moment later the rumble as a ball rolled down the chute from a pocket. The thin, abstracted whistling of Billy Hammond broke off, became words:

> *Annie doesn't live here anymore.*
> *You must be the one she waited for.*
> *She said I would know you by the blue in your eye—*

"Talk about one being your limit," his father said. "When we lived in Nebraska we used to put on some feeds. You remember anything about Nebraska at all?"

"A little," Henry said. He was irritated at being dragged into reminiscences, and he did not want to hear how many ducks the town hog could eat at a sitting.

"We'd go out, a whole bunch of us," John Lederer said. "The sloughs were black with ducks in those days. We'd come back with a buggyful, and the womenfolks'd really put us on a feed. Fifteen, twenty, thirty people. Take a hundred ducks to fill 'em up." He was silent a moment, staring across the counter, chewing. Henry noticed that he had tacked two wings of a teal up on the frame of the back-bar mirror, small, strong bows with a band of bright blue half hidden in them. The old man's eyes slanted over, caught Henry's looking at the wings.

"Doesn't seem as if we'd had a duck feed since we left there," he said. His forehead wrinkled; he rubbed his neck, leaning forward over his plate, and his eyes met Henry's in the back-bar mirror. He spoke to the mirror, ignoring the gobbling image of Schmeckebier between his own reflection and Henry's.

"You remember that set of china your mother used to have? The one she painted herself? Just the plain white china with the one de-sign on each plate?"

Henry sat stiffly, angry that his mother's name should even be mentioned between them in this murky hole, and after what had passed. Gabble, gabble, gabble, he said to himself. If you can't think of anything else to gabble about, gabble about your dead wife. Drag her through the poolroom too. Aloud he said, "No, I guess I don't."

"Blue-winged teal," his father said, and nodded at the wings tacked to the mirror frame. "Just the wings, like that. Awful pretty. She thought a teal was about the prettiest little duck there was."

His vaguely rubbing hand came around from the back of his neck and rubbed along the cheek, pulling the slack flesh and distorting the mouth. Henry said nothing, watching the pouched hound eyes in the mirror.

It was a cold, skin-tightening shock to realize that the hound eyes were cloudy with tears. The rubbing hand went over them, shaded them like a hat brim, but the mouth below remained distorted. With a plunging movement his father was off the stool.

"Oh, Goddamn!" he said in a strangling voice, and went past Henry on hard, heavy feet, down the steps, and past Billy Hammond, who neither looked up nor broke the sad thin whistling.

Schmeckebier had swung around. "Vot's duh matter? Now vot's duh matter?"

With a short shake of the head, Henry turned away from him, staring after his father down the dark pool hall. He felt as if orderly things were breaking and flying apart in his mind; he had a moment of white blind terror that this whole scene upon whose reality he counted was really only a dream, something conjured up out of the bottom of his consciousness where he was accustomed to comfort himself into total sleep. His mind was still full of the anguished look his father had hurled at the mirror before he ran.

The hell with you, the look had said. The hell with you, Schmecke-bier, and you, my son Henry. The hell with your ignorance, whether you're stupid or whether you just don't know all you think you know. You don't know enough to kick dirt down a hole. You know nothing at all, you know less than nothing because you know things wrong.

He heard Billy's soft whistling, saw him move around his one lighted table—a well-brought-up boy from some suburban town, a polite soft gentle boy lost and wandering among pimps and prosti-tutes, burying himself for some reason among people who never even touched his surface. Did he shoot pool in his bed at night, tempting sleep, as Henry did? Did his mind run carefully to angles and banks and Englishes, making a reflecting mirror of them to keep from looking through them at other things?

Almost in terror he looked out across the sullen cave, past where the light came down in an intense isolated cone above Billy's table, and heard the lugubrious whistling that went on without intention of audience, a recurrent and deadening and only half-conscious sound. He looked toward the back, where his father had disappeared in the gloom, and wondered if in his bed before sleeping the old man worked through a routine of little jobs: cleaning the steam table, ordering a hundred pounds of coffee, jacking up the janitor about the mess in the hall. He wondered if it was possible to wash yourself to sleep with restaurant crockery, work yourself to sleep with chores, add yourself to sleep with columns of figures, as you could play yourself to sleep with a pool cue and a green table and fifteen colored balls. For a moment, in the sad old light with the wreckage of the duck feast at his elbow, he wondered if there was anything more to his life, or his father's life, or Billy Hammond's life, or anyone's life, than playing the careful games that deadened you into sleep.

Schmeckebier, beside him, was still groping in the fog of his mind for an explanation of what had happened. "Vere'd he go?" he said, and nudged Henry fiercely. "Vot's duh matter?"

Henry shook him off irritably, watching Billy Hammond's oblivious bent head under the light. He heard Schmeckebier's big lip flop and heard him sucking his teeth.

"I tell you," the guttural voice said. "I got somet'ing dot fixes him if he feels bum."

He too went down the stairs past the lighted table and into the gloom at the back. The light went on in his room, and after a minute or two his voice was shouting, "John! Say, come here, uh? Say, John!"

Eventually John Lederer came out of the toilet and they walked together between the tables. In his fist Schmeckebier was clutching a square bottle. He waved it in front of Henry's face as they passed, but Henry was watching his father. He saw the crumpled face, oddly rigid, like the face of a man in the grip of a barely controlled rage, but his father avoided his eyes.

"Kümmel," Schmeckebier said. He set four ice-cream dishes on the counter and poured three about a third full of clear liquor. His squinted eyes lifted and peered toward Billy Hammond, but Henry said, on an impulse, "Let him alone. He's walking in his sleep."

So there were only the three. They stood together a moment and raised their glasses. "Happy days," John Lederer said automatically. They drank.

Schmeckebier smacked his lips, looked at them one after another, shook his head in admiration of the quality of his kümmel, and waddled back toward his room with the bottle. John Lederer was already drawing hot water to wash the dishes.

In the core of quiet, which was not broken even by the clatter of crockery and the whistling of Billy Hammond, Henry said what he had to say. "I'll be leaving," he said. "Probably tonight."

But he did not say it in anger or with the cold command of himself that he had imagined in advance. He said it like a cry, and with the feeling he might have had on letting go the hand of a friend too weak and too exhausted to cling any longer to their inadequate shared driftwood in a wide cold sea.

....

A GAME
OF BILLIARDS

BY *William Sansom*

Six months after reading this story, it will still creep into your mind. The narrator is trapped in a room with a madman who insists on playing billiards with balls that only he can see. Humoring him doesn't work, and implied threats make quitting seem too dangerous. What to do?

"A Game of Billiards" was first published in England by Hogarth Press in a collection of Sansom stories called A Touch of the Sun.

IT IS NOT EASY to say whether this is the account of how Patten met his wife or of why she in particular became his wife. Perhaps both.

In the mind or heart of everyone there is thought to exist an archetype to whom he or she inevitably is attracted—an archetype founded on the vision of some early strange face that once leaned down to entertain the pram with its first erotic shock. That is one belief. Otherwise—and one is tempted to think otherwise in Patten's case—a man's first meeting with a woman may coincide with a certain moment of distended nerve, of enlarged comprehension—and simply because of this the meeting assumes an exaggerated significance, personalities are photographed on a more deeply sensitive plate.

How many times do we meet and pass by those whom possibly we could love—because the moment of impact is dulled by circumstance, by a sloth of digestion, an empty pocket, a complacence of spirit! Yet—had the moment been propitious, a free moment of joy, of shock! . . . However.

That Monday Patten was forced to lunch late. It was already two o'clock by the time he had settled into his veal loaf and salad. By five past two this was finished. He refused the cheese and asked instead for a glass of beer. The saloon bar was empty—other lunchers had already left, a few weekend drinkers had dawdled finally away. About the enamel-white counter, the tired scarlet of the stools, the yellow plaster crabshell, the up-curling sandwiches, and a last strand of parsley on an empty plate—there hovered a ticking of long, clock-long tedium. Under dark Victorian overshelves a barmaid and a pale chef stood side by side, not talking. Upon everyone and everything was engraved one inevitable fact—that until three o'clock the room must remain open.

For Patten too there was an hour—a van was calling for him at three. Patten had no particular worry, nor was he unwell—but suddenly he saw the long, lonely prospect and saw it so clearly he clenched his hand till the knucklebones flushed in their white. There were things to do—he could get a haircut, he could walk out on to the Monday pavements of the red-brick suburb, he could look in shopwindows. But nothing seemed worth the effort. An afternoon neither hot nor cold, under a low sky, depressive and of no interest. He looked round him. Not a paper anywhere. Boredom on the barman's face—no small talk. No cat. And so it was with relish that as he sipped his beer he remembered he had not been to the Gentlemen's for some time. He welcomed the definition of such need, put down the beer, and made for the stairs.

The way to the lavatory, as with many such large Victorian houses, led through the billiards room. And on pushing the frosted glass door to this, Patten was surprised—in that emptiness almost shocked—to see there a man holding a cue. The room was never used now—it lay shrouded and in an upstairs manner deserted. He was in fact so surprised, feeling in some way an intruder, that he felt bound to greet the man—the greeting of two on a lonely road.

Like a townsman to a countryman, he turned away his face awkwardly as soon as he had spoken—vaguely perturbed too that he should have said "Good afternoon" instead of "Good morning"; it all depended on whether the fellow had taken his lunch or not. It seemed a long time after, when he had crossed the long linoleum past the table and had his hand already on the brass doorplate, that there came from behind him the words:

"*Good* day."

At first it sounded like a correction. But the words were most amicably spoken, with a pleased purr to the first of them, and Patten turned and nodded back. The man had straightened upright and was looking at him—he must have stood thus throughout Patten's long walk across the floor. He was a large man—in his first glimpse Patten called to mind a type of Dutch or Scandinavian sailor, large and pale-eyed, the evocation of the "big Swede" with solid breadth never quite controlled by his somber suit of Lutheran gray. But this man was plainly affable; he smiled and said across the room:

"You're not going, are you?"

Patten of course laughed and went on through the door. A few seconds later he looked up at the grilled window and frowned. An extraordinary thing? Hadn't the man been leaning over the table in an attitude of play? And had there been no ball? And wasn't the table under its dustcover? He tried hard to draw his mind back to the ball—he would have seen the polished round of white or red? It was odd? Then he shook his head—of course the man had been balancing the cue for weight, or measuring the floor space, or so forth.

But when he opened the door again there was the man crouched across the table, now almost lying across it, his cue reaching hard for nothing. And just then the gray-suited arm gave a short jab, the man sighed and, grunting his effort, lumbered down off the table. He shook his head at Patten.

"Sorry about that. But there isn't a rest anywhere."

Patten's eye turned to the wall bracket, looking automatically for the serrated head of a cue rest. He stopped himself and laughed. Then walking on toward the door said:

"I don't think your opponent will mind, anyway."

"Oh, but he does. Binder's very particular. And rules are rules after all."

To Patten, reasonably polite but in no lively mood, this was taking the joke a little too far. Irritating to underline the thing. So he said nothing further, merely nodded, not smiling. But now the big man had shifted himself round to the door; to pass, Patten was forced to move to one side. The man moved to one side, too, jumbling the approach as of two people meeting on a pavement. Above all now not wanting to raise his head or smile, Patten moved the other way. The man moved too. Patten struggled a "sorry" and then looked up into the pale eyes above him. The man simply stood there, eyes fixed on him, unconfused. It was plain that he was blocking the way.

As their eyes met, the big face smiled again.

"Please don't go. It's most fortunate, most fortunate indeed—you can score. It'll be a great help."

They were still some paces apart. Patten took a step backward—now snake-cold and alert, simultaneously conscious of the position of the door, its handle, the man's size, the bare extent of that great room, the drop from such first-floor windows, the grille of the lavatory skylight. For that large man had spoken in a voice too high, too small, too excited. A loving tone seemed to coax it high, his muscular bloodless lips stretched back wide with the smile of a man relishing food; the pale eyes shone hard with brilliant, sad desire. He was mad.

AT TIMES in the past Patten had daydreamed of this, of meeting a wild animal or a burglar or a madman. He had rehearsed his moves—and he had always shivered and sweated at the intense picture. He had always imagined that really in such a situation he would crumble instantly. But now—surprisingly—it was the opposite. He felt capable, alert, strong. After all, the rehearsals had been of use. Now he smiled as hugely, as fixedly as the man standing so still and eager above him.

"Billiards, eh? Now that sounds like something. What's the game—a hundred up?"

"That's right."

"And what's the score so far?"

"Score?"

"Yes—how many are you?"

The smile left the man's face, he looked sly—but as instantly a new smile came, faltering then pushing his lips forward in confidence. He whispered over:

"Twenty."

Patten nodded. He was going to change the subject, carefully, from billiards—somehow get the man interested and over toward the window. He went on:

"And the other chap?"

"Binder?"

Again the slyness, and this time a huge hand, gray-fleshed but strong as the rest of him, curved up to hide a high chuckle. He looked for a moment like a man with hiccups, absorbed with some physical movement inside him. Then the eyes glittered in amusement.

"Sixteen!"

"Good for you—"

"Shh!"

A pause, while again Patten nodded. He kept nodding automatically. Then suddenly he looked over straight at the window, made an urgent pointing movement. He shouted:

"Lord, look at that! A ship!"

The man paid no attention. He was squinting at the tip of his cue, measuring it.

"Did you see? A ship! Sails, flags!"

Patten thrashed his finger at the window. The man looked up, vaguely.

"How could there be a ship? It's a street, you're seeing things."

"But . . ."

"Couldn't we start now?"

Patten's arm lowered; it was no good, the man showed no interest at all. He looked only vague, as though he did not understand or that what Patten had said was so far from his world that it held no real meaning. It might take hours before the right diversion was found for such a mind. So Patten changed his tactics. He pulled up his sleeves and rubbed his wrists in energetic preparation.

"Good. Let's start. Over to the table with you."

But the man stood still, shaking his head. Patten tried again:

"Look, I'll just slip down and get a drink. Be right up. What's yours?"

Now the man frowned. With his fingers, with a slow, controlled movement, he balanced the cue in an arc so that it pointed to Patten's face. His fingers manipulated their stiff rotation, one protruded, a fetish of grace in the way muscular men, sailors and others of precise craft, hold with formal elegance a drinking cup. He spoke softly:

"You're trying to get out of it. It's not fair. I shouldn't if I were you."

His other hand had been holding the green chalk. Now—it was probably a thoughtless gesture; it was difficult to decide how much the man thought—he raised this hand to his face and with one extended finger rubbed the lid of his right eye. The slender cue was still pointed to Patten's face. The lid of the man's eye became smeared—absurdly yet with some of the sinister mask of all grease-paint—with an ill-chalked green.

Patten's assurance jumped like a gulp in the throat—and vanished. The man was violent. This had always been possible—but part of the old daydreams and the rehearsals had implied that all danger was superable and that the dream-Patten's tactics would know a walkover victory. Beyond this there were no resources. Now this man threatened; he imagined the point of the cue prodding into his soft eye—what had been self-command more than courage shriveled; he backed away from the big man, shrinking with the dispirit of youth before authority.

And like authority the great gray-faced man in his sober suit strode over to the table. Patten saw his size now not only as muscle, but as schoolmasters had once been bigger then he: monuments of reserve, voracious, at a move they would spring into sharp action—contempt cold in their knowing eyes, words of ridicule on their dry lips.

Yet this was momentary, an illusion of Patten's as his chest seemed to shrink and his eyes falter, as dutifully he backed to where the little score markers winked their varnish on the wall—for the man had already forgotten and was smiling excitedly as he stood to survey the position of balls that were not there. He shook his head and pursed his lips, acknowledging a difficult stroke. He bent over and with precision aimed his cue, paused, jabbed the air an inch from the cloth. Then straightened himself and turned to Patten in triumph.

"Cannon! My shot again, I think."

Patten marked up the score, only quickly glancing at the figure, not daring to turn his back.

THE MAN played on. And on and on. He made no mistake—the sequence of play became endless. He played slowly, with many pauses and much thought, with suppressed pursing of the lips as the invisible ball seemed nearly to miss its objective, with sudden chuckles of pleasure and a triumphant toss of the head when a difficult stroke was with ease achieved. He muttered to himself, grunted an occasional remark to Patten. The score rose—but slowly. Patten stood still and moved up the little markers. Sometimes now he looked at them; they took on an appearance of freedom; he envied the ease with which they bobbed so simply up and down the long slots. How different, this freedom of the little markers!

But with his captor absorbed, at least the hard tension of fear became relaxed—the room opened out again to him and he grew to know it too well. Deserted, upstairs, of solemn quiet purpose, its atmosphere hung veiled like a face from former years.

The table in the center shrouded like the emblem of an old feast; the walls recessive with long judicial seats dreaming from their raised platforms; a monstrous marble clock dead on the mantelpiece; the cold echo of carpetless, dust-aged floors; gaunt knob-headed coat stands guarding the corners, a frayed green curtain muffling the door, no blinds on windows strutted with machinery for the winding and opening of their upper lights. From these windows a gray north light paled into the room, the door curtain denied that there was ever a door. It might have been a room far away in an empty house, with time stopped.

But time? Time—Patten thought suddenly how it must be half-past two, how at three o'clock the last chance of someone coming up to the lavatory would be gone, the public house would close down on even the little unheard life it had, and he would be left with the long, silent hours of afternoon. And then suddenly he flinched at a new thought—what when the game was finished, when the steadily growing hundred was up?

"Pocket for the red! Mother'll be pleased as Punch. You should see her when she hears about *this*. . . . There we go again, cannon and in. . . ."

Muttering always in his high voice, he moved round the table. He stood back to chalk his cue, he clambered again on the table, he winked round at Patten with his one greenish eyelid. Once he came round to where Patten stood, aimed a shot from there—so that his back was turned, his head bent down, and Patten could see the gray solid neck with its blond ash of hair. So vulnerable. A moment— then! . . . but it passed; it could not be risked—one never knew the resources of strength such men might have.

Watching him, Patten felt himself seeing the balls, following the play as if it had been real. Only occasionally a noise came muffled through the window to bring him to his senses. A loud lorry passing, the excited quick clatter of a wood seller's donkey racing by, and once the distant cry—so forlorn a note of empty streets—of a rag-and-bottle man. How near the street was! And it was at a moment such as this—when life seemed again so absurdly close, just beneath the window which he dared not even approach—that a sudden and so simple idea occurred to him. He gritted his teeth for not thinking of it before. He began to move the markers backward instead of forward.

THUS AT LEAST a respite. Time now. And once more he began to look round the room. How much time? If no one came, then till five o'clock, six o'clock, later—until some man had drunk enough to have to come? The long hours of afternoon perpetuated themselves; the colorless middle daylight forecast their slow unshadowed monotony. A line of black electric meter boxes high up on the wall stared down at him and stated they would never move; the clock stayed uninterested under its veil of dust; the screen in the fireplace dozed its faded colors.

All these proclaimed themselves so reasonably of the everyday room, the parts of the house restful and undramatized—yet there pacing round the table, muttering, clicking his cue on the floor, winking and prodding, moved this one incongruous figure. Sometimes, over the distance of the table, he seemed insignificant and overshadowed by the stillness: but at others, when he came near and Patten could hear as well as the muttering a deep breathing and a near rustle of muscle straining in clothes, he grew again huge and in Patten's fear seemed to fill the room.

Then the door opened.

It moved slowly—uncertain whether to open itself or not. But Patten's eyes were on the curtain in the first instant. He glanced quickly back at the large man—he was leaning over the table with his back to the door, eyes concentrated on the table. The door swung suddenly in a wide curve open. A young woman stood on the threshold. She stood outlined in some sort of pink and dark blue, some blouse and suit and hat, against the dust of the passage outside.

She stood quite still, looking round the room, herself probably uncertain—but in the long exultant second she seemed to Patten to be standing for her own revelation; she had made some great entrance and waited now for the hushed moment of astounded eyes and raised hearts and then for the thundered release of applause. She stood like the embodiment of all heroic rescue—the figure of sudden salvation, the sworded angel, the wanded silver-shining Queen of Goodness. In her pink dressy blouse and her blue serge skirt.

He wanted to shout, but his breath was away. And when at last he caught it and opened his mouth, he had already realized that he must make no sound. The man was still leaning over the table. He would turn. She was a woman—she could only be the messenger for help. So quietly, opening his mouth wide and shining his eyes in a fixed large expression of greeting, he raised his left arm high at her and there held it. She saw the movement instantly. Her eyebrows made a sign of question. Patten made a little jigging of urgency with his body. He formed a soundless message with his mouth. Then with the raised hand he made large jabs of pointing to the passage behind her and downstairs.

She understood immediately. Her mouth opened in a horrified little O. She understood that she must not make a sound because the man at the table was taking his shot. So she made no sound and instead broke into a silent giggle, raised her hand to cup over her mouth, bent forward her body as if to contain further the dreadful sound, and then stopped—nodded to Patten meaningfully, grimaced, and backed quietly from the doorway, closing this behind her. She understood very well that this was the way to the Gentlemen's lavatory and that the Ladies' must be back along the passage.

BUT FOR PATTEN she was already hurrying down the stairs for help. His ears sang an excitement of praise for her, for a woman so quick to understand, so resourceful—yet calm enough to laugh! No fright, no fainting: in exaltation of relief she became impressed on his mind—as it happened forever—a figure of strength and color in the gray afternoon, after the gray fear, in the dark doorway.

He did not know what kind of help she would bring—warders and white attendants and straitjackets and leather-aproned barrel trundlers advanced together in his mind: but then as they massed and became more certain, they receded as rapidly into doubt and urgency . . . the large man had swung up from the table startled. The door had clicked. He jerked his head round to it, then moved it backward and forward looking or listening or smelling everywhere in startled animal jerks. He shouted high, stifled:

"What was that? Was someone there?"

Patten shrank into himself again, but managed:

"Nobody. You're hearing things."

The man's great muscular brows jutted together in a harsh-cleft frown, shading the eyes so that deeper back they glittered.

"My ears are all right."

Sound abruptly burst from everywhere. A great jangling amplified electric bell, earsplitting and mechanic. First silence, then abruptly starting nowhere this huge sound! The time bell! Still wired to the billiards room! It split into the large man's head; he threw down his cue clattering on the floor; he swelled his chest up and with one wide bent simian arm clutched the precious shroud and wrenched its placid surface into great troubled waves. Nothing remained of his game. The bell still ringing, he began to walk heavily toward Patten.

"So it's time, is it? Time to stop?"

Patten began to move away from him, backward, backward round the table. The man walked at every step a little faster.

"When the bell goes, it's time to begin. . . ."

At least the table was a protection. He could move fast enough. It could go on forever—it could only be a question of who first gave in—a dizzying vision came to him of minutes, hours spent circling that enormous table.

Then the bell as suddenly stopped. For the second time the door opened—this time it was burst open and there in his shirtsleeves stood the landlord's son—short, shirtsleeved, able, with a clipped black mustache. He was beginning to shout: "Time now . . . please!"—when he saw the large man and whistled.

"Lord—Moony! How in the hell did you get out? Come along, Moony, there's a good chap. . . ."

He walked easily over to the large man. And the large man seemed to have collapsed his strength. He looked embarrassed, and even in that great body, shy. He started to shuffle over to the landlord's son, dragging his hand grudgingly like a bad boy along the table cover.

"Just having a little game, a hundred up—"

The landlord's son took his arm.

"Now, now. You don't want to be playing today; you want to be in your room, nice and quiet—"

Big Moony let himself be led easily away: his face hung and his eyes looked down at his shambling feet. As they left through the door, the landlord's son turned his head round to Patten, screwed up his little mustache, and with his free hand gave three short taps to his forehead.

There are dreams of the condemned cell, of all hope lost, of a final situation where nothing at all more can ever be done and the dreamer faces nothing and absolutely nothing but the end. And then—perhaps—the weight is magically lifted; the walls recede, the pursuing beasts dissolve, the falling viaduct resumes its road. Free air returns, all is relief! But after the first sweet thankfulness, very soon after—

the dreamer looks round him and finds that there he is, indeed safe, but alone also, and with nothing and no one to use his freedom upon. The first need is for another person, someone to tell, someone upon whom to begin to exercise his newfound energies.

Thus with Patten in the billiards room. His chest drew in what felt like strong fresh air as those two left through the door and he looked round at the blessedly empty room. There was no question of not believing it was over—he believed it. He relished that empty room. Then gradually as he looked round, the furniture assumed other identities—the locked windows no longer looked so locked, the shrouded table shrank, the hat stands ceased to loom but simply stood plain as hat stands, the clock looked about to tick. He began to wonder how he could ever have been so enclosed. And then the room began to lose all significance; it became a worthless empty room, a silly place to be. Downstairs there would still be people, the second bell had not rung, he could hear distant laughter. He hurried to the door and to the stairs.

The stairs led straight down into the bar. There, spread out beneath, lay the familiar lighted place. In one corner two ladies laughed, emptying their last drinks. Looking down, he felt an irritation that his release had been so easy, that others had rescued him, that he himself had done nothing toward it. This agitated a greater need than ever to speak of it, to make more of it. He hurried on down: and then saw a third lady join the others—it was his savior in the satin blouse. He remembered her instantly. And he went straight up to her, flushed and smiling and powerful, to thank her and tell her the whole story.

At first the ladies were surprised, then awed, and finally the lady in the blouse broke down laughing. The barman laughed, too. Patten laughed. They all laughed in wonder and relief. Then the barman said how Moony had always been a bit touched, always a big boy for his mum; mum had died one night when Moony was having a game upstairs. He was strong; they gave him the cellar jobs in the pub.

"He wouldn't hurt a flea," the barman said.

In a way, instead of making him feel foolish, this made it even better for Patten. He felt that it had been all right after all. And he addressed himself seriously to the lady in the pink blouse.

1955

....

THE BIG HUSTLE

BY *Walter Tevis*

Walter Tevis was only twenty-eight years old when this story, one of his earliest efforts, was published in Collier's magazine August 5, 1955. Two years later, "The Hustler" appeared in Playboy, and the rest is history.

In a letter reminding me of "The Big Hustle," George Fels, consulting editor of Billiards Digest magazine, wrote: "I was about fifteen when I read it. I consider it to be an early inspiration that I could write about pool, too. Who can forget Ned Bales, Hot Springs Babe, and the first version of the 'I don't rattle, punk!' concept?"

Walter Tevis played good pool but never concentrated on it long enough to advance beyond intermediate status. According to Eleanora Tevis, his widow, he learned the game in his teens in Lexington, Kentucky, from Overton Chenault Kavanaugh.

For more on Tevis, see the introduction to "The Hustler," *page 121.*

NED BALES SAT next to the Chief and watched the kid shooting at the front table. He looked good. Ned guessed he was no more than twenty-five, but from the way he shot, practicing, he looked like a master. He was wearing a cardigan jacket, chartreuse sports shirt, brown-and-white shoes. At one point, he laid his cue aside and lighted a cigarette with an extremely thin, silver lighter. He blew the smoke out of his nose and went on shooting.

Finally the kid made a very difficult shot, and Ned Bales turned to the Chief and said, "So that's the Hot Springs Babe. He looks pretty good."

The Chief laughed, his gold tooth showing. "You said it, Ned Bales. He looks almost as good as you did twenty, twenty-five years ago, when you first came to Chicago."

"A lot of young hustlers *look* good."

"That's right." The Chief laughed again. "But you, Ned Bales, you *were* good. You were The Best."

Ned heard the emphasis in the Chief's voice and knew what was going on. The Chief was backing this kid. This was the first time in fifteen years that the Chief had been willing to back anyone against Ned.

The disturbing thing was that the Chief had always overrated him—as almost everybody had ever since they started calling him The Best—and so, if the Chief thought this Babe kid could take him, it was going to be rough. But Ned was still called The Best and there still wasn't anybody with nerve enough to try him in an even game, even though Ned guessed there were several who could beat him.

Except for an occasional kid—like this Babe—who would try him and lose to Ned's steadiness and experience, all of Ned's games for the last ten years had been with suckers; and now Ned himself wasn't too sure of what his game would be if he had to turn it on again. One of the big troubles with having a reputation was that if they knew how to play and still played him, they were bound to be pretty good.

The Chief stood up and looked toward the Babe. "Babe," he said, "I want you to meet Ned Bales. He's The Best."

Babe shot once more, made the ball, and looked up. "Hello, Bales," he said.

"Hello, Babe," Ned said. He tried to make his voice friendly, tried not to make it show the tenseness he felt.

"Ned Bales is pretty good at straight pool," the Chief said to Babe. "You think you can take him?"

"You putting up the money, Chief?" Babe said coldly.

"If you think maybe you can take him, I'll put up two hundred."

Babe's face was pale and smooth, but it was hard as he looked at Ned Bales. "I'll take him," he said.

The Chief grinned again. "Okay, Ned?" he asked. "You play my boy here? Straight pool, hundred twenty-five points for two hundred dollars? Or maybe you'd rather not? He's good."

Ned looked to the back of the room where the owner of the place was brushing off some tables. "Woody," he said, "come here and rack the balls." Ned nodded to the Chief, who was still grinning, but looked really happy now.

While Woody racked the balls, Ned walked over to the green cabinet in the corner and took out his private cue, a twenty-ounce stick with an ivory point, his name engraved on the little brass ring around the middle where the two sections joined together. It had been years since Ned had needed a cue that could be taken apart for traveling like a hustler from town to small town. But he still used the old joined cue stick. He was used to it, to its weight, balance, and stroke. . . .

Ned lost the toss and Babe elected to let him break. Ned placed the cue ball, aimed carefully, and shot. The break was good. He clipped the corner ball of the triangular rack one-third full and brought his cue ball back up the table to freeze on the near end rail. Two balls came out of the triangle, hit two cushions, and went back, not leaving a shot. It was a perfect rulebook break. The only thing for Babe to do was to try to play safe, to repeat the same shot.

But Babe didn't. He walked over to the foot of the table and looked closely at the balls, sighting carefully. One of the corner balls had not returned to exactly the right spot, and the triangle was a little out of line.

Ned couldn't see anything that looked open for a combination shot, except maybe the twelve ball, the one next to the misplaced corner ball, but that was a rail-first shot, much too tricky and dangerous for a money game.

But Babe walked back to the head of the table. "Twelve ball. Side pocket."

Ned glanced quickly at the Chief. He looked a little worried.

Babe drew his stick back sharply with a clean, cutting hit. The cue ball went a neat two rails and clipped the corner square and firm. The twelve rolled out across the table and fell into the side pocket. The rest of the balls spread wide. Babe had made it. Neatly and perfectly.

Ned sat down. There wasn't anything to do now but watch.

Babe was good. He was terrific. He ran the rest of the rack, then another and another. It wasn't until the score was sixty-two to nothing that Babe got a bad roll on his cue ball, kissed off a ball with it, and scratched.

Ned stepped up quietly and tried to do his best. He was able to score forty-one before he missed and left Babe a shot. Babe ran about fifty, played him safe, and then ran out, winning the game on his next shot.

The Chief looked sympathetic as Ned gave him two hundred dollars, but he didn't say anything.

As the afternoon passed by, Babe kept right on winning—not every game, but two out of three. He made brilliant shots, and his safe game was almost airtight. Ned shot well too, a calm, steady game, but by four o'clock his feet and head were aching, and he was twenty-six hundred dollars behind. A crowd had gathered around the table, and Ned could tell Babe was eating it up. When he'd make an unusually showy or difficult shot, he'd break his silence to make a remark about Ned's age or about the "old days" of the game. There was something cocky, terribly insulting about him. But he was beating Ned and beating him badly.

Ned wondered idly for a while why he didn't quit. He was beat, he knew it, and the surprised, silent crowd watching knew it. But he also knew, with a terrible sense of frustration, that he couldn't stop trying to beat this cocky kid, who shot pool like a wizard; until he'd lost every penny he had, all the money he'd put away in the bank, he couldn't quit. For thirty years, the other man had always quit him. Himself, he had never learned how to quit. Ned watched Babe shoot, running the game out, and he could see the thin little sneer on Babe's face as he won again.

There's only one way, Ned thought; if I keep playing this way, he's got me. There's just one way I might do it.

Ned walked over to the Chief. "How much is that, Chief?" he asked quietly.

Babe spoke before the Chief could answer. "Three thousand, Bales. You've dropped three thousand." He raised his eyebrows. "Wanta quit?"

"No." Ned looked at the Chief. "Want to go it?" he said, keeping his voice level.

For the first time, the Chief sounded doubtful. "What do you think, Babe? Can you go for three thousand?"

The corners of Babe's mouth twitched a little. "I can go," he said.

The Chief looked back at Ned. "I don't like it, Ned Bales," he said, "But I'll go with you. And then we quit, win or lose."

"Fair enough," Ned said.

It was the best way. His only chance was that the debt would rattle the kid. It wasn't too much of a chance; the kid had been around plenty and probably had what it took. So he, Ned Bales, would probably lose and be out six thousand dollars. In a way, it might be a good thing to get beaten badly, to forget about being The Best, and to quit wearing a reputation that had been awfully hard, lately, to wear. . . .

Woody racked the balls, and Babe broke. The break was perfect and there was nothing for Ned to do but play safe. They jockeyed back and forth for a while, both of them playing safe carefully, with precision and control.

Then it happened. It was Babe who hit a ball, just barely too full, leaving Ned an open shot, a slight chance. It wasn't an easy shot, but it was the kind a good hustler can cut in and then run the score way up.

Ned chalked his cue and bent down to shoot, taking aim carefully.

Then Babe spoke. He said softly, "Bales." His voice was slimy with insult and scorn, but with just the slightest trace of fear in it. "Bales. Don't miss that shot. If you do, you'll lose. Three thousand dollars, Bales."

Ned straightened up. He looked at Babe, then turned to the Chief. The Chief looked abashed.

Then Ned laughed. He threw back his head, leaned against the table and laughed. "Chief," Ned said, "he's trying to rattle me. This kid—this punk—is trying to rattle me."

Babe shifted in his chair nervously.

"You're in the wrong league, Babe," Ned said. "I knew there was something wrong with you. You're not playing anymore with the two-bit boys. You don't know who you're playing. Ask the Chief. Ask him about that yellow trick you just tried."

"That doesn't go, Babe," the Chief said. "Ned Bales don't rattle. I tried it once; I know. He's The Best."

Ned went back to the shot, aimed easily, and made it. He started running. He made seventy, and then he played it safe.

When Babe came up to shoot, Ned was trying to be calm and could see that he had him. Babe managed to run thirty-seven before he missed; but when he missed, it was an easy shot, and Ned could see his hand shaking. Ned stepped up to shoot.

Something made him feel like the old Ned, the Ned Bales whose game was like a legend in poolrooms everywhere, the Ned Bales who could always run a game out when the money was up. He shot easily, smoothly, clicking off the shots in his mind and then pocketing them on the table, forgetting his tiredness, forgetting how old he was, just shooting pool, shooting like The Best.

He did it. He ran the game out, ninety-seven points without missing. When he finished, the Chief took three thousand from his pocket and handed it to him. He didn't look at Ned.

"Chief," Babe said, "Let me play him another. I'll take him."

There was mild contempt in the Chief's voice. "No, you won't, Babe," he said. "You shoot good, but you don't play pool, kid. You shoot, but you don't play. You go back to Hot Springs. You do a lot better there."

Ned put the money in a roll and stuffed it in his pocket. "Better luck next time, Chief."

"Sure, Ned Bales," the Chief said. "You come back. Someday maybe I find somebody who'll beat you."

"Maybe you will," Ned said. "Everybody's got to get beat sometime."

As Ned walked out the door, he could feel the aching in his legs and feet and eyes coming back. The air outside was cool, and it was getting dark. Ned decided he'd better take a cab home. He was too tired to walk.

....

THE HUSTLER

BY *Walter Tevis*

You might not be reading this book if it wasn't for Walter Tevis (1928–1984). His short story "The Hustler," which first appeared in Playboy *in January 1957, was expanded into a novel of the same name in 1959 and made into the still-popular black-and-white film in 1961. A sequel to the novel,* The Color of Money, *was published in 1984, followed by a film two years later in which Paul Newman reprised his role of Fast Eddie Felson and won an Academy Award. The second film sparked a tremendous boom in the game—still going strong nine years later—which doubled the number of players in the United States and made books like the one you are holding economically feasible.*

Walter Tevis was born in San Francisco, received a Master of Fine Arts degree from the University of Iowa, and taught English at Ohio University from 1965 to 1978. I can enthusiastically recommend two of his nonpool novels, The Man Who Fell to Earth *(1963), which was made into a haunting film starring David Bowie in 1976, and* Queen's Gambit *(1983), about an orphan girl who is a chess prodigy.*

Note that the story that follows is not about a young hotshot named Fast Eddie Felson but an ex-con named Big Sam Willis. He challenges Louisville Fats, not Minnesota Fats. The characters in the story, novel, and movie are strictly imaginary, despite the claims of many pretenders. Tevis was particularly irritated by one

THEY TOOK SAM out of the office, through the long passageway, and up to the big metal doors. The doors opened, slowly, and they stepped out.

The sunlight was exquisite; warm on Sam's face. The air was clear and still. A few birds were circling in the sky. There was a gravel path, a road, and then, grass. Sam drew a deep breath. He could see as far as the horizon.

A guard drove up in a gray station wagon. He opened the door and Sam got in, whistling softly to himself. They drove off, down the gravel path. Sam did not turn around to look at the prison walls; he kept his eyes on the grass that stretched ahead of them, and on the road through the grass.

When the guard stopped to let him off in Richmond, he said, "A word of advice, Willis."

"Advice?" Sam smiled at the guard.

"That's right. You got a habit of getting in trouble, Willis. That's why they didn't parole you, made you serve full time, because of that habit."

"That's what the man told me," Sam said. "So?"

"So stay out of poolrooms. You're smart. You can earn a living."

Sam started climbing out of the station wagon. "Sure," he said. He got out, slammed the door, and the guard drove away.

It was still early and the town was nearly empty. Sam walked around, up and down different streets, for about an hour, looking at houses and stores, smiling at the people he saw, whistling or humming little tunes to himself.

In his right hand he was carrying his little round tubular leather case, carrying it by the brass handle on the side. It was about thirty inches long, the case, and about as big around as a man's forearm.

At ten o'clock he went to the bank and drew out the six hundred dollars he had deposited there under the name of George Graves. Only it was six hundred eighty; it had gathered that much interest.

Then he went to a clothing store and bought a sporty tan coat, a pair of brown slacks, brown suede shoes, and a bright green sport shirt. In the store's dressing room he put the new outfit on, leaving the prison-issued suit and shoes on the floor. Then he bought two extra sets of underwear and socks, paid, and left.

About a block up the street there was a clean-looking beauty parlor. He walked in and told the lady who seemed to be in charge, "I'm an actor. I have to play a part in Chicago tonight that requires red hair." He smiled at her. "Can you fix me up?"

The lady was all efficiency. "Certainly," she said. "If you'll just step back to a booth we'll pick out a shade."

A half hour later he was a redhead. In two hours he was on board a plane for Chicago, with a little less than six hundred dollars in his pocket and one piece of luggage. He still had the underwear and socks in a paper sack.

In Chicago he took a fourteen-dollar-a-night room in the best hotel he could find. The room was big and pleasant. It looked and smelled clean.

He sat down on the side of the bed and opened his little leather case at the top. The two-piece billiard cue inside was intact. He took it out and screwed the brass joint together, pleased that it still fit perfectly. Then he checked the butt for tightness. The weight was still firm and solid. The tip was good, its shape had held up; and the cue's balance and stroke seemed easy, familiar; almost as though he still played with it every day.

He checked himself in the mirror. They had done a perfect job on his hair; and its brightness against the green and brown of his new clothes gave him the sporty, racetrack sort of look he had always avoided before. His once ruddy complexion was very pale. Not a pool player in town should be able to recognize him: he could hardly recognize himself.

If all went well he would be out of Chicago for good in a few days; and no one would know for a long time that Big Sam Willis had even played there. Six years on a manslaughter charge could have its advantages.

In the morning he had to walk around town for a while before he found a poolroom of the kind he wanted. It was a few blocks off the Loop, small; and from the outside it seemed to be fairly clean and quiet.

Inside, there was a short-order and beer counter up front. In back there were four tables; Sam could see them through the door in the partition that separated the lunchroom from the poolroom proper.

There was no one in the place except for the tall, blond boy behind the counter.

Sam asked the boy if he could practice.

"Sure." The boy's voice was friendly. "But it'll cost you a dollar an hour."

"Fair enough." He gave the boy a five-dollar bill. "Let me know when this is used up."

The boy raised his eyebrows and took the money.

In the back room Sam selected the best twenty-ounce cue he could find in the wall rack, one with an ivory point and a tight butt, chalked the tip, and broke the rack of balls on what seemed to be the best of the four tables.

He tried to break safe, a straight pool break, where you drive the two bottom corner balls to the cushions and back into the stack where they came from, making the cue ball go two rails and return to the top of the table, killing itself on the cushion. The break didn't work, however; the rack of balls spread wide, five of them came out into the table, and the cue ball stopped in the middle. It would have left an opponent wide open for a big run. Sam shuddered.

He pocketed the fifteen balls, missing only once—a long shot that had to be cut thin into a far corner—and he felt better, making balls. He had little confidence on the hard ones; he was awkward. But he still knew the game; he knew how to break up little clusters of balls on one shot so that he could pocket them on the next. He knew how to play position with very little English on the cue, by shooting "natural" shots, and letting the speed of the cue ball do the work. He could still figure the spread, plan out his shots in advance from the positions of the balls on the table, and he knew what to shoot at first.

He kept shooting for about three hours. Several times other players came in and played for a while, but none of them paid any attention to him, and none of them stayed long.

The place was empty again and Sam was practicing cutting balls down the rail, working on his cue ball and on his speed, when he looked up and saw the boy who ran the place coming back. He was carrying a plate with a hamburger in one hand and two bottles of beer in the other.

"Hungry?" He set the sandwich down on the arm of a chair. "Or thirsty, maybe?"

Sam looked at his watch. It was 1:30. "Come to think of it," he said, "I am." He went to the chair, picked up the hamburger, and sat down.

"Have a beer," the boy said, affably. Sam took it and drank from the bottle. It tasted delicious.

"What do I owe you?" he said, and took a bite out of the hamburger.

"The burger's thirty cents," the boy said. "The beer's on the house."

"Thanks," Sam said, chewing. "How do I rate?"

"You're a good customer," the boy said. "Easy on the equipment, cash in advance, and I don't even have to rack the balls for you."

"Thanks." Sam was silent for a minute, eating.

The boy was drinking the other beer. Abruptly, he set the bottle down. "You on the hustle?" he said.

"Do I look like a hustler?"

"You practice like one."

Sam sipped his beer quietly for a minute, looking over the top of the bottle, once, at the boy. Then he said, "I might be looking around." He set the empty bottle down on the wooden chair arm. "I'll be back tomorrow; we can talk about it then. There might be something in it for you, if you help me out."

"Sure, mister," the boy said. "You pretty good?"

"I think so," Sam said. Then when the boy got up to leave, he added, "Don't try to finger me for anybody. It won't do you any good."

"I won't." The boy went back up front.

Sam practiced, working mainly on his stroke and his position, for three more hours. When he finished, his arm was sore and his feet were tired; but he felt better. His stroke was beginning to work for him—he was getting smooth, making balls regularly, playing good position. Once, when he was running balls continuously, racking fourteen and one, he ran forty-seven without missing.

The next morning, after a long night's rest, he was even better. He ran more than ninety balls one time, missing, finally, on a difficult rail shot.

The boy came back at 1:00 o'clock, bringing a ham sandwich this time and two beers. "Here you go," he said. "Time to make a break."

Sam thanked him, laid his cue stick on the table, and sat down.

"My name's Barney," the boy said.

"George Graves." Sam held out his hand, and the boy shook it. "Just," he smiled inwardly at the thought, "call me Red."

"You *are* good," Barney said. "I watched you a couple of times."

"I know." Sam took a drink from the beer bottle. "I'm looking for a straight pool game."

"I figured that, Mister Graves. You won't find one here, though. Up at Bennington's they play straight pool."

Sam had heard of Bennington's. They said it was a hustler's room, a big money place.

"You know who plays pool there, Barney?" he said.

"Sure. Bill Peyton, he plays there. And Shufala Kid, Louisville Fats, Johnny Vargas, Henry Keller, a little guy they call 'The Policeman' . . ."

Henry Keller was the only familiar name; Sam had played him once, in Atlantic City, maybe fourteen years ago. But that had been even before the big days of Sam's reputation, before he had got so good that he had to trick hustlers into playing him. That was a long time ago. And then there was the red hair; he ought to be able to get by.

"Which one's got money," he asked, "and plays straight pool?"

"Well," Barney looked doubtful, "I think Louisville Fats carries a big roll. He's one of the old Prohibition boys; they say he keeps an army of hoods working for him. He plays straights. But he's good. And he doesn't like being hustled."

It looked good; but dangerous. Hustlers didn't take it very well to find out a man was using a phony name so he could get a game. Sam remembered the time someone had told Bernie James who he had been playing and Bernie had got pretty rough about it. But this time it was different; he had been out of circulation six years, and he had never played in Chicago before.

"This Fats. Does he bet big?"

"Yes, he bets big. Big as you want." Barney smiled. "But I tell you he's mighty good."

"Rack the balls," Sam said, and smiled back. "I'll show you something."

Barney racked. Sam broke them wide open and started running. He went through the rack, then another, another, and another. Barney was counting the balls, racking them for him each time. When he got to eighty, Sam said, "Now I'll bank a few." He banked seven, knocking them off the rails, across, and into the pockets. When he missed the eighth, he said, "What do you think?"

"You'll do," Barney said. He laughed. "Fats is good: but you might take him."

"I'll take him," Sam said. "You lead me to him. Tomorrow night you get somebody to work for you. We're going up to Bennington's."

"Fair enough, Mister Graves," Barney said. He was grinning. "We'll have a beer on that."

At Bennington's you took an elevator to the floor you wanted: billiards on the first, pocket pool on the second, snooker and private games on the third. It was an old-fashioned setup, high ceilings, big, shaded incandescent lights, overstuffed leather chairs.

Sam spent the morning on the second floor, trying to get the feel of the tables. They were different from Barney's, with softer cushions and tighter cloths, and it was a little hard to get used to them; but after about two hours he felt as though he had them pretty well, and he left. No one had paid any attention to him.

After lunch he inspected his hair in the restaurant's bathroom mirror; it was still as red as ever and hadn't yet begun to grow out. He felt good. Just a little nervous, but good.

Barney was waiting for him at the little poolroom. They took a cab up to Bennington's.

Louisville Fats must have weighed three hundred pounds. His face seemed to be bloated around the eyes like the face of an Eskimo, so that he was always squinting. His arms, hanging from the short sleeves of his white silk shirt, were pink and doughlike. Sam noticed his hands; they were soft looking, white, and delicate. He wore three rings, one with a diamond. He had on dark green, wide suspenders.

When Barney introduced him, Fats said, "How are you, George?" but didn't offer his hand. Sam noticed that his eyes, almost buried beneath the face, seemed to shift from side to side, so that he seemed not really to be looking at anything.

"I'm fine," Sam said. Then, after a pause, "I've heard a lot about you."

"I got a reputation?" Fats' voice was flat, disinterested. "Then I must be pretty good maybe?"

"I suppose so," Sam said, trying to watch the eyes.

"You a good pool player, George?" The eyes flickered, scanning Sam's face.

"Fair. I like playing. Straight pool."

"Oh." Fats grinned, abruptly, coldly. "That's my game too, George." He slapped Barney on the back. The boy pulled away, slightly, from him. "You pick good, Barney. He plays my game. You can finger for me, sometime, if you want."

"Sure," Barney said. He looked nervous.

"One thing." Fats was still grinning. "You play for money, George? I mean, you gamble?"

"When the bet's right."

"What you think is a right bet, George?"

"Fifty dollars."

Fats grinned even more broadly; but his eyes still kept shifting. "Now that's close, George," he said. "You play for a hundred and we play a few."

"Fair enough," Sam said, as calmly as he could.

"Let's go upstairs. It's quieter."

"Fine. I'll take my boy if you don't mind. He can rack the balls."

Fats looked at Barney. "You level with that rack, Barney? I mean, you rack the balls tight for Fats?"

"Sure," Barney said, "I wouldn't try to cross you up."

"You know better than that, Barney. OK."

They walked up the back stairs to the third floor. There was a small, bare-walled room, well lighted, with chairs lined up against the walls. The chairs were high ones, the type used for watching pool games. There was no one else in the room.

They uncovered the table, and Barney racked the balls. Sam lost the toss and broke, making it safe, but not too safe. He undershot, purposely, and left the cue ball almost a foot away from the end rail.

They played around, shooting safe, for a while. Then Fats pulled a hard one off the edge of the rack, ran thirty-five, and played him safe. Sam jockeyed with him, figuring to lose for a while, only wanting the money to hold out until he had the table down pat, until he had the other man's game figured, until he was ready to raise the bet.

He lost three in a row before he won one. He wasn't playing his best game; but that meant little, since Fats was probably pulling his punches too, trying to take him for as much as possible. After he won his first game, he let himself go a little and made a few tricky ones. Once he knifed a ball thin into the side pocket and went two cushions for a breakup; but Fats didn't even seem to notice.

Neither of them tried to run more than forty at a turn. It would have looked like a game between only fair players, except that neither of them missed very often. In a tight spot they didn't try anything fancy, just shot a safe and let the other man figure it out. Sam played safe on some shots that he was sure he could make; he didn't want to show his hand. Not yet. They kept playing and, after a while, Sam started winning more often.

After about three hours he was five games ahead and shooting better all the time. Then, when he won still another game, Sam said, "You're losing money, Fats. Maybe we should quit." He looked at Barney and winked. Barney gave him a puzzled, worried look.

"Quit? You think we should quit?" Fats took a big silk handkerchief from his side pocket and wiped his face. "How much money you won, George?" he said.

"That last makes six hundred." He felt, suddenly, a little tense. It was coming. The big push.

"Suppose we play for six hundred, George." He put the handkerchief back in his pocket. "Then we see who quits."

"Fine." He felt really nervous now, but he knew he would get over it. Nervousness didn't count. At six hundred a game he would be in clover and in San Francisco in two days. If he didn't lose.

Barney racked the balls and Sam broke. He took the break slowly, putting to use his practice of three days, and his experience of twenty-seven years. The balls broke perfectly, reracking the original triangle, and the cue ball skidded to a stop right on the end cushion.

"You shoot pretty good," Fats said, looking at the safe table that Sam had left him. But he played safe, barely tipping the cue ball off one of the balls down at the foot of the table and returning back to the end rail.

Sam tried to return the safe by repeating the same thing; but the cue ball caught the object ball too thick and he brought out a shot, a long one, for Fats. Fats stepped up, shot the ball in, played position, and ran out the rest of the rack. Then he ran out another rack and Sam sat down to watch; there was nothing he could do now. Fats ran seventy-eight points and then, seeing a difficult shot, played him safe.

He had been afraid that something like that might happen. He tried to fight his way out of the game but couldn't seem to get into the clear long enough for a good run. Fats beat him badly—125 to 30—and he had to give back the six hundred dollars from his pocket. It hurt.

What hurt even worse was that he knew he had less than six hundred left of his own money.

"Now we see who quits." Fats stuffed the money in his hip pocket. "You want to play for another six hundred?"

"I'm still holding my stick," Sam said. He tried not to think about that "army of hoods" that Barney had told him about.

He stepped up to the table and broke. His hand shook a little; but the break was a perfect one.

In the middle of the game Fats missed an easy shot, leaving Sam a dead setup. Sam ran fifty-three and out. He won. It was as easy as that. He was six hundred ahead again and feeling better.

Then something unlucky happened. Downstairs they must have closed up because six men came up during the next game and sat around the table. Five of them Sam had never seen, but one of them was Henry Keller. Henry was drunk now, evidently, and he didn't seem to be paying much attention to what was going on; but Sam didn't like it. He didn't like Keller, and he didn't like having a man who knew who he was around him. It was too much like that other time. That time in Richmond when Bernie James had come after him with a bottle. That fight had cost him six years. He didn't like it. It was getting time to wind things up here, time to be cutting out. If he could win two more games quick, he would have enough to set him up hustling on the West Coast. And on the West Coast there weren't any Henry Kellers who knew that Big Sam Willis was once the best straight-pool shot in the game.

After Sam had won the game by a close score, Fats looked at his fingernails and said, "George, you're a hustler. You shoot better straights than anybody in Chicago shoots. Except me."

This was the time, the time to make it quick and neat, the time to push as hard as he could. He caught his breath, held steady, and said, "You've got it wrong, Fats. I'm better than you are. I'll play you for all of it. The whole twelve hundred."

It was very quiet in the room. Then Fats said, "George, I like that kind of talk." He started chalking his cue. "We play twelve hundred."

Barney racked the balls and Fats broke them. They both played safe, very safe, back and forth, keeping the cue ball on the rail, not leaving a shot for the other man. It was nerve-racking. Over and over.

Then he missed. Missed the edge of the rack, coming at it from an outside angle. His cue ball bounced off the rail and into the rack of balls, spreading them wide, leaving Fats at least five shots. Sam didn't sit down. He just stood and watched Fats come up and start his run. He ran the balls, broke on the fifteenth, and ran another rack. Twenty-eight points. And he was just getting started. He had his rack break set up perfectly for the next shot.

Then, as Fats began chalking up, preparing to shoot, Henry Keller stood up from his seat and pointed his finger at Sam.

He was drunk; but he spoke clearly and loudly. "You're Big Sam Willis," he said. "You're the World's Champion." He sat back in his chair, heavily. "You got red hair, but you're Big Sam." He sat silent, half slumped in the big chair, for a moment, his eyes glassy and red at the corners. Then he closed his eyes and said, "There's nobody beats Big Sam, Fats. Nobody *never*."

The room was quiet for what seemed to be a very long while. Sam noticed how thick the tobacco smoke had become in the air; motionless, it was like a heavy brown mist, and over the table it was like a cloud. The faces of the men in the chairs were impassive; all of them, except Henry, watching him.

Fats turned to him. For once his eyes were not shifting from side to side. He looked Sam in the face and said, in a voice that was flat and almost a whisper, "You Big Sam Willis, George?"

"That's right, Fats."

"You must be pretty smart, Sam," Fats said, "to play a trick like that. To make a sucker out of me."

"Maybe." His chest and stomach felt very tight. It was like when Bernie James had caught him at the same game, except without the red hair. Bernie hadn't said anything, though; he had just picked up a bottle.

But, then, Bernie James was dead now. Sam wondered, momentarily, if Fats had ever heard about that.

Suddenly Fats split the silence, laughing. The sound of his laughing filled the room, he threw his head back and laughed; and the men in the chairs looked at him, astonished, hearing the laughter. "Big Sam," he said, "you're a hustler. You put on a great act; and fool me good. A great act." He slapped Sam on the back. "I think the joke's on me."

It was hard to believe. But Fats could afford the money, and Sam knew that Fats knew who would be the best if it came to muscle. And there was no certainty whose side the other men were on.

Fats shot, ran a few more balls, and then missed.

When Sam stepped up to shoot, he said, "Go ahead, Big Sam, and shoot your best. You don't have to act now. I'm quitting you anyway after this one."

The funny thing was that Sam had been shooting his best for the past five or six games—or thought he had—but when he stepped up to the table this time he was different. Maybe it was Fats or Keller, something made him feel as he hadn't felt for a long time. It was like being the old Big Sam, back before he had quit playing the tournaments and exhibitions, the Big Sam who could run 125 when he was hot and the money was up. His stroke was smooth, steady, accurate, like a balanced, precision instrument moving on well-oiled bearings. He shot easily, calmly, clicking the shots off in his mind and then pocketing them on the table, watching everything on the green, forgetting himself, forgetting even the money, just dropping the balls into the pockets, one after another.

He did it. He ran the game. One hundred twenty-five points, one hundred twenty-five shots without missing. When he finished Fats took twelve hundred from his still-big roll and counted it out, slowly, to him. He said, "You're the best I've ever seen, Big Sam." Then he covered the table with the oilcloth cover.

After Sam had dropped Barney off, he had the cab take him by his hotel and let him off at a little all-night lunchroom. He ordered bacon and eggs, over light, and talked with the waitress while she fried them. The place seemed strange, gay almost; his nerves felt electric, and there was a pleasant fuzziness in his head, a dim, insistent ringing sound coming from far off. He tried to think for a moment; tried to think whether he should go to the airport now without even going back to the hotel, now that he had made out so well, had made out better, even, than he had planned to be able to do in a week. But there was the waitress and then the food; and when he put a quarter in the jukebox he couldn't hear the ringing in his ears anymore. This was no time for plane trips; it was a time for talk and music, time for the sense of triumph, the sense of being alive and having money again, and then time for sleep. He was in a chromium and plastic booth in the lunchroom and he leaned back against the padded plastic backrest and felt an abrupt, deep, gratifying sense of fatigue, loosening his muscles and killing, finally, the tension that had ridden him like a fury for the past three days. There would be plane flights enough tomorrow. Now, he needed rest. It was a long way to San Francisco.

The bed at his hotel was impeccably made; the pale blue spread seemed drum-tight, but soft and round at the edges and corners. He didn't even take off his shoes.

When he awoke, he awoke suddenly. The skin at the back of his neck was itching, sticky with sweat from where the collar of his shirt had been pressed, tight, against it. His mouth was dry and his feet felt swollen, stuffed, in his shoes. The room was as quiet as death. Outside the window a car's tires groaned gently, rounding a corner, then were still.

He pulled the chain on the lamp by the bed and the light came on. Squinting, he stood up and realized that his legs were aching. The room seemed too big, too bright. He stumbled into the bathroom and threw handfuls of cold water on his face and neck. Then he dried off with a towel and looked in the mirror. Startled, he let go the towel momentarily; the red hair had caught him off guard; and with the eyes now swollen, the lips pale, it was not his face at all. He finished drying quickly, ran his comb through his hair, straightened out his shirt and slacks hurriedly. The startling strangeness of his own face had crystallized the dim, half-conscious feeling that had awakened him, the feeling that something was wrong. The hotel room, himself, Chicago; they were all wrong. He should not be here, not now; he should be on the West Coast, in San Francisco.

He looked at his watch. Four o'clock. He had slept three hours. He did not feel tired, not now, although his bones ached and there was sand under his eyelids. He could sleep, if he had to, on the plane. But the important thing, now, was getting on the plane, clearing out, moving West. He had slept with his cue, in its case, on the bed. He took it and left the room.

The lobby, too, seemed too bright and too empty. But when he had paid his bill and gone out to the street, the relative darkness seemed worse. He began to walk down the street hastily, looking for a cabstand. His own footsteps echoed around him as he walked. There seemed to be no cabs anywhere on the street. He began walking faster. The back of his neck was sweating again. It was a very hot night; the air felt heavy against his skin. There were no cabs.

And then, when he heard the slow, dense hum of a heavy car moving down the street in his direction, heard it from several blocks away and turned his head to see it and to see that there was no cab light on it, he knew—abruptly and lucidly, as some men at some certain times know these things—what was happening.

He began to run; but he did not know where to run. He turned a corner while he was still two blocks ahead of the car and when he could feel its lights, palpably, on the back of his neck, and tried to hide in the doorway, flattening himself out against the door. Then, when he saw the lights of the car as it began its turn around the corner, he realized that the doorway was too shallow, that the lights would pick him out. Something in him wanted to scream. He pushed himself from his place, stumbled down the street, visualizing in his mind a place, some sort of a place between buildings where he could hide completely and where the car could never follow him. But the buildings were all together, with no space at all between them; and when he saw that this was so, he also saw at the same instant that the car lights were flooding him. And then he heard the car stop. There was nothing more to do. He turned around and looked at the car, blinking.

Two men had got out of the backseat; there were two more in front. He could see none of their faces; but was relieved that he could not, could not see the one face that would be bloated like an Eskimo's and with eyes like slits.

The men were holding the door open for him.

"Well," he said. "Hello, boys," and climbed into the backseat. His little leather case was still in his right hand. He gripped it tightly. It was all he had.

....

CHAMPS

BY *Pedro Juan Soto*

Pedro Juan Soto was born in Puerto Rico in 1928, served in the army during the Korean war, earned an M.A. in English from Columbia University, and returned to Puerto Rico in 1954, where he still lives. "Champs" appeared in a collection of his short stories called Spiks *(1957), published in English in 1973 by Monthly Review Press.*

Señor Soto is the author of four novels, three short story collections, and two plays. One of his novels, Hot Land, Cold Season *(1961), was published in English by Dell in 1973.*

Concerning his pool playing, he writes: "I play once in a while when my wife and I travel to the Puerto Rican countryside. It has always been a good way to make friends or enemies and influence people. I had to learn it in order to keep track of my youngest brother, a good pool player who was murdered in a South Bronx poolroom."

THE CUE MADE one more sweep over the green cloth, hit the cue ball, and smacked it against the fifteen ball. The plump, yellowish hands remained still until the ball went clop into the pocket, and then they raised the cue until it was diagonally in front of his acned and fatuous face: his vaselined little curl fell neatly over his forehead, his cigarette was tucked jauntily behind an ear, his glance was oblique and mocking, and the fuzz on his upper lip had been accentuated with a pencil.

"Quiubo, man. Wha's up?" asked a shrill voice. "That was sure a champeen shot, eh?"

He started to laugh. His squat, pudgy body became a gaily trembling blob inside his tight jeans and sweaty T-shirt.

He contemplated Gavilán—his eyes once alive now no longer so, his three-day beard trying to conceal the ill humor on his face and not succeeding, the long-ashed cigarette gripped between lips behind which swam curses—and enjoyed the feat he had perpetrated. He had beaten him two games in a row. Of course, Gavilán had been in jail for six months, but that did not matter now. What mattered was that Gavilán had lost two games to him, and these victories placed him in a privileged position. They put him above the others, above the best players of the barrio, above those who had thrown the inferiority of his sixteen years, his childishness, in his face. No one now could deprive him of his place in Harlem. He was *el nuevo*, the successor to Gavilán and other respected individuals. He was equal. . . . No. Superior, because of his youth: he had more time and greater opportunity to surpass all their deeds.

He felt like going out in the street and shouting: "I won two games in a row off Gavilán! Now say somethin', go ahead an' say somethin'!" But he didn't. He merely chalked his cue and told himself it wouldn't be worth it. It was sunny outside, but it was Saturday and the neighbors would be at the market at this hour of the morning. His audience would be snot-nosed kids and indifferent grandmothers. Anyhow, some humility was good in champions.

He picked up the quarter Gavilán had thrown down on the felt and exchanged a self-satisfied smile with the scorekeeper and the three spectators.

"Take wha's yours!" he said to the scorekeeper, wishing that one of the spectators would move to the other tables and spread the news, comment that he—Puruco, that fat kid, the one with the pimply face and the funny voice—had made the great Gavilán look ridiculous. But apparently the three were waiting for more proof.

He put away his fifteen cents and said to Gavilán, who was wiping the sweat from his face: "Wanna play another?"

"Sure," said Gavilán, picking another cue from the rack and chalking it meticulously.

The scorekeeper took down the triangle and set up for the next game.

Puruco broke, starting immediately to whistle and stroll elastically around the table, almost on the tips of his sneakers.

Gavilán approached the cue ball with his characteristic slowness and aimed at it, but he did not shoot. He simply raised his bushy head, his body leaning over the cue and the cloth, and said: "Lissen, quit whistlin'."

"Okay, man," said Puruco, and swung his cue until he heard Gavilán's cue stroke and the balls rolled and cracked once again. Not one was pocketed.

"Ay bendito." Puruco laughed. "Man, I got this guy licked."

He shot at the one ball, made it, and left the two ball lined up with the left pocket. The two ball also went in. He could not keep from smiling at all corners of the pool hall. He seemed to invite the spiders, the flies, the various numbers runners among the crowd at the other tables to witness this.

He studied the position of each ball carefully. He wanted to win this game too, to take advantage of his recent reading of Willie Hoppe's book and all those months of practice taunted by his rivals. Last year he was no more than a little pisser; now real life was beginning, a champ's life. With Gavilán beaten, he would defeat Mamerto and Bimbo. . . . "Make way for Puruco!" the connoisseurs would say. And he would impress the owners of the pool halls, he'd get good connections. He'd be bodyguard for some, intimate friends of others. He'd have cigarettes and beer for free. And women, not stupid girls who were always afraid and who wouldn't go further than some squeezing at the movies. From there to fame: the neighborhood macho, the man with a hand in everything—numbers, dope, the chick from Riverside Drive slumming in the barrio, the rumble between this gang and that to settle things "like men."

With a grunt he miscued the three ball and swore. Gavilán was behind him when he turned around.

"Careful—doncha gimme that evil eye," he said bristling.

And Gavilán: "Aw, cuddid out."

"Naw, don' gimme that, man. Jus' 'cause yer losin'."

Gavilán didn't answer. He aimed at the cue ball through the smoke, which was wrinkling his features, and shot, pocketing two balls on opposite sides.

"See that?" said Puruco, and he crossed his fingers to ward off evil.

"Shut yer mouth!"

Gavilán tried to ricochet the five ball, but he missed. Puruco studied the position of the ball and decided on the farther but better lined-up pocket. As he was aiming, he realized he would have to uncross his fingers. He looked at Gavilán suspiciously and crossed his legs to shoot. He missed.

When he looked up, Gavilán was smiling and sucking his sick upper gums, to spit out the bloody pus. Puruco no longer doubted that he was the victim of an evil spell.

"Don' fool aroun', man. Play clean."

Gavilán looked at him surprised, stepping on his cigarette casually.

"Wassa matter with you?"

"Naw," said Puruco, "don' go on with that *bilongo*, that evil eye."

"Jeezus," laughed Gavilán. "He believes in witches!"

He brought the cue behind his waist, feinted once, and pocketed the ball easily. He pocketed the next one. And the next. Puruco got nervous. Either Gavilán was recovering his skill or that *bilongo* was pushing his cue. He had to step it up, or Gavilán would win this game.

He chalked his cue, knocked on wood three times, and waited his turn. Gavilán missed his fifth shot. Then Puruco gauged the distance. He dropped the eight ball in. He did a combination to pocket the eleven with the nine ball. Then he got the nine ball in. He cannoned the twelve ball into the pocket and then missed on the ten ball. Gavilán also missed it. Finally Puruco managed to make it, but for the thirteen ball he almost ripped the felt. He added up to himself. Only eight points missing now, so he felt he could relax.

He moved the cigarette from his ear to his lips. As he was lighting it with his back to the table so that the fan would not blow out the match, he saw the scorekeeper's sly smile. He turned quickly and caught Gavilán in the act: his feet were off the ground and his body rested on the edge of the table to make the shot easier. Before he could speak, Gavilán had pocketed the ball.

"Lissen, man!"

"Watsa matter?" Gavilán said calmly, eyeing the next shot.

"Don' gimme that, kid! You ain' gonna win like that!"

Gavilán raised an eyebrow to look at him and sucked in his cheeks, biting the inside of his mouth.

"Wha's botherin you?" he said.

"No, not like that." Puruco opened his arms, almost hitting the scorekeeper with his cue. He threw down his cigarette violently and said to the spectators: "You saw' im, dinchya?"

"Saw what?" asked Gavilán, deadpan.

"That dirty move," shrilled Puruco: "You think I'm a fool?"

"Aw Jeezus Christ," laughed Gavilán. "Don' ask me 'cause I might just tell you!"

Puruco struck the table edge with his cue.

"You gotta play clean with me. It ain' enough you make magic first, but then you gotta cheat too."

"Who cheated?" said Gavilán. He left his cue on the table and approached Puruco, smiling. "You tellin' me I cheat?"

"No," said Puruco, his tone changing, sounding more like a child, his body wobbly. "But you shouldn' play like that, man. They seen you."

Gavilán turned around to the others.

"Did I cheat?"

Only the scorekeeper shook his head. The others said nothing, just looked away.

"But you was on top uh the table, man!" said Puruco.

Gavilán grabbed the front of his T-shirt almost casually, baring Puruco's pudgy back as he pulled him forward.

"Nobody calls me a cheat!"

At all the other tables the games stopped. The others watched from a distance. Nothing but the hum of the fan and the flies could be heard and the shouts of the kids in the street.

"You think a pile uh shit like you can call me a cheat?" said Gavilán, pushing into Puruco's chest with the fist that gripped his shirt. "I let you win two games so you could have somethin' to brag about, and you think yer king or somethin'. Geddoudahere, you miserable . . . ," he said between his teeth. "When you grow up I'll see you."

The shove pushed Puruco against the plaster wall, crashing him flat on his back. The crash shattered the silence. Someone laughed, snickering. Someone said, "Wadda boaster!"

"An' geddoudahere 'fore I kick yer ass," said Gavilán.

"Okay, man," stammered Puruco, letting the cue drop.

He walked out without daring to raise his eyes, hearing again the cue strokes on the tables, the little laughs. In the street he felt like crying but he didn't. That was sissy stuff. The blow he had received had not hurt him; what hurt was the other: "When you grow up I'll see you." He *was* a man. If they beat him, if they killed him, let 'em do it forgetting that he was sixteen. He was already a man. He could make trouble, lots of trouble, and he could also survive it.

He crossed the street furiously kicking a beer can, his hands in his pockets pinching the body nailed to the cross of adolescence.

He had let him win two games, said Gavilán. Liar. He knew that from now on he would lose all of them to him, the new champ. That's why the witchcraft, the cheating, the blow. Ah, but those three guys would spread the news of Gavilán's fall. Then Mamerto and Bimbo. No one could stop him now. The neighborhood, the whole world, would be his.

When the barrel hoop got caught between his legs, he kicked it to one side and slapped the kid who came to pick it up.

"Wachout, man, I'll split yer eye."

And he went on walking, ignoring the mother who cursed him as she ran toward her crying child. He breathed deeply, his lips closed tight. As he moved along he saw streamers fall and cheers rain from the deserted and closed windows.

He was a champ, walking along ready for trouble.

BEYOND THE SUNSET

BY *Jesse Hill Ford*

Almost every billiard room has a player who prefers playing alone. You can see him or her off in the corner, practicing, practicing. Mr. Clarence Perks, in the following story, has played by himself during his lunch breaks all his life, never drinking, never gambling, never competing. One day he is forced into a game with a stranger; the results are surprising to all concerned.

Jesse Hill Ford received an M.A. from the University of Florida in 1955 and attended the University of Oslo as a Fulbright scholar in 1961. His writings have won him an Atlantic Monthly Award (1959), an O'Henry Award (1961), a Guggenheim Fellowship (1966), and an Edgar Award (1975). His 1965 novel, The Liberation of Lord Byron Jones, *a Book-of-the-Month Club selection, was made into a movie in 1969.*

"Beyond the Sunset" was first published in the Atlantic Monthly *in 1960, later in a collection of Ford stories entitled* Fishes, Birds, and Sons of Men, *published by Atlantic Monthly Press in 1968.*

As PEOPLE SAID, Mr. Clarence Perks looked like a man who would skin a flea for its hide and tallow. It was his nose, too long and too thin and too snoopy; it was his eyes, restless and gleaming hard as flint. Below his eyes two red spots marked his cheekbones, and the rest of his face was pale and tinged yellow, like a toad's belly.

When he spoke, his voice was no better, for it whined like an old hound under the porch on a winter's night.

As a result, his only way of making friends was to listen to people, and all the winter, after he came to Somerton from east Tennessee, he listened to the west Tennesseans talk. Mostly they told him what a regular ringtail tooter Billy Turnbull had been, how everybody loved Billy, what a fast car Billy had, and what a sweet wife Billy had left without any insurance to support her, so that she had bought a couple of hair dryers on credit and curtained off half the front room at Billy's house for a beauty parlor business.

And Mr. Clarence listened and said almost nothing because he was at a disadvantage in Somerton, having taken Billy Turnbull's place as manager of the People's Dandy Store, a dry-goods establishment on Main Street across from Alf's Service Station. Alf's, Mr. Clarence soon learned, sold almost anything liquid you could name except gasoline and oil, and it had been Alf's where Billy was last seen alive. Although Billy had had on him a sweet face, the truth was that Billy had been a pretty terrible drinker about once a month, and when he drank, Billy's thoughts always wandered to his car, which was blue and had a souped-up engine, until finally Billy would get in his car and shake the cobs out of it in the general direction of Memphis. The last time Billy had lit a rag for Memphis, he had died trying to cross the Forked Deer River about six feet to the left of the highway bridge, thereby leaving the Somerton People's Dandy without a living manager. Here was where Mr. Clarence Perks came in, a stranger from east Tennessee, and under a cloud because he was replacing a very popular fellow.

When they asked Mr. Perks why in the world *he* was sent to Somerton, the old man would turn white around the mouth and try to reel off the explanation as fast as he could, for merely thinking of *why* gave him a deep sensation of regret. The People's Dandy was a chain of stores operating in fifty Tennessee counties, and they had bought Mr. Perks out lock, stock, and barrel up in Cherokee Gap, near the state line, where he had owned a small store. Then, like a fool, Mr. Perks had gone to work for the People's Dandy folks, managing what had once been his own store. The next thing he knew they had transferred him to Somerton. The reason they transferred *him*, they said, was because he didn't have any living family. His wife was dead. So one day, sure enough, his orders came, and Mr. Perks got on the bus in the sunset of his life, for he was sixty and hadn't felt well in years, and he came to live far, far away from everything he loved.

But anyway, he said, he had survived. He had a room two blocks back off Main Street in the Somerton Tourist Home. What he didn't tell was that every night when he couldn't sleep for thinking about home, about Cherokee Gap, he would raise his window and put the light out and lie on his bed listening to them break half-pint bottles out behind Alf's Service Station.

He would listen to the bottles breaking and finally the sounds of shattering glass would get his mind off all his wrong decisions, and he would think how they were over at Alf's mourning for Billy Turnbull. Half-an-acre-of-broken-glass, Mr. Perks would think, hearing a bottle break. For Mr. Perks himself was not a drinking man. And presently, counting the bottles as they broke, Mr. Perks would be lulled to sleep, if he didn't think about his wife, Lura. But if he happened to think about his wife, he would lie wide awake and begin to blame Lura for dying, for Lura's death was what he figured had caused all his troubles. If Lura had lived, he would not have sold his store in Cherokee Gap. Lura wouldn't have let him do it. If Lura had lived, Mr. Clarence Perks would never have been transferred into the midst of strangers just at a time in his life when the idea of going beyond the sunset should have been a comfort.

"Beyond the Sunset." It had been a favorite song of his, for he had secretly planned for twenty-five years to die before his wife, Lura, and thus to have some time to himself in heaven before she got there. Well, that was all ruined. She was there now, waiting for him, and so he didn't write in to the radio stations on his birthday any more to request them to play "Beyond the Sunset" for Clarence Perks. No. He had only one remaining pleasure in life, and when he finally got around to thinking about *it,* he could get some little bit of satisfaction. His mind would feed on it, and then, while the sound of bottles breaking behind Alf's drifted in his window upstairs at the Somerton Tourist Home, Mr. Perks would drop off to sleep. And not infrequently, he would dream about his one remaining pleasure, shooting pool.

So the winter passed, and Mr. Perks was still listening, trying hard to make friends with the People's Dandy customers, and they began to dingdong at him in March, saying everybody in cotton country had to have credit for spring hats and shoes and work clothes, and how in the hell did he expect to stay in business being so tight on credit? And Billy Turnbull, now, *he* had let everybody have credit because *he* knew come the fall and cotton season that the accounts would be settled up. And all the while Mr. Perks just stood there with a letter in his hind pants pocket from the People's Dandy Chain, from the headquarters office in Nashville. And the letter said that, other than certain names on the letter in black, credit would be limited to twenty-five dollars per customer family, and that names on the list in red—the worst of it being that so many of the red names were Billy Turnbull's own flesh and kin—that the red names were to have no credit at all.

So, whenever he got a chance, Mr. Perks nearly wore the letter out that spring by unfolding it in the stockroom at the back of the store, checking to see who could buy what, if anything, and in what amounts.

And when summer, which fell in like the roof was on fire in June, instead of creeping up gradually sweet the way it did up east in Cherokee Gap, when summer came they commenced to complain how the store wasn't even air-conditioned and said they never knew the People's Dandy to be so hot back whenever Billy was manager, back when it was a *real* store where somebody could buy something without he had to sign his name six times. For, as they said, it hurt a man or a woman having to go through standing there while some point-nosed hill rabbit like Mr. Clarence Perks called up the bank and shouted so loud in the telephone he could be heard clean across the street and into the dime store if you happened to be over there.

"Well," Mr. Perks would sometimes say, slyly, "the dime store's strictly cash, so why would anybody in Sligo County be over there anyhow?" Mr. Perks couldn't help saying *something* back now and then, for he was dead tired of trying to sleep under an electric fan, a thing never needed where he had come from, and the hot weather lit a little blaze of anger in him that he could not hide all the time.

And finally, in September, the cotton bolls started turning brown. That was when Mr. Perks discovered they didn't have enough cotton sacks in stock, long funny things he had never seen, things the cotton pickers were supposed to drag behind them as they went through the fields. So Mr. Perks put through a rush order and ended up with several gross too many in stock, many more than could be sold. For that mistake he got a birthday letter from People's Dandy, addressed in red ink. All it said was: "Happy birthday with regard to seven gross cotton sacks too many in which People's Dandy money tied up."

Of course, his clerks found out about the birthday letter by taking it out of the wastebasket before throwing the trash out back of the store, and they told the birthday story on Mr. Perks all over town. For several days afterward store customers would come in and try to explain to Mr. Perks how to merchandise his store. And he just sat by the hour and listened and never uttered a word, for at noon every day he got some relief.

As long as he could remember, nearly, since he first went to work in a dry-goods store in Cherokee Gap at eleven years of age, Mr. Clarence had played pool on his lunch hour. So now, every day at noon, he took his two baloney and mustard light-bread sandwiches to the Somerton Pool Hall, down a side street and up over the bus station, and there Mr. Perks gobbled his sandwiches down. When his sandwiches were gone he would buy a Powerhouse candy bar and a Pepsi, and finally, swigging on the Pepsi and eating the candy, he would shoot a game or two of pool.

He had always played against himself—all his life. And nobody in Cherokee Gap had cared, for the pool hall was nearly always empty at noon anyway. And probably nobody in Somerton would have ever noticed if the pool hall manager on this particular day had not been fresh out of detective magazines to read. What the Somerton pool hall manager saw over Mr. Perks's shoulder was that the new manager of the People's Dandy was a pool-playing shark. He was more than that, he was a maestro. Old Mr. Perks was so good that the sight caught the pool hall manager completely off guard and he swallowed his spit backward and nearly strangled before he could quit coughing. As he said later, Mr. Clarence Perks just didn't look like a pool shooter, he didn't act like a pool shooter, he didn't smell like one— but he was. So when Mr. Perks had cleared all the balls off the table and racked himself up a new game, the pool hall manager, who made it quite a practice never to say a word if he could possibly get around saying it, spoke up.

"You shoot pretty fair," he said.

His coughing and gagging hadn't startled Mr. Perks a bit, but his speaking voice did. Mr. Perks long since had assumed that the pool hall manager was a deaf-mute, for he had never heard him say a word or seen him even come from behind his counter, not for ten months, six days a week, fifty minutes each day. Not even "Hello."

So Mr. Perks felt his heart begin to pound and he took a swig of

Pepsi to calm himself. Then he said, "Well, many thanks," and put his drink down and broke the triangle formation of balls and swiftly cleared the table again. Just to be friendly he made some of his hardest shots with the cue stick behind his back. And then he sank a few shooting left-handed, thinking the pool hall manager might say something else, but he didn't. The manager just stood there. So when the last shot was sunk Mr. Perks ate the last bit of Powerhouse and downed the final swig of Pepsi and went back to the People's Dandy. Hardly anyone noticed him as he went swiftly up to Main Street, and at one o'clock sharp he was in the back of the store again, checking his black list before phoning the bank. But that was the last day hardly anybody noticed Mr. Perks on his lunch hour.

It was the last day because the next day the pool hall manager went downstairs to the bus station and bought four secondhand mystery magazines from the ticket agent for a dime. The bus drivers saved the magazines for the ticket agent, collecting what passengers left behind when a bus was emptied. So at noon, when the ticket agent saw Mr. Clarence Perks pass and when he heard footsteps on the stairs leading up to the pool hall, something in his brain connected up the noise going past his ear with what his eyes had just seen. In other words, as he later said, he put two and two together to get four, that the noise on the stairs and the sight of Mr. Clarence Perks going by with his sack of two baloney sandwiches were connected.

The ticket agent put his hand in his pocket then and fingered the dime which the pool hall manager had paid for the four magazines, and fingering the dime he remembered what the pool hall manager had said about Mr. Perks. So in five minutes, when he couldn't get it off his mind, for not being able to believe it, the ticket agent was upstairs eating a stale pack of Cheez-It snacks and drinking a grape soda which he bought with the dime. He stood beside the pool hall manager and they both watched Mr. Perks.

For his part, Mr. Perks tried to start up a conversation. He tried twice. The first time he said it was a nice day, and the second time he said it was a shame the way candy bars got littler every year. For example, he went on, say the clothing business tried something like that, making all the shirts littler. But neither the pool hall manager nor the ticket agent wanted to talk, so Mr. Perks concentrated on his game and ignored them. And the day following he had ten people watching him. And the next day following that, which was Friday, there were a dozen, including a sort of slick-faced young man in electric-blue peg trousers, who identified himself as a champion pool shooter from Colliertown, over in the next county. He wanted to shoot Mr. Perks a game, he said, for ten dollars. He looked relieved when Mr. Perks said flatly, "No thanks." Everybody there knew Mr. Perks could have beat the out-of-town man hands down, and by reputation the Colliertown hotshot was the best pool player in west Tennessee, or had been, until Mr. Clarence Perks was transferred to Somerton.

Mr. Perks thought very little more about it. He had always played against himself, not against others. And as far as he was concerned, that was that. Besides, cotton season was going now in dead earnest, and they were really busy at the People's Dandy.

When he locked up the store that evening to go home, tractor-drawn cotton trailers were piling into Main Street like an endless circus parade, and little rollers of cotton lint about the size of Mr. Perks' thumbs were blowing along the sidewalk, picking up dust and trash as they went. The little thumbs of cotton tickled Mr. Perks some way, making him almost smile, seeing them. They made him think of a barbershop in Somerton where they were cutting off all the long gray whiskers of all the old men in the whole world. Whiskers, thought Mr. Perks as he walked to the tourist home. Cabbage, he thought, as he went inside the home and climbed the stairs to the hallway bathroom and washed up for supper.

And it was sure enough cabbage he had smelled as he came in the door. At supper Mrs. Dillworth, the landlady, talked her customary steady stream and let the others at her table—the three railroad men, the two salesmen, the tractor mechanic, the new high school agriculture teacher, and Mr. Perks—eat in peace. Mr. Perks was inwardly observing, as was his habit, that the fat-faced salesman ate twice as many biscuits as the others at the table. And then he wondered why the mere fact that the high school ag teacher took cream in his coffee but no sugar set him apart from the rest of them somehow, identified him, in fact, as an educated man. But-it-does, Mr. Perks thought, helping himself to more cabbage as the bowl came by, and as he replaced the serving spoon, the sound of it rapping against the bowl reminded him that the room had gone silent. Looking at Mrs. Dillworth, he realized dimly that she had spoken to him.

"I beg your pardon?" said Mr. Perks to the landlady.

"—that you play pool?" she said. "Do you go to the pool hall after lunch each day, Mr. Perks?"

"Why, yes," said Mr. Perks, "I do." He had it in mind to explain that he had been doing just that for years, playing pool against himself on his lunch hour, and to add that it was his one remaining pleasure, but something about the set of Mrs. Dillworth's mouth drained that notion out of him, and he corrected himself, lamely saying, "Well, I— I don't often go if it's raining."

"They sell beer there," said Mrs. Dillworth. "It's a gathering place for drunkards, trash."

"But I don't drink," Mr. Perks said. He looked about him, at the other men.

"Beer and billiards go together like ham and eggs," Mrs. Dillworth said firmly. "I don't like the name of the Somerton Tourist Home being mixed up with the pool hall, Mr. Perks."

"Anybody who goes to a pool hall is asking for trouble," the tractor mechanic said. He was a very religious man, and his voice quavered as he spoke. Three years before he had tracked down his young wife and her lover and had killed them both with a ball-peen hammer, in self-defense. Mr. Perks had always been a little frightened of the mechanic, and sometimes, meeting him coming out of the bathroom in the morning, Mr. Perks had noticed the mechanic's white muscular arms. The man was a violent enemy of everything sinful and was capable of nearly *anything,* so they said, when he lost his temper. "Asking for trouble," the mechanic repeated. "First it's a sip of beer. Next you start smoking. Then you spit on the floor. One bad habit leads to another one until, until you— you—" The next sin was so terrible that the tractor mechanic did not even talk about it. He turned very pale instead and was silent a moment before he said, "I don't know if I'd want to live under the same roof with anybody that went in a place like that pool hall."

"Well, wait a second," Mr. Perks said. "Now you take this fact, now, I'm sixty-five years old." He made himself five years older than he really was. But-I-have-to-protect-myself, he thought. Certainly the mechanic wouldn't try to throttle a weak little old man and send him beyond the sunset. But the mechanic was still glaring at Mr. Perks.

"It's *never* too late for sin," the tractor mechanic said in a threatening tone. "Never too early and *never* too late, Mr. Clarence. If it happens to be one thing I know out of experience, it's just that."

"Aw, I don't see nothing so wrong in it," said the fat-faced salesman tolerantly, buttering a biscuit. "If Mr. Perks wants to run upstairs over the bus station on his lunch hour at noon and shoot hisself a little pool. Especially so long as he don't bother nobody. Maybe has him a candy bar and a Pepsi. Now I wouldn't *know*, of course, what Mr. Clarence does, for, as you all know, it is my policy to keep my nose out of other folks' business and never to listen at no idle gossip.''

"No sugar, thanks," said the ag teacher automatically as he reached out and got the cream pitcher.

Sizing up things, Mr. Perks saw that, except for Mrs. Dillworth and the tractor mechanic, none of the others cared. And the fat sales-man was the star boarder, since he took the three-dollar room which looked out over the parking lot of the Methodist Church. So the matter was more or less settled. But as they left the table, embarrassed and silent for the sake of Mr. Perks, the tractor mechanic growled one last time. "You'll end up getting in trouble, Mr. Perks. You'll see," he said.

Mr. Perks opened the store Saturday morning, not sure whether he would go to the pool hall or not. He thought of his wife, Lura, and he thought of Cherokee Gap. He thought of "Beyond the Sunset." No-escape, he thought.

At lunchtime he grabbed his paper sack and walked on down to the pool hall. He finished eating and took down the cue stick he always used, an old model, one end of which appeared a little charred, as though someone years before had poked a fire with it. Turning to the table, he saw the ticket agent coming through the screen door, followed by two farmers in overalls. Mr. Perks chalked his cue stick and had just prepared to break the wedge of balls at the other end of the pool table when a weather-gnarled hand appeared in his line of sight. The hand held a brown bottle of beer, and when it drew back it left the beer bottle directly in front of the cue ball. The entire action reminded Mr. Perks of a television advertisement, so he looked up at the farmer and grinned. But when he saw the farmer's face he felt the pink dawn of something warn him, deep in his belly. The other man had a sour, milky odor, and his face was curiously reptilian, with a blunt, curved mouth.

"Play you for that there beer," the farmer said. "And then my brother, he wants to play you." He turned and took down a cue stick from the rack and turned back to Mr. Perks, as though the match were arranged.

"I don't play for beer," Mr. Perks said.

"Ain't you the champeen?" the farmer asked.

"I never play—"

"Ain't you the new People's Dandy man?"

Mr. Perks nodded. "But I don't play for beer," he said. "I just don't."

The farmer's brother stepped in from behind Mr. Perks then. "We come up here to play you," the brother said. He turned to the ticket agent. "He's the one they been talking about, ain't he? Looky there at what a nose."

"Oh, he's the one," said the ticket agent. "He's the champ."

"I come on my lunch hour. I don't drink beer nor gamble," Mr. Perks said. He spoke calmly, trying not to show his anger.

"That's right, boys. No call to take offense," said the ticket agent. "Just because Mr. Perks is particular about who he plays with ain't no cause for you to go and bust an old man's face in with them beer bottles."

Mr. Perks felt himself go pale.

The farmer turned angrily to the ticket agent. "You mean to say I ain't got the right to ast anybody I want to about shooting a pool game with me? Is that what you're a-trying to push off on me?"

"I ain't in this argument, mister," the ticket agent said. "It's between you and him, between Mr. Clarence Perks here and yourself."

The farmer turned back to him, and Mr. Perks saw again that his mouth was curved upward toward the center, like a snake's. "You think I ain't got the money to play you, ain't that it, Mr. Dandy?"

"Mr. Perks gets awful mad if you don't call him by his right name," the ticket agent said.

"Think I ain't got it," the farmer went on, moving his right hand slowly up the front of his overalls to a center zipper pocket over his chest. Mr. Perks expected to see a pistol, but instead money came out of the pocket, a great wad of it.

"Boys, he's going to bet his cotton money against Mr. Perks," the ticket agent said.

Mr. Perks looked around at the crowd, surprised at how quickly it had gathered. Then he looked at the farmer. "I'll shoot you for a dollar," he said briskly. "You want to break them?"

The farmer nodded and the game started. Mr. Perks won the dollar and then five dollars, and then the bets were doubled each time, because the crowd insisted that it was only fair for Mr. Perks to give the farmer a chance to win his cotton money back. Just when the bet got up over two hundred dollars, Mr. Perks began to warm up. He beat the farmer, shooting all his shots with the cue stick behind his back. Then he beat him shooting left-handed. And finally the farmer laid down the entire roll, seven hundred dollars. Mr. Perks shot the last game left-handed with one foot off the floor and his left eye closed, and the farmer got five shots and missed three of those. Then Mr. Perks clasped his hands together and cracked his knuckles. My-dander's-up, Mr. Perks thought. "Now, where's your brother?" he asked.

"I done thought this over, and I don't guess I'll play," the brother said. "I never could stand the sight of a cheater, nohow."

"Are you saying I cheat?" Mr. Perks said sternly. My-dander's-up, he thought again. It-really-is-up. He had felt the same way only once that he could remember, once near Cherokee Gap when the car he was riding in with its owner lost its brakes on a mountain road and finally plowed into a hay wagon, killing a mule and the man driving the wagon and breaking Mr. Perks's collarbone. It was a queer giddy feeling, and for the second time in his life he was feeling it. He noticed his unfinished Powerhouse and calmly took a bite of it. Then he swigged a little Pepsi. Finally he looked at the man he had beaten fairly. Seven-hundred-dollars-and-forty-six-cents, he thought. And then he felt the warning. The farmer's hand came out of his overalls pocket slowly, this time with a little hook-bill knife, which the farmer opened. Seeing the dark little yellow-tarnished blade gave Mr. Perks a sensation he sometimes had when he went outdoors and saw the sunset after working hard indoors all day. It was exhilarating, like stepping outside into the cool fresh air and looking west, at the last pink glow of the sky, like knowing suddenly how you've spent your whole life. Your-whole-form-life, thought Mr. Clarence Perks, looking at the knife blade.

"He's gonna cut the old man," said the ticket agent, marveling. "He's gonna spill Mr. Perks's guts—he's going to—looky!"

The farmer came on slowly and Mr. Perks backed away. It was like a dance, but the music was mostly silent except for the scrape of Mr. Perks's shoes and the sudden scuffle of the farmer's shoes as he lunged forward. Mr. Perks reversed the old pool cue and brought it down briskly on the farmer's head. When the cue didn't break he swung it sideways and caught the man just above the left ear. First the farmer's knife fell, and then the farmer himself went down. He appeared to sit down at first, but then, with the blood running freely over his ear where the scalp was split, he fell backward, hard. He lay there very pale and still, the first man Mr. Clarence Perks had ever felled. Oh-Lord-my-dander's-*sure*-up, thought Mr. Perks. It's-up-for-a-fact!

While the pool hall manager phoned the police, the ticket agent squatted down beside the bleeding man and spoke up. "It was the purest case of self-defensing I ever seen," he declared. "I wish you'd looky how this guy's a-bleeding."

The cue stick, which Mr. Perks still held, was broken like a corn stalk. And-it-was-my-favorite-one-too, he thought sadly. It's-ruined.

"Clovis is kilt," said the bleeding man's brother. "Clovis? Are you dead, Clovis?"

"Huh?" Clovis replied in a weary voice.

"I ast if you was dead."

"Naw, but hell, I'm hurt. My head's done broke." The wounded farmer sat up then, and with a final effort he stood, leaning against his brother and groggily pressing a faded bandanna handkerchief into the gash on his head. "You're a mean little bastard, ain't you?" he said to Mr. Perks.

"Mean?" said Mr. Perks, as though the notion never had occurred to him. He took the wad of bills out of his pocket and laid them primly on the pool table. "I never wanted your money in the first place," said Mr. Perks. "You keep it." Then he spun on his heel and went back to the store, late getting back to work from lunch for the first time in his life that he could remember.

By closing time the clerks were giving him queer looks which told him they knew. But he ignored them as best he could, and when he finally locked the People's Dandy and rattled the door for good measure before starting home for supper, he found he was not feeling bad, not feeling good. Just-feeling-about-the-same-as-always, he thought. He still missed Cherokee Gap, and yet for some reason he did not miss it quite as much, it seemed, not as much as he had missed it before. Getting-used-to-this-place-maybe, he thought, rounding the corner. The cotton gin was going full blast, and Mr. Perks saw the giant tube that sucked the cotton out of the trailers and up into the ginning machines. The tube, called the "suck," was being guided into a fresh load of cotton by the man whose job it was to handle the unloading. Mr. Perks was still conscious of the gin's operation while he washed up for dinner in the lukewarm tap water. He thought of the farmer's head, remembering how the doctor had phoned him just before closing time to say the wound had required eighteen stitches. Drying his face, Mr. Perks went back to his room. He sat down in the wicker rocking chair to think. He began to rock, slowly at first, and then faster, in time with the swelling and subsiding of the sounds from the cotton gin. He felt a curious elation. And when the dinner bell rang, he went downstairs briskly and sat at the dining table. He was followed by the salesmen, the ag teacher, the three railroad men, and finally the tractor mechanic. Mrs. Dillworth came in last, from the kitchen, and sat down. "Hello," said Mr. Perks. But she answered him coldly, with a tight-lipped nod. As the biscuits came around, the fat salesman took two.

"I don't hardly know of a person in Somerton that don't sorely miss Billy Turnbull," the tractor mechanic began pointedly, addressing himself to Mrs. Dillworth with a righteous stare. "Billy managed that store and minded his business. And Billy never thought of hurting nobody. But some in this world are always trying to hurt others. It's the trouble with some. But now, Billy, he wouldn't of hurt a fly." The tractor mechanic turned his gaze on Mr. Perks. Ball-peen-hammer, thought Mr. Perks.

"He was a sweet, sweet boy," Mrs. Dillworth mourned. "Such a way to die, and such a sweet little wife to leave behind."

The star salesman, who sold hardware, cleared his throat. "And she's already took up with another man, so they say," he said. "Not that I'm the one to spread a mean story. I wouldn't know whether it's true or not that this guy is seen very regular, while in the act of crawling out of her bedroom window late at night, at, say, two A.M. in the morning. I don't spread mean stories. Some say he's on the police force."

The tractor mechanic gave a crestfallen grunt and began to eat wolfishly. Mr. Perks helped himself to the fried chicken as it came by and took two spoons of gravy for his mashed potatoes, feeling an uneasy satisfaction at seeing the tractor mechanic crestfallen at last. The man appeared to have lost all interest in life now, outside of eating.

"Naw," one of the railroad men put in. He was the tallest and leanest of the three, and he smoked a pipe. "It ain't anybody on the police force. You got it wrong, for it's this new guy, some drifter from Arkansas working down at the fire hall. I forget the pecker-wood's name."

"That's the one," said Mrs. Dillworth. "They say he's got this tattoo over his right elbow and he drinks paregoric. He used to be a sailor and once married this German woman, but later got him a divorce." She shook her head disapprovingly. "And he's not the *only* one, I hear."

"No sugar," said the ag teacher, taking advantage of the pause during which Mrs. Dillworth drew her breath. Mr. Perks stole another glance at the tractor mechanic. To his surprise, the other man was no longer pouting. He sat looking raptly at Mrs. Dillworth instead, his mouth half open, as though drinking in, in advance, the horror of what the landlady would say next. Safe, thought Mr. Perks. I'm-safe-at-last.

THE CROSSROADER

BY *Don Carpenter*

Don Carpenter (1931–1995) was born in Berkeley, California, and earned degrees from Portland State College and San Francisco State University. His first major literary success came in 1966 with the publication of the novel Hard Rain Falling, *which contains a vivid pool scene set in the old Palace Billiards in San Francisco. Carpenter wrote ten novels as well as dozens of short stories and screenplays, including especially the screenplay for* Payday, *a 1972 film featuring a bravura performance by Rip Torn as a hard-drinking country singer.*

"The Crossroader" was written in 1964 and appeared in The Murder of the Frogs and Other Stories, *published by Harcourt Brace & World in 1969.*

See also Carpenter's evocation of a player who gets hot playing one pocket on page 225.

NOBODY EVER DID find out where he stayed while he was in town. Some thought down among the Indians on the other side of the river, but that wasn't likely, because the Indians didn't like Negroes, either. Not many Negroes came to town, and the one or two families of them in eastern Oregon lived farther north, in Bend, and didn't travel around. Once, a couple of years back, the U.S. Air Force made a mistake and assigned a Negro to the radar station out on top of Raincloud Butte, but he got off the bus at the depot around eleven o'clock one night and got on another one before noon the next day and went back to Tacoma, after the mayor and the chief of police drove up to the station and explained things to the major in charge, and the major telephoned to his headquarters there in Tacoma and explained things to them. That one solitary Negro Air Force man wouldn't have been happy stationed here because he would have had to stay on the station and not come to town. Not because anybody would say anything to him, just that nobody in the bus depot would serve him and he wouldn't get waited on at the barbershop and there would be no seats left at the movie. Things like that.

So when the other Negro showed up and stayed around for three days, everybody wondered where he slept and ate. Nobody saw him do either, and there weren't any strange cars in town, and besides, he was seen to get off the bus from Bend with his two little pieces of luggage, one a faded brown canvas overnight bag and the other what looked like a black leather fishing-rod case, although nobody around here had ever seen a fishing-rod case that looked quite like it. He was slim and small, this Negro, and looked almost white, a lot whiter than the Indians, but with that kinky hair. Most of us first saw him when he came into Bud's Billiards on Walnut Street, but we had already heard about the overnight case and the fishing-rod case, and he wasn't carrying either of them. So he must have put them down someplace, and wherever it was, he must have slept and ate there, too, and probably counted his money, because nobody ever saw him do that, either, and from time to time that money needed counting. And putting away.

Nobody quite remembers how it got that way, but Bud's Billiards is about the only place in town where the Indians can come and go as they please, and maybe that's why this Negro just didn't get the cold shoulder right away and leave town; but anyway, he didn't. We all saw him come in, and after a while we all looked away from him, not forgetting him at all, but just not looking at him, and pretty soon Otis Cranmer said, "He's back there playing pool by hisself," and some of us turned to see how good he was. You couldn't tell. He would just put the balls out on the table and shoot at them like anybody else, sinking a few and missing a few, walking around the table slow and easy, not worried, just passing the time.

He played and played and time passed and some of us went to

dinner and came back and he was still there playing by himself and it was almost ten at night before anybody thought to play a game with him just to see what would happen. We only have three good pool shooters in town, and it was one of them, Lew Bagge, who got up from the horseshoe bar and went back there and challenged the Negro to a game of rotation. Lew worked out at the lumber mill, used to be a logger but got his leg broken some time back and now limped a little, favoring the hurt leg more and more as the evenings passed and he got more liquor inside him; not a bad man, just a little mean, not from the accident but always just a little mean, a tall thin man with reddish-yellow hair and red skin, and right where you would expect a big nose hardly any nose at all. He had a wife and five children but he never spent any time with them as far as anybody could tell. He was in Bud's every night, and you sort of wondered where those five children came from. But not out loud.

Some of us moved over by the pool tables to watch the game, sitting at the two poker tables that were empty at this time of the month and would be empty until tomorrow night, when the mill and most of the ranches paid off.

"Tom, you rack those balls," Lew said. The Indian had been letting the Negro rack his own, but when Lew called out to him he came over and slapped the rack triangle down on the table and asked what game.

"Ro-tation," the Negro said, and he almost smiled while he said the word, as if it was a joke. He and Lew tossed for the break and played. It was easy to see after the first couple of games that Lew was no match for him. They started out playing for fifty cents a game, and then Lew raised it to a dollar, his face all red and his mouth tight, and by the time they were playing for two dollars a game Lew wasn't winning any of them. He drank all the time he played and got to limping more and more as he went around the table, and finally, he just went broke and couldn't play anymore. He just stood there at the end of the table, leaning on that cue of his and staring at the Negro, who just waited. "Tom," he said finally, "you just put that on my bill."

"That's all?" the Negro asked.

That was all. Lew left, and the Negro kept on playing by himself and nobody came up to challenge him. When it was time to close most of us left together and nobody saw the Negro leave. One minute he was there, and the next he was gone. Bud said later he paid his time and walked out about the same time as the rest of us, but we didn't see him. Lew was outside, sitting on the bench in front of the bus depot on the corner, and he asked a couple of men where the nigger was, but nobody knew.

He was back the next afternoon. It was payday, and after a while all the poker tables and pool tables were in use, and the Negro just sat in a chair out of the light and watched. He didn't ask to get into any of the nine ball games, he just sat. And nobody asked him to get in, until Lew showed up a little after dinnertime. Lew was drunk, and he stood over by the door to the men's room, leaning against the wall and watching one of the nine ball games that had his two fellow good pool shooters in it, refusing to get in the game and just laughing or drinking out of his glass as he watched.

"Come on, Lew, get your stick," Billy Hagstrom said. He was probably the best pool shooter in town, a little fat man who worked in the hardware store, and he and his wife raised chickens. He hadn't been there the night before and hardly ever came in except on payday or Saturday nights. But he couldn't help but know what had happened the night before.

"No, you go ahead," Lew said. "You and Fergis win all the money. Then we'll see." He looked over toward where the Negro was sitting in the dark and laughed. "Maybe later we'll get up a good game."

Fergis had been there last night. He said, "You mean, he beat you, and now you're gonna watch while he beats us."

"That's right," Lew said.

"Who?" said Billy.

"The little man who wasn't there," Lew said. "You'll see."

Fergis said, "Well, I won't see anything. One more game and I'm going home."

"You ain't goin' noplace," Lew said.

"Mind telling me why?"

"You'll try him," Lew said. "You got to."

"I saw you and him last night, remember? I don't have to drink poison just because I saw you do it."

That got to Billy, and he walked right over to where the Negro was sitting. "Well, you're so good, why don't you play? You want a special invitation?"

"I'll play," the Negro said.

Lew laughed. "I'll get my stick, too," he said. "Let's us just play three-handed."

The game was for a dollar a nine ball. Billy shot first, then Lew, then the Negro. It wasn't long before everybody could see what was going on: Billy was shooting as well as he could, but if he didn't see a chance to make the ball, he'd shoot badly and leave a good shot for Lew. If Lew couldn't make the ball easily, he just shot safe, to leave the Negro where he couldn't make a shot at all. It was the old whipsaw. By all rights, the Negro didn't stand a chance. He lost eight or ten dollars before things changed, and by this time Billy and Lew were too far in to get out. Or maybe they were too stubborn, or maybe, since they had made up their minds to cheat the Negro, probably deciding on it before either of them got to the pool hall that day, couldn't back out because when you cheat you're supposed to win, otherwise there would be no point in cheating. At first, Lew made it look like he was really trying to win, so the Negro wouldn't catch on that he was being cheated, but after a while, after the Negro started winning his own money back, and then some of Billy's and Lew's, he even stopped that and just plain shot safely without ever trying to sink a ball, and the hell with what the Negro thought.

The Negro didn't seem to notice anything, or if he did, he didn't let on. He just kept playing, and no matter where Lew left the cue ball, the Negro would move around the table, slow and easy, sighting the balls and the angles, and finally come up with a shot that would either sink the ball he was after or leave Billy so bad he couldn't even make a bad shot, let alone sink a ball. It got to be a pretty ugly contest, with none of the players saying anything. When the Negro won the game he would break for the next game, and that sometimes meant he would just run all nine balls and break again, and after a while, he had won a considerable amount of money, always picking up the bills and tucking them in his shirt pocket. After a while the game was over and he had all the money.

"What'er you gonna do with all that money, nigger?" Billy said. He looked mad, and his skin was white all around his mouth.

"All what money?" the Negro said. "This few dollars?"

"Around here, boy, a few dollars is still money," Billy said.

"I reckon I'll get in this here poker game, if you'll let me," the Negro said.

"Go ahead," Lew said. "Let him in the game. It don't matter. Let him win all the money he wants." Lew was grinning again, and I doubt if there were two people in that room who didn't know what Lew meant. Some of us looked pretty uncomfortable, and after the Negro sat down at the stud table and bought chips, a lot of us left, not just not wanting to see what happened, but not even wanting to be around when it happened.

We heard later how the poker game turned out. There was no cheating—Bud wouldn't allow that—but it didn't matter, because they never had any intention of letting him get out of there with the money anyhow. He won a good deal of money playing poker, some said over a hundred dollars and others said closer to two hundred, but a lot, anyway. "We should of known," Billy said the next day, behind the counter at the hardware store. "When he cashed in his chips we should of known he wasn't dumb enough to come out the front door and walk right into us. No, all he did was say something about washing the grime off his fingers and got up and went into the toilet and didn't come back out. He must of noticed the window earlier. Some of us waited around nearly a half an hour, and Lew I don't think got any sleep last night at all, but spent the whole night roaming around town lookin' for the nigger. He even went over to the Indians, but they said they hadn't seen any strangers."

But sure enough, there he was again, Saturday afternoon. Ready to play pool again, or poker, or anything anybody wanted to play. That was the funny part. We all thought he'd have enough sense to get out of town now that he had won so much money, but here he was back again, fooled people twice and going to try it for the third time. But this time nobody was going to let him get out of any men's room window or anything of the kind; in fact, nobody was going to let him get out of sight. Nobody would play him any more pool, since he had beaten the experts even when the experts were trying to cheat him, and so he sat down at the stud table and played poker all afternoon. When people came back from dinner he was still there, still playing, and still winning. Pool is one thing—you can win at pool if you have more skill than anybody else—but poker is another game entirely. How he continually won at poker was a real mystery. He couldn't have been cheating, because everybody watched him so closely. One thing was certain, just having him at the table upset most of the players, and they were so busy watching him that they might not have had time to play good poker against him. And he would talk in that Southern accent of his, and that was pretty irritating.

Anyway, he kept winning all day and most of the night. Lew and Billy were both there at night, but neither of them played. They sat together at the bar and drank and talked quietly together and waited. Because sooner or later the Negro would have to make his move. He would have to try to get out of there and get out of town with all that money. It was close to five hundred dollars by now, pretty nearly every loose nickel in this part of eastern Oregon. Not very many of the regular hangers-out at Bud's Billiards felt like letting him leave with the money, and a good few of them probably would have liked to lynch him. But nothing like that ever happened here and wasn't likely to. So they waited, and while they waited the Negro just kept on winning all the money.

And it was worse than that. Nobody is trying to make any excuses for this town, or at least for some of the men who hung around Bud's; it's here in the telling, the way we behaved when we were put off balance by that Negro coming to town and winning all that money; but it was worse. Somebody talked to the chief of police, Bob Dickey, and what was going to happen was that Bob was going to find the Negro after the men got through with him and put him in jail for vagrancy.

But he saved us. Not Bob Dickey, he was probably willing to pretend to himself that he was doing his duty by putting the Negro in jail after he caused so much trouble. No, it was the Negro saved us. At least, you could look at it that way.

You see, he had a real problem. He not only had to cash in his chips, which would be a signal that he was getting ready to go, he also would have to get out of the place, go to wherever he hid his bags, and then go to the bus depot. Because there just wasn't any other way for him to get out of town. So he couldn't just cash in and then make a run for it, because no matter how fast he ran, he would have to end up at the bus depot, and that was not as much as a block away. Besides having to wait for a bus—any bus—leaving town. That was his problem. And he sure couldn't get police protection, and he didn't have any friends waiting around for him, or we would have noticed. He was all alone. It was quite a problem. Some of us probably even hoped he would get away and save us from what we thought we had to do. Because it wasn't just Lew and Billy and the boys who lost to him in poker, even though it started out that way. It was all of us, counting our police department. That was the worst part. We knew it, we felt it, and even felt smug about it. We were protecting ourselves from that one outsider, Negro or not, and if we lost, if he saved us, it was through no fault of our own. He did it by himself, and we could see then how a small thin fellow like that, Negro or not, could manage to survive in the dangerous business he was in, of coming into small towns like ours and collecting all that loose money and getting out again. There must have been times when he didn't make it, when the boys of whatever town it was caught him, beat him half to death, and got that money. And towns where they took the money from him right in the jail. So maybe the reason he pulled it off was because he had the practice and we didn't. That and even the courage to try, or if it wasn't courage, the hatred, because even that was possible; the hatred and the ability to hide it.

It happened so quick that it was a couple of days before we understood how completely we had been taken, before all the facts and suppositions got themselves straightened out and fell into place. At first it was just confusing.

He got up from the table and cashed in his chips at a little after midnight, and that left him only four minutes or so to catch his bus, only we didn't know this last part. He tucked the money into that shirt pocket and instead of going to the toilet or heading toward the door, he came over to the bar, to where Billy and Lew were sitting drinking. We were all watching by now, but nobody was close enough to hear what it was he said to them. We all saw Billy and Lew get up, Lew kind of smirking, and we all saw the three of them leave the bar together, and when the door closed there was a kind of universal sigh, because we knew now that whatever was going to happen, we weren't going to have to do it. Not actively participate. Billy and Lew, being the first and worst stung, would do it for us.

It was over twenty minutes before Billy and Lew came back into the bar, and by that time the Negro was fifteen minutes at least out of town. The first thing Billy said was, "Where is he?" He looked all around the room. "Where the hell did he go?" Then we began to understand, as Billy and Lew stood there, tall and thin, and short and fat, with their faces frozen in unbelief. Understand not how, but what. It was quiet for a minute, and then Lew began to swear, and he and Billy and a few of the rest of us poured out of the place and down the street to the bus depot, to find out what we already knew. The woman at the depot, Mrs. Callisher, said yes, he had the little brown overnight case and the black leather fishing-rod case with him when he got on the bus.

Back at Bud's, Otis Cranmer said to Billy, "Well, what did he offer to sell you? The Empire State Building?"

"He didn't sell us nothing," Billy said. He finished his drink and went home. Lew was already gone. For a while, some of us thought he might have offered to divide up the money with them, but that wasn't it, either, because that didn't explain how he went one way and they went the other way, just as soon as they got outside. Finally, though, it came out.

"It sounded too good to be true," Billy finally said. This was on Monday, and Billy was behind the counter in the hardware store. He didn't look too pleased. "He just asked us if there was some place out on the edge of town, some secluded place, he called it, where he could start up a little crap game."

"Just the three of you?" Otis asked. He could ask that because he doesn't gamble and didn't have anything to do with anything.

"No," Billy said. "Anybody who wanted to play. I told him we could play out in my barn, and he said that would be fine. This was all right there at the bar."

"Well, how did he convince you two to escort him outside?"

"That's the hard part," Billy said. "It was our idea. He said he had to go get his bag, that had some more money in it, and had his dice in it. So we said we'd go with him. He didn't like that, but he let us come with him anyway."

"He let you," Otis said.

"Well, we thought—never mind what we thought. You didn't hear him. You weren't there."

"So the three of you were going out to your nice lonely barn and shoot dice," Otis said. "With the chickens."

That was all we could get out of Billy, and Lew wouldn't talk at all, just limped around town as if he had a wooden leg, and so we mostly had to guess at the rest, supplied with a few hints, what you might call tangible evidence found in the alley back of the pool hall, and a few other ideas, as to how, once outside and in the dark of the alley, the Negro must have explained that he didn't want anybody to know where he kept that bag and that fishing pole, and that, so nobody would think he was trying to cheat anybody, he would give them something to prove his good intentions, and the guesses ran that he must have slipped the bundle to Lew, taking it out of his shirt pocket in the dark and putting it into Lew's hand—not Billy's, because Billy would have taken it out into the light and looked at it—and disappeared into the dark. Because that must have been the way he did it, preparing that wad of cut-up notepaper beforehand, maybe even before he came to town, and then when nobody happened to be looking exchanged the wad of money from his shirt to his pants and that wad of cut-up notepaper from his pants to his shirt, so it would look natural for him to reach into his shirt pocket and put the whole wad into Lew's, not Billy's, hand—a man in that kind of business has to be a good judge of human nature—knowing Lew would slip it fast into his own pocket and already be trying hopelessly to figure some way he could cheat Billy out of his half. And that would make it Billy who demanded that they wait for the Negro to come back with his bag, because Billy didn't have the money yet and wanted the Negro to get it back so the two could take it from him together. It must have happened that way. There is just no other explanation for all those pieces of notepaper, all rumpled and wrinkled, scattered around the alley back of the pool hall that more than one of us happened to notice the next day, Sunday, on the way to church.

THE SNOOKER SHARK

BY *William Harrison*

Novelist William Harrison was born in 1933 in Dallas, Texas, graduated from Texas Christian in 1955, earned an M.A. from Vanderbilt, and has spent many years teaching at the University of Arkansas. His recently published novel Upriver *is his fifth set in Africa. Harrison is perhaps best known for adapting his short story "The Rollerball Murders" into the 1975 movie* Rollerball, *which featured James Caan, Ralph Richardson, and John Housman. Unlike cue sports, Rollerball is a violent game used as a substitute for war in the twenty-first century to slake the blood lust of the masses.*

Gentler is the following story, which appeared in the Saturday Evening Post *in 1967 and the following year in* The Best American Short Stories. *The protagonist is a college student preparing for an academic career in history. But he has a problem: he happens to be a terrific snooker player.*

The story is not autobiographical. In response to my question, Harrison wrote: "I am known to run as many as three balls in snooker."

THERE WERE no lettered archways, no inscribed monuments, nothing which properly announced that this was the University, his dream. Sammy looked in vain for a single Latin phrase cut into the façades of the buildings.

The dormitories, the battered columns of the building where most of his classes were held, the worn tables of the Student Center disappointed him, as did his fellow students, who slouched along beneath the campus trees at an indifferent pace, coming to life only at rallies when the varsity paraded onto the amphitheater stage. His professors, too, frustrated him; they stood mechanical and grim beside their desks. One, a graduate student who taught Sammy's first English class, had a spark of enthusiasm, but misspelled two words in writing the first assignments on the board.

In the library he had expected miracles, expected to find himself lost in a maze of impressive shelves, deep in an intellectual ecstasy. But the rules prevented him from penetrating beyond the checkout desk; prim, bored girls brought him the books he requested. "Lose yourself in that wonderful place, Sammy," his mother had told him. "Lose this little town, the life in your daddy's pool hall, every shackle. Do it, honey, and never forget that you've got a mama who can let go, who can tell you how to let yourself go too!" Good advice, the expression of a dream. But only teachers or graduate students with special permits could proceed beyond that miserable checkout desk.

His father had added a warning. "Put your cue stick away," he had said. "You haven't got a talent. More like a curse. And never let anyone up there see how good you are, or you'll be in trouble. I seen it happen to too many guys, and I know."

Yet that first semester, before September was gone, he went down to McNeil's Pocket Billiard and Snooker Parlor, turning in his dismay to this familiar concentration, this therapy. At one of the back tables, he broke a rack of snooker balls and shot the table clean—the fifteen one-point red balls, the six two-through-seven-point "color" balls— missing scarcely at all. He broke two more racks, played them equally well. When he was finished, he pulled on his frayed corduroy jacket, paid his bill, and went back to his dormitory room.

IN HIS FATHER'S pool hall, Sammy Stahl had long ago forsaken the more popular game of pocket billiards for the larger table, the smaller balls and pockets of the game of snooker. At the age of nine he could beat anyone in Westedge except his father. At thirteen he could beat him, and after his fifteenth birthday none of the old men who came down to watch him, who came to fondle a beer and talk sports, ever saw Sammy in defeat. It didn't matter what handicap his opponents had; he made fantastic runs, left them impossible angles. He turned everyone, finally, into an admirer of the game as it ought to be played.

Only twice during his high-school years did Sammy gamble, both times at the urging of his father, and only to get rid of undesirables who had drifted into Westedge to hustle a few dollars. Except for those two times, money was never part of his game. Snooker remained for Sammy an athletic skill. Long-legged, baby-faced, wearing bright white sneakers, he moved around the table like a junior-high basketball player, innocent and eager.

But snooker was never the dream. In the Stahl house knowledge was always the dream, the vision which kept Westedge in its proper small corner of the world. Sammy's parents carefully kindled the dream with overstatement. "The University, Sammy, ah, there's nothing like it," his mother told him. "A crossroads for ideas. People going someplace, doing things, talking exciting subjects!"

Educational institutions were shrines to his uneducated father and to his mother, who had once, during the Depression years, worked as a waitress in order to stay a few months at that very university. In their Westedge house—a clapboard bungalow near the fields of truck gardens south of town—his mother scrimped the grocery money to provide Sammy with installment-plan culture: a set of encyclopedias, a phonograph, a tolerably good microscope, subscriptions to magazines. In the pool hall T. R., his father, preached a gospel of concentration. "Think!" T. R. would cry out. "Snooker is a subtle game. How you gonna get me hooked this time? How? Think about your game! Will you go for the hook, or will you shoot for points? You haven't thought about it yet! Put down that cue stick for a minute and use your head!"

Their urging that he educate himself had not been necessary. He came to the University eager to read, to major in history, to buttonhole his professors. He came in all his innocent confidence, believing that education, like snooker, would be difficult but possible. He would become a storehouse of information, a citadel of insights; he would travel, absorb, digest; he would teach those who followed after him. His father, the son of a Belgian farmer, had seen, in the schoolyards of his childhood, boys carrying young valedictorians on their shoulders, celebrating their accomplishments, and T. R.'s approval for enthusiasm of this sort was shared by Sammy. "I'm a serious man," he sometimes warned his high-school girlfriends. "Ambitious and serious. Take me that way, or leave me." If the girls hadn't heard from their father and brothers about Sammy's famous runs on the big snooker tables in Stahl's Recreation Hall, they might have laughed at him.

HIS GIRL at the University that year was named Sterrett. She was tall, like Sammy, and wore sneakers like his. Their early dates went well, but by the Thanksgiving recess they had argued, parted, exchanged a series of silly notes, dated again, parted again. They didn't know what to make of each other. He wanted her to understand his intellectual dream; she wanted him to be her provider, with a clear and lucrative ambition.

"Vague," she said once. "You've got no goals. I mean, what kind of major is *history,* after all? What'll you do with it?"

Or again: "Who do you think you *are?* Take stock of yourself! Just a boy from a small town downstate who imagines he doesn't need to pledge a fraternity. But you can't just *study*—you've got to *live* too. I love you, Sammy, but what in the world do you want?"

"To be an intellectual," he answered. Simply, as always, just like that.

"But you can't want *that!*"

"Why not?"

"Because that's like wanting—well, uh, *fame.* It happens, but you just can't want it *per se!*"

"Sure I can!"

"Oh, sweet, no! Sammy, love, you're so *good.* And I adore you. But why can't you just be premed or something sane like that?"

So Sterrett, in her way, became part of his dismay. Often that first semester, wrapped in her cashmere embrace, he suspected that he was inadequate, that his dream was unsubstantial. His parents, he thought, had never guessed how difficult things would be.

One November weekend afternoon Sterrett lured him from his books to a picnic at a river resort sixty miles from the campus. They nibbled hot dogs and sang campfire songs with the sorority sisters and their dates; they lay on blankets, Sterrett's warm breath against his ears; they went for a long stroll in the pine forest. Standing on the canoe dock that afternoon, he delivered an earnest speech to Sterrett.

"I'm treated with condescension," he complained. "My adviser gives me idiotic smiles. Have they stopped believing in education? Have they given up on teaching? I corner them in their offices, you know, and they put me off. I want to ask questions and have my say about Livy and de Tocqueville and Will Durant. I want to hear their cynicisms—if that's all they have to say. Let 'em say that history is just a makeshift art, an illusion. But they clam up on me! Why? And why should I care so much? I think the system is against serious boys like me, Sterrett. Ah, hell, I could jump in this slimy river and float away!"

"Your chin," she answered. "It's a lovely, melancholy chin, Sammy, it really is." This was his Sterrett: the materialist, the enemy of critical thought.

Had he been able to communicate with her in any other way, he wouldn't, finally, have taken her down to McNeil's Pocket Billiard and Snooker Parlor. But he had to show her, make her glimpse the depth and passion of his academic monasticism. At least that was what he told himself as he led her into that place of stale beer odors where few females had ever trespassed. Perhaps some residue of adolescent pride lingered in him as he led her between those rows of green-felt tables, but he imagined that from his performance Sterrett might come to understand his determination, his ascetic flight from the hard physics of the snooker table, that she might somehow embrace his abstract dream.

But she couldn't comprehend what she saw. Sammy, frowning with concentration, ran an amazing seventy-seven points off the table, and only McNeil himself, lurking by the door to the men's room, offered any appreciation. "Gawd," he sighed, when the run was over. "I can't believe it!"

Sammy replaced his cue stick in the wall rack and rolled down his sleeves.

"Well, what of it?" Sterrett asked.

"Nothing," Sammy told her flatly. "It's just that I'm probably one of the greatest snooker players in the world."

"Oh, you *silly*," she said.

He shrugged. "It's true."

Then McNeil stepped up. "What's your name, son?" It was the only identification he asked; he had seen enough.

During the ensuing conversation, Sterrett, slightly confused and embarrassed by McNeil's bursts of enthusiasm, drifted away. For Sammy, as she slipped on her coat and left the poolroom, a vision blurred, a dream ebbed. "Yeah, yeah," McNeil was saying, "I heard about you. I know you now. I heard about you from two hustlers who toured downstate. Sure!"

IN JANUARY, when Sammy returned from the Christmas holidays, Sterrett was still at home with the flu. Trudging across the icy campus, he felt terribly alone. The library remained a great stone fist closed against him. The students threw snowballs and were frantic about basketball.

Sighing, he turned again to his books, studied hard. On his narrow dormitory bed, propped up so that he could see the trees beyond his window all heavy with ice, he turned even to Thomas Wolfe. *Naked and alone we come into exile . . . we come into the unspeakable and incommunicable prison of this earth . . . O lost, and by the wind grieved, ghost, come back again.* It was just too damned lovely, too true. He wanted to weep. He went to the small mirror in his room and examined his chin—it did seem a little melancholy. Sterrett was right, and she was right about his indecision, his lack of direction and identification. He stood before the mirror, chin jutted out, remembering the most exciting snooker games with his father, how the crowds had gathered, how silence and cigar smoke had filled the room. McNeil, he decided. He might understand. At least he'll know what I've given up.

"OH, SON, YEAH, I seen 'em all," McNeil drawled, pulling the wide brush across the snooker table. Sammy watched him intently. McNeil was certainly no demonic figure, no scowling hustler. He wore a dirty T-shirt, and his jolly keg-sized stomach hung over his belt. A perpetual smile creased his face, a smile without malice or design.

"Who's the greatest you've ever seen?" Sammy asked. "Minnesota Fats? Mosconi?"

"Don't even know his name," McNeil said. "Came in this very place wearing a bus driver's uniform. He sat quiet until he spotted Todd Ragsdale, about the best local shooter we ever had. Drank a soda and just watched Todd. Then he challenged him to a game of straight pool. I knew right away he was hustling when he wouldn't play call shot. The really good shooters try to make their shots look accidental, you know. Well, he had ninety dollars and some odd cents, and he lost eighty-five dollars to Todd. Sat back down over there with another soda. Looked like he might bust out cryin'."

"What happened then?"

"After a time he got up and started playing around the other tables with that last five dollars. Cleaned everybody in the place, then got back to Todd Ragsdale. It was a setup all the way."

"He beat Todd, I guess?"

"Son, he must've walked out of here with a thousand dollars. And his shots—hell, I can't describe 'em! Great, only he'd make it look like he was just slopping 'em in, and he'd shake his head and say, 'Be damned, look at that! Am I ever lucky!' Best I ever saw, but I'll tell you this: He couldn't beat you at your game. No, sir! Here, play me a few racks."

They played. Time and time again Sammy left the cue ball kissed behind a cluster of other balls or half snugged in a corner pocket, an impossible challenge to McNeil. Then, at the proper moment, he ran the table.

"Genius!" McNeil cried. "You're something, Sammy! Have a beer!"

"I never drink," Sammy said, smiling.

It went this way for weeks. Sammy came more and more to McNeil's, practiced his game, basked in McNeil's encouragement. He could hardly bring himself to answer the letter from his father which arrived in late February.

Sammy:

I see you took your personal cue stick back to school after Xmas vacation. Didn't see it missing until this week. Yr not minding what I said. Are you drinking hard liquor too? Smoking stogies? Dating experienced girls? Send the stick back, Sam, please. It won't do you no good up there at school, just make trouble. Enclosed is my little check for $20. Study hard.

Yr dad, T. R.

One evening as he sat with Sterrett in the parlor of her sorority house, he learned that she was afraid of him.

"Afraid of me? Why?" he asked.

"Because you're *different* nowadays. And I know it's that *place*, Sammy, and whatever you're doing there!"

It was true.

Standing idly with his monogrammed cue stick by the great green snooker table in the center of McNeil's, watching his opponent bungle through a few points, feeling the crowd tense and expectant around him, he was learning his identity. Nearby, on the bench where he seldom had time to sit before his opponent missed a shot, there would be a textbook, a marker stuck among its pages. Occasionally, glancing at it, he would ask himself: Is it so good to know who I am? Will I be a snooker shark forever? Who knows me? Ah, professors, Dad, Sterrett, if you could only know! Call me dunce, call me anything, but know me.

His game improved shamefully, and by April he had begun to take on visitors, out-of-town shooters who came weekends at McNeil's invitation.

Yet snooker remained just an avocation in his thoughts. Around him at McNeil's bets went down, but he had no share in them and accepted only soft drinks and cashews as rewards for his winning performances. Late in the evening, his feet aching and his clothes rank with the stale smoke of McNeil's, he would trudge back to the library and slump at one of the long oak tables behind a wall of books. Sterrett, who had come to regard him with increasing awe and curiosity, would go with him, often just to sit and watch him as he read.

"The good student can simply overcome a dull school," he said one evening, turning to her abruptly.

"That's right, Sammy." She smiled, detecting a lack of affirmation in his voice. He was her Sammy now, her companion of campus reputation, her man. His small confusions didn't matter because of his mastery at McNeil's tables; the game of snooker—though Sterrett had never fathomed it—had relieved all her anxieties. He'd go through life a champion of sorts, full of assurance, she told herself.

In May a shooter from Ohio came to town at McNeil's invitation, and Sammy agreed to play him. Word got around. On the evening of the match, boys poured out of the fraternity houses to watch; McNeil's big room bulged with spectators. Even Sammy's adviser, Professor Whitson, was among the first-row spectators, an old straw hat jammed down on his wide forehead. Sterrett and a girlfriend stood watching the expanding crowd for a few minutes, then departed. Moments before the match was to begin, while McNeil's boys were still arranging chairs and benches and serving big schooners of beer, Sammy saw his father push through the onlookers.

"I didn't expect you," Sammy managed to say.

"So then we surprised each other," T. R. Stahl replied grumpily.

The Ohio shooter was a thin, hawklike man with long fingers that formed a delicate bridge for his cue stick. He gambled and won at the very first, breaking the rack with a hard shot and scoring. Sammy saw his father squirm in his chair, and walked slowly around the table to him. "Ah, Sammy, Sammy," T. R. whispered. Sammy bit his lower lip and said nothing.

The Ohio shooter was taking his time and not missing, but Sammy couldn't concern himself with the game. He wanted to say something to T. R., something like: *Our dream wasn't a true dream, wasn't realistic, and I couldn't wait for another. I wanted to be somebody. I had to. It's a petty compensation, T. R., but that's what I needed.* He watched his father remove his coat. The familiar gray garters held his sleeves. Vest open. Tie, as usual, slightly askew. The same old T. R., Sammy thought. My mentor and tormentor. He imagined a sadness in the curve of his father's mouth.

A slow ten minutes passed, and the Ohio shooter still hadn't missed. The red balls were all gone now, and the two, three, and four balls; everyone watched the Ohio man draw a bead on the blue five ball, saw it topple slowly into a corner pocket—no chance now for Sammy to win. "That's game," McNeil announced. He had lost one hundred dollars before his protégé even had a turn at the table, and though it was a long match—ten games at one hundred dollars each—he seemed a little grave.

Sammy's father went to the bar and drank a small glass of beer. Nervous, his hands fussed with his collar and vest. He tipped over the empty beer glass when he set it back on the bar.

Sammy opened the second game with a safe shot, then went and stood beside T. R. again.

"Snooker!" T. R. said with derision. "What's gotten into your head? What're you thinking about?"

"I'm thinking about everything," Sammy said dolefully. "My whole life."

T. R. winced and looked down at his shoes. Reaching out, he patted his son on the ribs. "But you shouldn't be here," he said uncertainly.

"It's not only snooker," Sammy said, fumbling. "It's school too. It's people and what's expected of me. All those ideas we had about the University were too idealistic."

T. R. frowned, trying to understand. "You were going to study hard," he protested.

"I *did*. I still do. Only no one wants that from me. This is what they expect of me instead. That's one of my professors sitting over there!"

T. R. shook his head sadly and watched in silence as Sammy and the Ohio shooter traded safeties.

Between shots, all the questions and doubts of the recent weeks buzzed in Sammy's head. Does a talent always possess its owner? Do I owe my arms and concentration to the world's silly snooker tables? Pondering, he stared into the soft blue cloud of cigarette smoke hovering overhead. Sterrett. It's partially her fault, he thought. But excuses— No. I'm mostly to blame. Me.

The crowd broke into applause as the Ohio shooter made a difficult shot and broke up a defiant cluster of red balls on the table. The game was suddenly wide open again, and everyone could see that it was going to be another good run for the visitor.

Sammy leaned on his cue stick, waiting. Across the silent room, suffering, T. R. rested his chin on his fist. Occasionally he looked up at McNeil and the other spectators, rubbed his eyes, then let his head sink down again.

Another burst of applause from the crowd brought a thin smile to the lips of the Ohio shooter. Then, on his next shot, he missed.

With great deliberation, Sammy chalked the tip of his cue. The Ohio shooter stepped back, and for a moment there was no sound in the room except the soft scrape of the chalk. Sammy sighed. T. R. was taking everything so hard. If only I could stand up on the table and make a long speech explaining everything, he thought. A long speech with a slide projector, enough pictures so that T. R. would understand—Sterrett, the library, old Professor Whitson asleep under his old straw hat.

T. R. got to his feet again and came over to Sammy. "You're not thinking," T. R. said. "Don't you know some men in here have bets on you?" They took a long look at each other. A faint hope was suddenly aroused in Sammy that communication had been established, that T. R. knew him. In a moment he was sure that T. R. did, for his father wagged a finger at him and said in a low whisper, almost a hiss: "Concentrate!" Then, turning to McNeil, T. R. produced a thick roll of bills from his pocket. In a voice loud enough for the entire room to hear, he asked, "Any particular limit on the side bets in here?"

"Well, how much?" McNeil drawled. He looked at T. R. with suspicion.

"Oh, two hundred on this game." Having said this, T. R. swallowed hard.

McNeil took a long look at the table and scoreboard. Though the Ohio shooter had missed, he was forty points ahead and there were only the four, five, six, and seven balls left. "Hell, I'll give you six to one on the boy," McNeil said. "On the Ohio feller, I'll—"

"Never mind about him," T. R. said. "I'll take your odds on the boy. I'll take 'em because this kid is maybe just the greatest snooker player in the world."

It was too much, a grandstand wager. Something profound stirred in Sammy, and he wanted to reach out and touch T. R.'s slumping shoulders.

The Ohio shooter complained about the delay, but the bet had been made. Sammy came slowly up to the table then, his tennis shoes squeaking on the floor. His fuzzy adolescent whiskers were illumined in the harsh slant of light from above the table. He looked such a mere boy that several in the crowd allowed themselves small derisive smiles.

Sammy took his stance—feet together, body low, cue stick leveled like a rifle, head slightly tilted. With his easiest touch, he left the cue ball behind the black seven ball.

"Your shot," he told his opponent.

The object ball was the four, and the Ohio shooter studied the angles for more than a minute, then tried a two-cushion shot and missed, losing points.

"The name of the game," whispered T. R. Stahl to those around him, "is snooker."

Sammy glared down his cue stick at the table, hoping that this sudden capitulation on T. R.'s part was genuine, that his father somehow understood. Then, measuring his stroke carefully, he hid the cue ball again, this time behind the blue five ball. When the Ohio shooter missed again, Sammy gave the scoreboard a quick glance. He was still far behind but knew he would win.

Eight times in a row Sammy forced the Ohio shooter to miss and forfeit points. Then, with a great sigh, he rammed in the remaining, the winning, balls. "Game!" McNeil shouted hoarsely, and the crowd broke into shouts and applause.

Sammy watched his father. A faint smile had edged into the corners of T. R.'s mouth, but it wasn't a smile of relief at having won the bet. It was not a smile of satisfaction of any sort. A sad smile, Sammy thought. Resignation.

He didn't lose again. Methodically, wearing down the Ohio shooter with hopeless table problems, he won the rest of the games in the match, and McNeil, for the first time in anyone's memory, offered drinks on the house.

That evening, in the town's leading restaurant, Sammy devoured a huge meal: sirloin steak, potatoes, three glasses of milk. His father and Sterrett sat beside him, T. R. describing the match for his son's girlfriend, Sterrett saying things like, "Oh, it must've been wonderful!" and "I'd love to have seen it!"

But the next day, before his father went back to Westedge on the train, when he and Sammy were alone together, there was almost no mention of snooker. "Your mama is always going to adjust to anything you do," T. R. said. "She can let go. She told you so herself."

The afternoon vexed Sammy. A strange uneasiness had grown between them; his father, sitting with him in the dorm room, then lunching with him at the Student Center, had offered no admonition, no regret, nothing more than an unexpected piece of advice before he stepped onto the train at dusk.

"Don't let them guys play you free anymore," he said. "Go ahead and take your cut. Play the game."

Sammy still hadn't wanted to hear that. He had wanted to throw out his arms and shout: "But—the library! It's still there! I can't just give it up! I can't get what I want from it, and I can't forget it either!" And he had wanted to shout: "All the big stimulation I was going to find, it isn't here! Some of it's in me, but buried way down where I can't dig it out!" But he had known that such cries would be ridiculous, and he had felt abandoned. Abandoned and alone, an exile. He was full of poetic argument, but kept silent because he sensed—and knew T. R. did too—the inevitability of his destiny.

That night he sat on the edge of his bed and stared out at the dark, fragrant trees. He wished that T. R. hadn't said those things, that he had come into McNeil's poolroom resolute against this inevitability. *Don't let them play you free* . . . It was just T. R.'s way,

Sammy knew, of letting him know that he was a talent and therefore a property of the world.

He settled back across the bed and fell asleep. When he woke the next morning he was thinking about his next match, and Sterrett, and the excitement of the coming weekend.

....

LEM THE BARBER

BY *Danny McGoorty,*

AS TOLD TO ROBERT BYRNE

Dapper Dan McGoorty (1901–1970) told me the story of his life—and a colorful, knockabout life it was, too—on his deathbed in 1969. My notes and tape recordings led to the book McGoorty, the Story of a Billiard Bum, *which was published in hardcover by Lyle Stuart in 1972 and as a trade paperback with a photo section added by Citadel Press in 1984. A short-lived mass market paperback edition was published by now-defunct Curtis Books in 1973. The book in one form or another was in print for twenty-two years, slipping out of print in 1994.*

McGoorty was a wonderful storyteller with a sense of structure, an eye for amusing detail, and an ear for the language of his hidden world, as the following excerpt from the book attests.

The year is 1933.

WHENEVER I TELL people about riding freights they always seem amazed that as many as a hundred people might be on a train at once. Hell, that was nothing. I've been on freights that were carrying *two* hundred hobos, two hundred and fifty, even. All kinds of people. In the Depression an awful lot of people were broke and were going someplace else hoping to find better luck, or to run out on debts, or to go live with relatives. Without money, riding the rails was the only way to go, especially in the West. Hitchhiking was too slow. There weren't enough good roads or fast traffic.

It got to be a way of life for some guys—always on the move. Always looking for something—they couldn't have told you what. They didn't even know where they were going exactly, most of the time. Ask them and they would say, "West," or, "East." That's all. Not the name of any place.

There were migratory workers, following the harvest. Heading for Washington in the fall to pick apples, stuff like that. But then there were guys who would be going in the opposite direction, trying to get as far away as possible from where the work was being done. Time to pick lettuce in California? Then they would be in North Carolina. I was pretty much like that myself. Work was strictly a last resort. Things had to be awful tough.

Things *did* get awful tough. I did just well enough hustling to stay alive, but not much more. I used the lemonade, the dump, the double dump, every trick in the book, but the pickings were slim.

One reason the hustling was hard was because I had so little money. I had no chance to gamble away a few bucks to set a guy up for a kill. Lots of time I had to play on my nerve, without a penny in my pocket. I would wake up in the morning in some flophouse kicking the wolf in the mouth, flat broke. Not even enough for a cup of coffee and a sinker. The minute the local pool hall was open I would be there and I would be hitting somebody up for a game of pool. Hungry, so hungry sometimes I could hardly stand it.

"Sure, I'll play you a game, mister," a guy says to me one morning, "but not for money. Let's just play for fun."

Jesus Christ, my stomach is screaming for food, and he wants to play hee-haw! But that's the sort of thing you run into in those one-turd towns.

Eventually I started making some scores. The best one was in El Dorado, Kansas.

I had smartened up considerably, knew how to travel. It was about ten at night when I wheeled off a "mop." "Mop" is what we called the Missouri-Pacific Railroad. I wheeled off a side-door Pullman and hiked down to the depot. They didn't stop freights in front of the depot to make it easy for the bums, you know. Christ, sometimes we were *miles* from the depot. I was wearing coveralls, with the sleeves and pants cuffs tied with cord to keep the dirt out, and the neck tied tight with a bandanna. In the depot can I peeled off the coveralls.

Underneath I was wearing a complete suit of clothes—white shirt, tie, handkerchief in the chest pocket, the whole works. All I had to do was wash my face and hands and wipe off my shoes and I was ready for anything. The whole process took me only about ten minutes, including stashing my coveralls, razor, and toothbrush in the bushes.

I walked up the main drag. About three thousand population, I figured . . . not big enough to have a player that could give me any trouble. Into the pool hall I went. Every town had one. Now I was hungry, understand what I mean? Hadn't eaten for pretty near a day. Didn't have a penny on me.

The room was like a lot of others, a long line of beat-up pool tables with low lights over them, each one with a green metal shade. Spittoons in the corners covered with crust. To the guy behind the counter I said, "You got anybody here who wants a game of pool?" I had no time to fuck around. I needed a score fast.

"Some of the boys in the back might want to play a little pastime," the guy said.

"Listen," I said, "I don't play hee-haw. I'm looking for somebody who wants to make it interesting."

"Ohhhhhhhhh. You're a good player, is that it?"

"I sure as hell am." The direct approach. Somebody would be curious enough to play me a game just to see if I was kidding.

"Get Lem," the bartender said, nodding to a bunch of guys who were standing there eyeing me. Lem was the local shark, a barber by trade, best player in seven counties, and people flew out the door looking for him. Everybody wanted to see some action. This was El Dorado, Kansas, remember, where not a hell of a lot happens.

Fifteen minutes later in walked a guy, tall and thin. He looked like he could be a player.

"I hear you want to play a little pool," he said.

"That's right," I said, "but not for less than three dollars."

Three dollars was quite a bit in the Depression. For three dollars you could get ham hocks and beans, a fifth of giggle soup, a hotel room with a window, and maybe a hoor or two besides.

"Get your cue," he said.

He didn't seem afraid at all. He picked out his favorite table, one where he knew all the hills and dales, while I tried to find a decent cue in the rack. It took me quite a while to find one that wasn't left behind by W. C. Fields. Fifty points of lineup straight pool, we decided. For three dollars, and me without a red cent. To show you how cocky I was in those days, I bummed a cigarette off the guy.

I won the lag and made him break. As I was chalking my cue, who walked in the door but the town clown. The constable. The door shaker. He was probably the only cop the town had, but he was *big* . . . about six foot six . . . and he stood three feet from the end of the table, looking me over. He wasn't wearing a uniform, just a police cap and work clothes, and a long billy club that he *held in his hand*. He rocked back and forth, back and forth. I missed my first shot so far I banked it in the side.

Everything started running through my mind. I would be tarred and feathered and run out of town on a rail. Or they would put me on the chain gang to do roadwork for a few years. First thing I knew I was behind forty-three to eight, my shot with nothing open. It was hopeless, so I decided to take a powder, get the hell out of there. I would head for the hobo jungle down by the tracks and hope that they would give me a bite to eat. I hated to go into a jungle empty-handed, though. You were supposed to contribute something to the stew.

I laid my cue on the table. "I have to take a leak," I said. "Where's the pisser?"

It was in the back end of the room. I didn't have to take a leak, but I walked up to the urinal and stood there. My idea was to go out the back window, but it was barred. Bars the size of your finger. There was no way, I mean there was no way to get out. The back door, I thought. I would come out of the pisser and shoot through the back door. With a head start of fifty feet, fleet-footed Dan could lose himself in the night. But the back door had a huge plank nailed across it. Nailed solid. With the right tools I could have pried it off in about a week.

On my way back to the table I thought, "Well, you dumb bastard, you got yourself into it this time. Your luck has run out." I had played on my nerve many times before and always was fortunate.

I shot a deliberate safety. That put him off a little, because he fouled when trying to return it. Then I took a deliberate foul, just touching the tip of my cue to the ball. He scratched again, trying not to break up the balls. I took another deliberate, leaving him corner-hooked. Trying to play safe—which was not his game at all—he scratched again, and that cost him fifteen points. There was a little argument about that, but it is right in the rule book: three scratches in a row costs you fifteen points. That dropped the score to 25–6; I was back in the ball game.

I got another lucky break then—the town clown left. He wasn't interested in games where the players jacked off playing safe. That made me feel better, and I started to make balls. All the other action in the joint stopped; everybody was watching our game. I really didn't know if I would be better off losing or winning. That crowd didn't look very friendly.

The final score was 50–40—I beat him after needing forty-two when he only needed seven. But the amazing thing was this: when I made the last ball, the place went wild—cheering and yelling, everybody shaking my hand, slapping me on the back, telling me how great I played. It was fantastic. Turns out that everybody *hated* Lem the Barber. Lem had been taking their money for years. They had been *waiting* for somebody, *hoping* for somebody to come to town who could beat him.

One young kid came over to me and grabbed me and shook my hand and said, "Jeez, that was great. Where you headed?"

"West."

"Are you in the local hotel?"

"Well, no, I haven't had a chance to check in yet."

"Come on out to the house, then. How would you like a home-cooked meal and a warm bed? When pa hears what you did tonight he'll kill me if I don't bring you home." Oh, how they hated the barber in that town.

I went with that kid and met his family. They honestly seemed to like me. Of course, they hated the barber. I stayed with them for five days, eating all I could and sleeping late. Then one day the father came home with a big smile and said to me: "Wonderful news, Dan! I've got a job for you with Standard Oil. You start tomorrow."

"Gee, thanks," I said. "That certainly is wonderful news."

Before dawn the next morning I was tiptoeing out of the house on my way to the railroad yard. An hour later I was on a rattler headed for El Paso.

DE ORO'S BLADDER

BY *Danny McGoorty,*
AS TOLD TO ROBERT BYRNE

Like the previous selection, this is an excerpt from my book McGoorty, the Story of a Billiard Bum, *first published in 1972.*

Alfredo De Oro was born in Cuba in 1863, spent most of his life in New York City, and died in 1948 at the age of eighty-five. His win at age seventy-two over Welker Cochran, described here, came in the first round of the world three-cushion billiard tournament of 1934. The loss prevented Cochran from repeating as champion, the title going instead to Johnny Layton. Willie Hoppe finished fourth, De Oro eleventh.

THE ALL-TIME MASTER of the psychological hustle was a Cuban: Alfredo De Oro. He was a foreigner, but he spoke fine English—not with a limp like so many of them. When I first saw him in 1925 he was sixty-two years old but looked older. Because he had lost some of his skill, he had learned every possible way to irritate the other fellow and throw him off his game.

In his time he was quite a player. The record book shows that he won the world's title in pool in 1887 and won it fifteen more times after that. He won the three-cushion title at least six times, back around the turn of the century.

He complained constantly. He objected to the referee's calls. He went to the can and stayed there forever, but if the other guy took

183

a quick piss he raised the roof and demanded the game by forfeit. He shot deliberate safeties and then argued that he had tried to score, walking around the arena looking into the audience for support. "Is there a man here who can honestly say I didn't try to make that shot?"

He was a rib artist with a million irritating remarks. If you ignored what he said to you, then he would mutter to himself on the sidelines. While his opponent was trying to shoot, Alfredo was polishing his cue, or chalking it with loud squeaks, or filing the tip, or dropping it on the floor, or coughing, or sending up clouds of talcum powder. If the referee told him to stop doing those things, he would start doing a whole raft of *other* things. I've seen him change shafts just for one shot, taking all day about it.

You see players today whipping out a handkerchief just when the man at the table is about to shoot, but you should have seen the way Alfredo did it. It was masterful. He kept his handkerchief folded like an accordion, with the tip sticking out so he could grab it without fumbling. It was big, a big brilliant white handkerchief. When he snaked it out of his pocket he always sort of shook it to the right and left like a long scarf before putting it to his nose and honking.

And the way he lit a cigar in the other guy's line of sight! His timing on striking the match was terrific. I used to sit in the stands trying to second-guess him. The man at the table would be stroking, just about ready to pull the trigger. Alfredo watched him like a hawk, holding a big kitchen match against a box ready to strike it. "Now!" I would think to myself, leaning forward, anticipating him, but he would wait. "Now!" Not yet. Alfredo waited, watching the man stroke, studying him, then suddenly he would strike the match just as the guy was bringing his cue forward to hit the cue ball. It was beautiful.

He played defense at the table and offense on the sidelines, and the fans crowded in to watch his antics.

In 1934 he managed to claw and scratch his way to win over Cochran in the days when Cochran could shoot the lights out. That crusty, bent old man won a game from the great Cochran, who was one of the flashiest, most brilliant players of all time. It was a sensation when it happened, and old-timers still talk about it. Cochran had an excuse, though, that has never been put in print before. He told it only to the members of his immediate family.

Here is what Welker said:

"I knew the old man would have to take at least six piss breaks during the game. I couldn't complain about it because of his age, and I wasn't going to let it bother me if he took a lot of time. Halfway through the game he hadn't yet asked for permission to leave the table, and I started worrying about him. Started worrying about his bladder. After an hour he still hadn't gone to the can. Was he all right? Was he going to go in his pants? Was he in pain trying to hold it back? I got so worried about his bladder I couldn't concentrate on what I was doing. That old man did not take one piss the whole game, and that is what beat me."

THE HUNGARIAN CINCH

BY *Bill Pronzini*

Randolph GQ-XIV, an extraterrestrial with orange skin and hairy legs who has never played pool before, challenges Fancy Fontana to a game of one pocket for $50,000. Is this the mortal lock Fancy has long dreamed of, or is something fishy afoot? Bill Pronzini sends a curving cue ball our way in this bizarre science fiction tale.

Pronzini, author of such novels as Panic!, Snowbound, The Vanished, *and* Undercurrent, *has written hundreds of short stories and compiled dozens of anthologies of crime fiction. He has played pool for thirty-five years but claims to lack "the eye, the patience, and the mathematical turn of mind to shoot a proper stick." He and Marcia Muller, his mystery-novelist wife, live in northern California.*

I AM HAVING a poached egg and a glass of skimmed milk in my office at Fancy's Billiard & Pool Arena when No-Balls Rinker comes in big-eyed. He is a bantam type with a jillion freckles on his face and is what you call my aide-de-camp and general factotum.

"Fancy," he says, "you will never guess who is outside to see you at this moment."

"So I will not bother," I say. "Tell me."

"It is one of the alien types."

I frown. "I have nothing to do with the alien types since they come down here on the Cultural Exchange Program one year ago. My duodenal ulcer does not get along with orange skin."

"This particular alien type has come with a proposition."

"I am not interested," I say. I have discovered a piece of shell hiding in the broken yolk of my egg. "Give him the double door."

"You will be interested when I lay the nature of the proposition on you," No-Balls says. "Which is that the alien type wishes to set up a game."

"A game?" I forget about the eggshell. "Since when do the alien types learn to shoot pool?"

"He does not tell me. All he tells me is he represents one of his brothers who wishes to challenge you to a game of one pocket."

"One pocket!"

"The alien type is a genuine hairy leg, Fancy. He mentions a little sweetening to this game of one pocket." No-Balls leans closer. "Fifty big ones," he says.

I blink. "Do you say fifty big ones?"

"That is the figure he quotes."

This is a horse of another hue, as the poet says. Since I am recognized many years back as the greatest player and hustler in the history of pool, almost no one will play me for gold. Finally I am forced to come off the hustle, which I have been on most of my life and is the only thing makes me truly happy, and that is when I open Fancy's Billiard & Pool Arena. Once in a while some lamb who thinks he is good enough to beat the master comes in and lays down a challenge, and I proceed to whack him out. But propositions are few and far between of late. I am getting stale and depressed. Now at least, if things work out, I will have this new proposition to perk me up for the time being, even if it is only a game with an alien type.

"No-Balls," I say, "show the hairy leg in."

He hurries out and comes back again with the alien type in tow. It is the first time I see one of them up close. I feel my duodenal ulcer quiver. The alien type looks the way all the rest of them do, which means he has got fluorescent orange skin and a big furry column, like an upside-down beer bottle, on top of his head. He is about four feet tall and is wearing the loincloth which the United Nations puts down they have to wear. When they first come here they are in the altogether, and half the women at the new spaceport in Washington, D.C., faint when they appear.

"Mr. Fancy Fontana," No-Balls says, "I would like for you to make the acquaintance of Mr. Cleve FX-VII, alien type."

I and Cleve say to each other that it is a pleasure. He gives me one of his orange paws, which is cold and damp. My duodenal ulcer quivers again. "Take a seat for yourself and put it down, Cleve," I say to him.

He does this on the chair in front of my desk. I look at No-Balls, who departs. Then I say, "No-Balls says you wish to set up a game of one pocket."

"That is correct," Cleve says. "As I was telling him, I am prepared to wager the sum of fifty thousand of your dollars that my compatriot, Randolph GQ-XIV, can defeat you in a game of one pocket pool. Just a single game, Mr. Fontana."

"Cleve," I say, "since you are an alien type perhaps you do not know that I am the greatest player in the history of pool."

"I am quite well aware of your reputation, sir. That is precisely why I have chosen you as the opponent for Randolph GQ-XIV. Do you accept my challenge?"

I do not answer this right away. Instead I say, "Where do you alien types learn to shoot pool? I am curious."

"Since we arrived on your world," Cleve says, "and learned your various languages, we have become voracious readers of your printed matter. Many of us have become extremely interested in your games of chance and your sporting events upon which wagers may be placed. Randolph GQ-XIV was taken by the game of pool and has read every book written on the subject."

"You are telling me you think this Randolph GQ-XIV can beat the great Fancy Fontana in a game of one pocket just because he reads a few books?"

"He has practiced somewhat, of course. We are also rapid assimilators of technical skills."

Now I have heard it all, I think. One pocket is the hardest of all to master; it takes me twenty years before I am good enough to play the big names and another ten to become the greatest of all time. Along comes this alien type who has read a few books—none of which are written by Fancy Fontana—and wishes to challenge a game for fifty big ones. These orange lambs must be the woolliest I ever see.

I rub my hands together. "Cleve," I say, "you have made yourself a deal. I will shoot your Randolph GQ-XIV the game of one pocket for fifty big ones."

"Excellent. Would you care to suggest a location, Mr. Fontana?"

"If you do not have any objections to Randolph playing on my home territory, we will hold the game right here in my private room."

"I have no objections," Cleve says. "However, I would suggest you limit the attendance to as few as possible. You understand that such ventures would be frowned upon by certain officials."

"Of course, Cleve," I say. "No eyeballers."

"Is Saturday evening agreeable? Eight o'clock?"

"This is most agreeable."

We shake again, and I show him to the door. When he is gone I grin wide and happy, like the fox in the henhouse. I am already thinking how I will spend the fifty big ones I am going to take off Cleve FX-VII, for if ever I encounter an absolute Hungarian Cinch in my long and illustrious career, this is it.

THE ALIEN TYPES show up right on time Saturday night. No-Balls, who is waiting out front, ushers them into my private room. I am there, and Fat Leo, and The Brain. That is all. Fat Leo is a tall, skinny dude who does not weigh a C in his skivvies. I do not know why he is called Fat Leo, and Fat Leo does not know either. He is a tush hog, which is a muscle-type guy who is kept around to see that things do not get out of line. He does not look like any tush hog you ever come across, and this is his advantage. He is a very tough boy.

The Brain is a guy who has been to a zillion colleges and who collects degrees like I collect pool cues when I am a kid. He could be a lawyer or a professor, like that, but he grows up when the hippie types are the vogue. He is down on the Establishment and prefers (he says) to associate himself with the more base elements of our society. I do not comprehend this, but I take it as a compliment. The Brain is a very handy dude to have around, for he helps me to cheat the government on my income tax and advises me when I am in need of advising.

I go forward to meet the alien types. I cannot tell which is Cleve FX-VII and which is Randolph GQ-XIV, since all alien types look alike to me. But one of them pumps my hand, and I surmise this is Cleve. "Mr. Fontana," he says, "Randolph GQ-XIV."

The other alien type gives me his paw. I say, "So you are Randolph. I am looking forward all day to the pleasure of making your acquaintance."

"And I as well," Randolph says. "I consider it a great honor to compete with such a master as yourself, sir."

"You are too kind," I say, and smile inside myself. This is what is known as the soft con. We are buttering each other up, for this is a good strategy when you are about to play for such gelt as fifty big ones. You do not wish to make your opponent, no matter who he is, feel what is called animosity toward you, for this could charge him up enough to give him an edge. I wonder which book Randolph GQ-XIV reads to learn about the soft con.

I snap my fingers, and No-Balls steps up and removes the gold I have given him earlier. Cleve produces his own wad of green from inside his loincloth. Then they exchange the wads, count them, and both are satisfied it is all there.

I say, "No-Balls will hold the stakes, if this is agreeable."

"It is," Cleve says, and hands over my green.

"Now," I say, "let us commence."

We step up to the table. "Medium size," Randolph says. "Four and a half by nine. Very good."

I open my case, which I have nearby, and produce the two halves of my cue. I screw them together. Then I remember that Randolph GQ-XIV is not carrying a case. "You have forgotten your cue, Randolph," I say to him.

"I have no cue," he says.

"No cue?"

"Randolph does not feel the need for using a professional model," Cleve says. "He prefers a simple house cue."

I blink. Why are these alien types not around when I am young? I am then a zillionaire today and not bothered by a duodenal ulcer.

Fat Leo gets Randolph a house cue, and the alien type does not even check to see if it is warped. I say, "We will toss a coin to see who will break."

Randolph nods. Fat Leo takes a coin from his pocket and tosses it. "Heads," Randolph calls. The coin bounces on the felt, spins, and comes up heads.

"You have got the honor, Randolph," I say.

Fat Leo racks the balls. I and Cleve and No-Balls and The Brain sit on the folding chairs which are facing the table on the left. Randolph GQ-XIV picks up the cue ball and walks to the break end, and I notice he does not bother to dust powder on his hands, nor does he bother to chalk his cue. I smile again inside myself.

I will tell you now, in case you do not know, how the game of one pocket pool is played. The rules are very simple. You use the standard fifteen balls, such as you do in the games of 14.1 and rotation. They are racked in no special order. Whoever is the one to break has the choice of which pocket he will shoot for. If the break is made from the left side of the table, it is the far right pocket; if the break is made from the right side, it is the far left pocket. All you must do to win a game of one pocket is to make eight of the fifteen balls, in whichever order you wish to make them, in the pocket which is yours.

But it is not so easy as it may sound. You must be able to have unlimited control of the cue ball and know what type of stroke to use and when to use English and when not to use English. You must be able to make kiss shots and cluster combinations, and two- and three-cushion banks. You must know when and where to play the defensive—when to sacrifice a ball for a safety so that your opponent will not be in position to run out. What I am saying is that you must know everything there is to know about how to play the game of pool in order that you are a good one pocket player, and you do not learn this by reading books and practicing somewhat. Unless you are born with what they say is the silver cue in your hand, as I am, you probably do not ever learn this.

So this is why I am so confident as I wait for Randolph GQ-XIV to commence the game. I take a cigar from my pocket and bite off the end. I cannot smoke them since I have learned of my duodenal ulcer, but the doc says nothing about how I cannot chew them.

Randolph is ready to break. He sets the cue ball to the left of center, which means the far right pocket is his. What he must do on the break is to send the balls toward his pocket, so he will have position advantage at the beginning. He does this by applying right English on the cue ball, making a thin hit on the first ball in the rack and a pretty solid hit on the second ball from the left. If he does not make a ball on the break, the cue ball must touch a rail for a safety.

I watch Randolph lean over the cue ball. He is using an open bridge, which is a sure sign of the amateur. He does not even seem to be concentrating. But I change my mind fast about this when he breaks, and bite down hard on my cigar. It is perfect. He puts right juice on the cue ball and it hits thin on the first ball in the rack and heavy on the second from the left. The rack slides to the right, nice and easy, and the Nine drops in his pocket.

"One," Fat Leo, who is referee, says.

No-Balls whispers to me, "Just luck, Fancy."

I am silent.

Randolph walks around the table, studying position. "Twelve ball," he says after a time, and leans over and whips the cue ball into the Twelve, which is an easy kiss and a shot any kid can make. But the cue ball juices off the end rail and then stops on a dime.

"Two," Fat Leo says.

"Seven ball," Randolph says. It is a straight-in shot, and he makes it with no effort. I watch the cue ball draw and roll to the far center of the table.

"Three," Fat Leo says.

I edge forward in my chair. Now is where Randolph GQ-XIV falls apart, I say to myself. He has the choice of only one good shot, which will leave him in position for a possible run-out. It is a three-ball combination Six off the Two off the Fourteen, which I spot with my practiced eye.

I side-gaze No-Balls. He nods and winks at me. He has seen it too, for he has been around almost as long as I have. The alien type will not see it, I think. And even if he does, he cannot possibly make such a combo; it is a very difficult shot and takes a mastery of proper English.

"Six ball," Randolph says. "Combination off the Two off the Fourteen."

I stare. Randolph strokes. Fourteen into the Two into the Six. The Six drops in his pocket.

"Four," Fat Leo mutters.

"Goddamn!" No-Balls says.

"Nicely done," The Brain says, which is for him some kind of compliment. Usually he is what is called your reticent type.

I note there is sweat forming on my forehead. I take out my handkerchief and wipe it off. My throat is suddenly like somebody pours hot sand down there.

"Fifteen ball," Randolph says. "Cross-bank."

The Fifteen drops. Again, the cue ball stops on a dime.

"Five," Fat Leo says.

"Two ball," Randolph says.

"Six," Fat Leo says a second later.

"Eleven ball," Randolph says. "Kiss off the Thirteen."

"Seven," Fat Leo croaks.

"Jesus Christ," No-Balls says, awed.

My hands have commenced to shake. I do not believe it. If Randolph GQ-XIV makes one more ball, I am out fifty big ones and I do not even get a shot. My duodenal ulcer is on fire. Fancy Fontana, the greatest player and hustler in the history of pool, beaten by an alien type. Should such a thing leak out to the likes of Carbuncle Harry, who is a filage (fraud, like) that claims *he* is the greatest player and hustler in the history of pool, even though I have whacked him out many times over the years, I will be what is called the laughingstock and everyone will think I am headed for Tapioca.

Randolph is walking around the table again. It is so quiet in there you can hear a cockroach pass wind. Even The Brain is sitting on the edge of his chair, and I do not ever know him to get excited.

Randolph stops walking. "Thirteen ball," he says. "Combination off the One off the Eight, three-cushion bank."

I nearly drop my cue. There is no doubt I have underrated Randolph GQ-XIV, for he has shot a very fine stick so far. But the shot he chooses to win the game and my fifty big ones, while it is not impossible, is the next thing to it. As great as I, Fancy Fontana, am, it is extremely difficult for even me to make such a shot. The lie of the balls which remain on the table is an obstacle course. Randolph must juice the cue ball off three cushions, with a great deal of hard right English to bring it around the Five ball, which is blocking part of his path to the One. If he does this much, it is a fine shot. But after the cue ball clears the Five, it must hit the One full on the left side, driving it into the Eight. The Eight must then roll soft to the Thirteen, which is almost frozen on the rail near his pocket, kiss it gently, and send it home.

No-Balls leans toward me. "Fancy," he says, "I think you are about to receive your initial shot. The odds on a combo like that must be—"

"Eight hundred to one," The Brain says.

"Right," I say, and I relax a little. But I am still sweating.

Nobody breathes as Randolph strokes the cue ball. I watch stupefied as it snaps around the table. Side rail, end rail, side rail—three cushions. Never do I see such perfect right English. The cue ball hooks around the Five like the curves Sandy Koufax throws when I am a pants-tugger, and hits the One full on the left side. The One rolls straight into the Eight with a soft kiss. The Eight rolls easy toward Randolph's pocket.

And hangs on the lips.

And drops in.

I collapse backward in my chair. It is like every bone in my body turns to jelly. Fat Leo's eyes bulge like a frog's; he does not even say, "Eight" and announce the game is concluded. The Brain is a statue in his chair, and a tic stutters on No-Balls' jaw.

Cleve FX-VII bounces to his feet. "We have won," he says to me. "I assume, naturally, that you will want a rematch, and we agree to this. But the stakes must be one hundred thousand Earth dollars. I will contact you shortly for your decision, Mr. Fontana."

I am staring at a spot on the ceiling which I do not really see. I cannot speak.

Cleve turns to No-Balls and collects all the gold and puts it away in his loincloth. Randolph lays the house cue he has used to win my fifty big ones on the table. Both of them bow to us, and then out they go.

I and Fat Leo and No-Balls and The Brain do not say anything for a long time. Finally I push myself out of my chair and stand. My legs are wobbly. "No-Balls," I say in a voice which does not sound like my own, "get me a fifth of gin and a large bottle of Maalox liquid."

He stares up at me.

"I wish to get drunk at this time," I tell him, "but I do not care to have my duodenal ulcer perforated in the process."

IT IS THREE days later, and I am brooding in my office. Cleve FX-VII comes by to see me that morning and we set up the rematch for the coming Saturday night. I am eager to have this rematch, but I am also very nervous about it for three good reasons.

The first reason is that while there is no doubt that Fancy Fontana is still the greatest player and hustler in the history of pool, never do I face an opponent with more skill than Randolph GQ-XIV; he has belted me out once, and if he wins the coin toss it is not impossible that he will belt me out again. The second reason is that I am afraid word will leak out to Carbuncle Harry and some of the other boys that I have already been whacked out by an alien type, though this has not yet happened; if it does, I will still be the laughingstock even though I win this rematch. The third reason is the stakes. After I have lost the fifty big ones, I have only about a hundred big ones left in my safety deposit box, which is just enough to cover the rematch bet. Win, and I am ahead by fifty big ones and that is sweet. Lose, and I am tapped out and will have to sell Fancy's Billiard & Pool Arena— and without I change my name and my face I cannot even go on the hustle again, where I am truly happy, since no shooter who is what The Brain calls *compos mentis* will play Fancy Fontana for gelt. It is Tapioca for sure, then . . .

There is a knock on the door, and No-Balls shows The Brain in. The Brain puts it down in front of my desk. No-Balls stands over against the wall.

"Well, Brain," I say morosely, "where have you been the past two days? I do not see you in that time."

"I am a suspicious type by nature," he says, "and I am out making certain discreet inquiries. Prepare yourself to receive a shock, Fancy."

"Hah," I say. "After the alien type chiselers take my fifty big ones, there is nothing which can shock me."

"You are wrong there, for I discover in the course of my discreet inquiries that certain of the alien types possess a power which we do not heretofore know they possess."

"Power?" I say. "What power is this?"

"The power of limited mass hypnotic suggestion through means of telepathy," The Brain says. "I discover this after reading a scholarly tome which is written on the alien types by some professor on the Cultural Exchange Program."

My eyelids rattle. "I do not comprehend."

"On the night you play Randolph GQ-XIV for the fifty big ones," The Brain says, "we are all hypnotized before the game begins. They do this, apparently, as soon as they come in. Then, when they leave, they release the hold."

"Brain, what are you laying down?"

"The game which we see take place does not actually take place at all," he says. "All that happens is planted in our minds by the alien types. Randolph GQ-XIV does not make those fantastic shots to run you out. Cleve FX-VII does not put up fifty big ones. Only *you* put up fifty big ones, Fancy."

I grapple with this, and finally it comes through to me. "I am taken!" I roar.

The Brain nods. "The big con, alien-type style," he says.

"Fancy Fontana, victim of a sting," No-Balls says, disbelieving.

I shout, "I know from the beginning we should not allow the orange bastards down here on the Cultural Exchange Program!"

"Do not judge all the alien types by Randolph and Cleve," The Brain says. "The world Establishment knows of the hypnotic powers they possess before they are allowed to come here, and they are made to promise not to practice same on the people of Earth. The alien types, who are for the most part honest and friendly such as we are, agree to this."

"Honest and friendly? It is honest and friendly to take me for fifty big ones?"

"There are thousands of the alien types down here at this moment, Fancy. Do you not think out of that number, two bad apples may have snuck in unbeknownst?"

"You are telling me that all the alien types are not con artists? Only Cleve and Randolph?"

"This is my presumption."

"But why do they do it? I am not able to comprehend it, Brain. What good is all the American Earth green to them?"

"It is too bad you do not think of this when you accept the challenge Cleve lays down."

I scowl at him.

"But this is past history," he says quickly. "It is my theory that the fifty big ones are not even important to the alien types. They perform the sting simply because that is their profession. After all, if two American Earth con artists manage to get to their world, would they not try to con the alien types out of something?"

"I will not stand for being stung!" I shout, and bang my desk. But then I remember Cleve's visit earlier, and the rematch we have set up for Saturday night, and I am much calmer. I tell The Brain about the rematch and then I say, "When Cleve and Randolph show up, we will put the arm on them and use a little muscle to find out what they have done with my fifty big ones—"

"This will not work, Fancy," The Brain says sadly. "If we try to muscle them, they will only use these telepathic powers which they possess to keep us from doing it. I am quick to add, also, that the bureaucrats of the corrupt Establishment have passed stiff laws against any muscling of the alien types."

I sag back in my chair, for I know The Brain is laying down the true goods. "What do we do, then?" I ask him.

"I do not see anything we do. I suspect the names they give us are nom de plumers, and because all the alien types look alike to us, we cannot even go to the boss alien types. We cannot go to the piglets in blue or to the corrupt bureaucrats, either, for gambling is illegal and we also have no proof that we are conned."

I put my head in my hands. I must have the horns put on me, I think. Such a thing can only happen to someone who has had the horns put on him.

No-Balls is silent all this time, but now I hear him say, "I have perceived a possible solution, Fancy. I do not know if it will work, but perchance it is worth trying."

"What possible solution is this?" I say, raising my head.

"Well," No-Balls says, "what if we are to pretend we have not discovered the sting and allow the rematch to come off as planned. Only this time we make sure it is legit. In a legit match you are the General and will have no trouble winning."

I stare at him. "You have gone loony, No-Balls," I say. "How do we make sure the game is legit? We do not know we are hypnotized by the alien types the last time, which means they are able to hypnotize us as they please and we do not know it until it is too late."

"Not if we bring in an alien type of our own, one of the honest and friendly ones who do not wish anything but goodwill. This honest and friendly alien type will be present at the game, hidden like out of sight. When Cleve and Randolph hypnotize us, the honest-and-friendly *un*hypnotizes us. Then the game continues legit, and you will whack out Randolph."

I look at The Brain. He says, "This might just work, Fancy. I am surprised I do not think of it myself."

So I ponder for a moment. "I have questions," I say finally. "First question: Why does an honest and friendly alien type agree to assist against two of his orange brothers?"

"Because he is honest and friendly," The Brain says, "and does not wish to have bad relations develop between our respective races. He is glad to see justice done, for according to the scholarly tome I read, the alien types are gung ho for justice."

I am satisfied with this. I say, "Second question: Since Cleve and Randolph do not need gelt because they hypnotize us into believing they have it, they will not bring my filaged fifty big ones on Saturday night—so how do we recover this green?"

"Perhaps they do bring it," No-Balls says. "Who can tell with alien types? But if they do not, we instruct the honest-and-friendly to shadow them and/or turn them over to the boss alien types. Either way, we recover your fifty big ones sooner or later."

Which makes sense to The Brain, for he nods. I nod too. "Third question," I say. "Why do we need to let the rematch come off at all? Why do we not just sic the honest-and-friendly on Cleve and Randolph the minute they show their orange faces?"

"Because," The Brain says, "then the honest-and-friendly has no proof there has been a sting."

"He has our word," I say.

"The corrupt Establishment and the boss alien types will not accept the word of even a great man like Fancy Fontana," The Brain says. "This is a hard fact of life. No, we must allow Cleve and Randolph to attempt to sting you again. That way, the honest-and-friendly *knows* we are victims of the big con and is so righteously indignant he works gung ho for us."

I am able to think of no more questions, so finally I decree it is a good plan and we will put same into operation. I am still worried about my last hundred big ones and about Carbuncle Harry and the boys—it is even worse for me if they learn I am stung, not belted out legit, by the alien types—and my duodenal ulcer is complaining very loudly. But I know this is the only way I will ever hope to see my filaged fifty big ones again, and I do not feel so bad as I do a few minutes ago.

No-Balls says, "There are always alien types hanging around the city hall, which I know my way around through past frame-up rousts by the piglets. I will go there and recruit an honest-and-friendly and bring him back for a confab."

"Make sure he *is* an honest-and-friendly," I say.

"I will make sure," No-Balls promises.

When he is gone, I say to The Brain, "Brain, I feel the need for some practice time. Since it is visiting day at the women's slammer and Fat Leo has gone there to see his mother, you will have to do my racking and scorekeeping."

We go to my private room and I commence playing 14.1 to warm up. Then I switch to one pocket. I am ashamed to say it, but the great Fancy Fontana shoots a very poor stick for the first time in so long as I remember.

THE HONEST-AND-FRIENDLY No-Balls recruits is named Theodore RJ-XXI. He is very indignant about the "alleged" (this is his word) sting which Cleve FX-VII and Randolph GQ-XIV have laid on me and says once he witnesses their con artistry for himself he will do everything in his power to see justice is done and I am returned my fifty big ones.

I ask Theodore, "Are you alien types able to hypnotize each other like you hypnotize us Earth-type people?"

"To some extent," Theodore says, "though telepathically projected objects, while appearing to be three-dimensional, may be detected by us for what they really are when the nerve sensors in the appendages you call fingers fail to register a response."

I look at The Brain. "What does this mean in English?"

"It means the alien types can hypnotize each other," The Brain says, "but when they touch something and cannot feel it, they know they are hypnotized."

"So Theodore here cannot hypnotize up my hundred big ones, and I must lay out the real gelt."

"I am afraid so," Theodore says.

No-Balls says, "There is no way you will lose it, Fancy. This time we have got a Hungarian Cinch for sure."

"Now that I am stung once," I say, "I do not take anything for granted anymore. But all right. Leave us now plan our strategy for the second coming of Cleve and Randolph."

NEVER DO I see time go so slowly, and never does my duodenal ulcer give me such a hassle. I am always very cool before a big game or match, but this is not the same thing. Still, I practice long and heavy and I am very much on my stick again; if Theodore RJ-XXI does what he is supposed to, I will have no trouble whacking out Randolph GQ-XIV and keeping my hundred big ones safe in hand.

Saturday night finally comes. Theodore shows up at seven o'clock, like I have told him, and I install him behind the curtains which cover the hallway where the johns are. We are not bothered by eyeballers, since we manage to keep the lid on about the sting and the rematch, and Carbuncle Harry and the boys have no idea of what is coming down; for this I am very relieved.

I and The Brain sit quiet in our chairs. No-Balls and Fat Leo pace forth and back, working off what The Brain calls your nervous energy. I have my eyes fixed on the wall clock. But except that my duodenal ulcer quivers now and then, I am cool like a church deacon waiting for the Sunday services.

Right at eight o'clock the doors open and in comes Cleve FX-VII and Randolph GQ-XIV. We do the greet-and-shake number, though I am thinking it is the necks of the alien types I prefer to grasp in my hand, and then we soft con each other like before. Randolph says it is an honor and a privilege to play the great Fancy Fontana again. I say I am very impressed by the stick he has shot the last time. Cleve says we are both brilliant practitioners of the art of pool. There is more of this sheizola, until finally I say to Cleve, "Let us get on with business. One hundred big ones apiece, to begin."

Cleve and No-Balls exchange fat wads of green. I look closely at Cleve's bills, but I cannot tell if it is real gold or hypnotized gold. Neither can No-Balls, for he looks at me and shrugs.

When No-Balls is holding all the stakes, I and Randolph and Fat Leo go up to the table. I say, "House cue, Randolph?"

"House cue," he says.

Fat Leo brings him one. I screw my own cue together and chalk the tip. Randolph just stands there with the house cue.

"Toss the coin, Fat Leo," I say to my tush hog.

Randolph calls, "Heads" when the coin is in the air. It bounces and flips over on the felt, and I see that it has come up heads. My duodenal ulcer quivers again.

"It is your break, Randolph," I say. "But before we commence, I discover I have to use the john. I will be back in fast time."

I cross to the curtains and push through. Theodore RJ-XXI is standing against the wall. I say to him, "Well, Theodore?"

"They used their telepathic powers as soon as they came in," Theodore says. "I have already counteracted the hypnosis."

"Do I see Cleve give No-Balls real gold or hypnotized gold?"

"Hypnotized gold, as you term it."

"So they have not brought my fifty big ones," I say. "But we will recover this green later, will we not, Theodore?"

"Absolutely, Mr. Fontana," Theodore says. "I am convinced now that they have used their powers to cheat you, and I will see to it that restitution is made to you and that they are punished."

"Since you have unhypnotized us, the coin toss I just see is legit?"

"Yes."

"You are sure Cleve and Randolph do not know we are unhypnotized?"

"They will realize something is wrong when the game begins and does not proceed as they have planned," Theodore says. "They will attempt to reestablish matters in their favor, but I will prevent that from happening."

I nod. When I push out through the curtains again, I see Fat Leo has racked the balls and Randolph is ready to break. I sit in my chair, take out a cigar, and commence to chew it. "Any time you are ready, Randolph," I say to the alien-type filage.

Randolph sets the cue ball to the left of center, as he does the last time, and breaks the rack: perfect right English, thin on the first ball and heavy on the second from the left. The balls slide toward his pocket. The Four rattles between the pocket corners, then drops.

"One," Fat Leo says, side-glancing me.

I mangle the end of my cigar. Can it be Randolph GQ-XIV really does know how to shoot pool, and what I just see is also legit? This must be, for Theodore RJ-XXI says we are unhypnotized. . . .

"Nine ball," Randolph says, which is an easy cut. The Nine disappears into his pocket.

"Two," Fat Leo says.

Randolph walks around the table, one full turn. Then he stops and says, "One shot, six-ball combination. Twelve off the Ten, Ten to follow. Reverse English to the Six. Cue ball off the right rail, Eight ball off the Fifteen, Fifteen to follow. Cue ball off the end cushion to the Three."

I and No-Balls and The Brain are on our feet. This shot Randolph has called is impossible, and I do not mean maybe. Not even Fancy Fontana, as great as I am, could come close to completing such a shot. This is the end of Randolph GQ-XIV, all right.

Unless—

Randolph strokes, and when he does Fat Leo gasps and we are all frozen in what you call your state of incredulity. The Ten ball slides into the Twelve, and the Twelve drops, and the Ten follows. What the cue ball does then is come spinning off with crazy English—the kind you cannot put on a ball even with a massé stroke, which Randolph has not used anyway—and curls around the Six and kicks it home. Then the cue ball, still acting crazy, juices off the right cushion, herky-jerks to the Fifteen, sends the Fifteen into the Eight, and they drop one after the other, *plunk, plunk.* After which the cue ball juices off the end rail, angles to the Three, taps it, stops dead like it is tired from all this freaky work, and sits there as the Three rolls home.

Cleve FX-VII jumps up immediately and says, "We have won." He grabs the gelt out of No-Balls' hand and shoves it inside his loincloth. While he is doing this, I fling down my cigar and my face is so hot there must be smoke coming out my ears and nose.

"We are still hypnotized and I am stung again!" I bellow, for this is the only possible explanation for what I just see. "Fat Leo, No-Balls, put the arm on these two alien-type chiselers!"

Fat Leo and No-Balls react very fast; my tush hog makes a grab for Randolph and my aide-de-camp lunges for Cleve. But all they come up with is air, because in that instant both alien types disappear. I mean, one second they are there and the next they are gone, *poof!*, like in one of those magical acts you see on the TV.

I whirl around, so confused and so mad I feel funny in the head, and start over to the curtains. But before I take two steps, the curtains part and out comes Theodore RJ-XXI. He flashes me a grin and lifts his hand—and then goddamn if he doesn't vanish just like Cleve and Randolph.

"What the hell is going on!" I roar. No one answers me. No-Balls' mouth is hanging open, and Fat Leo looks groggy, the way I see guys look after they have been popped on the head with a bung starter. Only The Brain, who is always cool, looks close to normal.

I glare at No-Balls. "Do you not tell me you have found an honest-and-friendly in Theodore RJ-XXI? He is as big a con artist as Randolph and Cleve!"

"I cannot understand it, Fancy," No-Balls says. "I think all along he *is* an honest-and-friendly. Perhaps the tome The Brain reads is not so factual, and all the alien types—"

He does not finish what he is saying. The reason he does not finish it is because the door opens right then and in comes a pool cue with arms and legs.

I think I am having delusions and rub my eyes, but it is still there: a pool cue with arms and legs and nothing else, like a giant-size stickman of the type I draw when I am in the fifth grade at P.S. 15, my last year in the public school.

I have freaked out, I think. I am ready for the straitjacket and the padded cell. But the others see it too, and they gawp like I do. No-Balls lets out a yip and his face turns the color of vanilla ice cream. Fat Leo says something that sounds like "Urk!" He puts a hand inside his coat but does not draw his piece. He looks at me, helpless. How can you shoot a pool cue? his eyes say.

The cue walks up to where we are and stops. A little hole opens up near the tip and a little stalk comes out. At the end of the stalk is a mouth, and the mouth says, "I am the instrument of vengeance, for I know the truth about everything. I have come for the man who conceived the sting against Mr. Fancy Fontana."

"What is this?" I say. My voice comes out like I am being strangled. "The man? Do you say the *man?*"

"No-Balls Rinker," the cue says.

No-Balls yips again and looks around all wild and panicked. "I . . . I do not know what you are laying down," he says, trembling.

"Of course you do. You recruited Cleve FX-VII and Randolph GQ-XIV and Theodore RJ-XXI; it was your idea from the beginning to cheat Mr. Fontana out of his one hundred and fifty thousand dollars."

"*No*-Balls?" I say.

"The proof is in his coat pocket," the cue says. "That is where your money disappeared to tonight, Mr. Fontana, not away with Cleve FX-VII."

No-Balls claps a hand to the pocket of his coat. Then he pulls the hand away and looks at The Brain and at Fat Leo and finally at me. What he sees in my face makes him yip a third time, and suddenly he spins and commences to run for the door.

But the cue steps in front of him, and No-Balls skids to a halt. Very fast, the mouth on the end of the stalk grows and keeps on growing until it is bigger than the cue itself, until it is so big as a doorway. Inside I see two rows of teeth, very sharp and gleaming, and a tongue like an elephant's trunk. "I am going to bite your head off, No-Balls Rinker," the mouth says, and advances.

No-Balls screams and faints dead away.

And the mouth and the cue disappear, *poof!,* just like Cleve and Randolph and Theodore.

"Fat Leo," The Brain says, "investigate the contents of No-Balls' coat pocket."

Fat Leo comes forward, shaky, and bends down beside No-Balls. His hand goes inside the pocket, and when it comes out again he is clutching my wad of green.

I do not say anything. I still feel funny in the head.

The Brain turns and looks over to the storage room behind my private bar. "All right, Bartholomew," he says.

And the storage room door opens and out comes another alien type.

My legs are so wobbly now I think I am going to fall down any second. I lean against the table and hang on to one of the rails, watching this new alien type come up. When he reaches us, The Brain says to me, "Fancy, I wish for you to make the acquaintance of Bartholomew TZ-III, who is an honest-and-friendly I brought in to sting the stingers. Bartholomew, Mr. Fancy Fontana."

The alien type bows. "Pleased to meet you, sir."

I shake my head several times, until I am able to clear away some of the fog which is inside. I tell the honest-and-friendly I am happy to make his acquaintance. Then I look at The Brain, respectful. "Brain," I say, "do you know all along No-Balls is behind the stings?"

"Not all along," he says. "But I have my suspicions ever since he comes up with his solution for getting back your fifty big ones. In all the years I know No-Balls, he never comes up with a solution to anything. Also, it seems to me he is not happy when I learn about the telepathic powers the alien types possess and tell same to you; and he is very eager to have the rematch come off as scheduled. When he offers to find an honest-and-friendly himself and comes back with Theodore RJ-XXI, I am even more suspicious. So I go out and hunt up Bartholomew here, who is not only an honest-and-friendly but a boss alien type as well. I know I can trust him."

"I must confess," Bartholomew says, "that I was not convinced at first. But, of course, what I saw here tonight eliminated all doubts. You were all hypnotized by Cleve FX-VII and Randolph GQ-XIV as soon as they came in, and Theodore RJ-XXI not only failed to un-hypnotize you but added his own telepathic illusion. The person you call No-Balls, during the course of the 'game,' transferred the currency to his pocket. He had nothing in his hand when Cleve FX-VII appeared to take the bills from him just before they vanished."

"How are they able to disappear like they do?" I ask him.

"They didn't," Bartholomew says. "They were already gone, all three of them. What they did, you see, was to wait until they were outside before dissolving the illusions—first the one cast by Cleve and Randolph, then the one cast by Theodore. This made it seem, in the instant you were released, that they had disappeared."

"And the walking, talking pool cue?"

"A telepathic projection of my own. When it had served its purpose, I released you all from *my* hold and it vanished too."

"But you allow Cleve and Randolph and Theodore to escape," I say. "Or do you?"

"Not really. I intend to report them to our chief emissary. They will be deported immediately and severely dealt with at home."

"Then you know their real handles?"

"No, but I have their descriptions."

"Do you say you are able to tell them apart?"

Bartholomew smiles. "Certainly," he says. "Although I must confess I have difficulty telling you Earthlings apart."

I look down at No-Balls, who is still unconscious on the floor. Who would have thought him for a filage? I think. "There is no more loyalty in the world," I say. "Even your friends turn out to be bastards sometimes."

"This is sad but true," The Brain says, "and is the fault of the corrupt Establishment. Still and all, I always lock up my valuables when No-Balls is around, for I often see he has a funny gleam in his eyes when he is near gelt and things worth same."

I am feeling almost normal now. I say to Fat Leo, "Haul No-Balls into the back and wake him up and ask him about my fifty big ones. Tell him if I do not get every penny back he will vanish, *poof!*, like the three alien types do."

Fat Leo nods and carts No-Balls out of the room. I say then to Bartholomew TZ-III, "Well, Bartholomew, you have done a fine job, even though I almost have a heart attack and a perforated duodenal ulcer while you are doing it. If there is anything which I am able to do for you in the way of a favor, do not hesitate to ask."

"As a matter of fact, Mr. Fontana," he says, "there is one thing. I find your game of pool fascinating, as I have discovered a great many of our race do; we are quite sports-minded, you know. I wonder if you would show me how it is properly played?"

I am taken unawares, and I say, "This is the straight goods about you alien types being fascinated by pool?"

"Oh yes. In fact, I would not be at all surprised if the game quickly spreads to our home world, and we sign an import agreement for equipment quite soon."

I have a vision of a jillion alien types hunched over a jillion pool tables. Then, suddenly, I see myself, Fancy Fontana—a jillion of me—hunched over these same tables. And I think: Why not? I have hustled pool in every state in the Union and in foreign-type countries which have names I cannot pronounce—for gelt mostly, though there are plenty of other things which are acceptable stakes. No one will play me now, here on Earth, because I am the greatest, but on an alien-type planet that is gung ho for pool . . .

I say to Bartholomew TZ-III, "Bartholomew, I am delighted to teach you the finer points of pool playing. Perhaps, if it can be arranged, I and The Brain and Fat Leo will even come to your alien-type planet and teach your orange brothers as well."

"I think that can be arranged, yes," Bartholomew says. "It is kind of you to make the offer, Mr. Fontana."

I grin like the Cheshire cat as I pick up my cue and lead him to the table. In all my dreams I do not ever expect I will find such a true Hungarian Cinch: a jillion orange lambs all eager and waiting for the return to the hustle of the Big Mahah . . .

....

GREAT BIG BOFFS
THEY ARE

BY *Ken Mitchell*

*The best con games, scams, and stings—like pool hustling—depend
on the greed of the mark. What happens when the mark is a nice
person who has the hustler's best interests at heart? If you are now
or ever have been a hustler, you know how frustrating it can be.
Canadian writer Ken Mitchell describes a case in point in the
following story.*

*Mitchell, a professor of English at Saskatchewan's University of
Regina, has written plays, poems, short stories, novels (see especially*
Wandering Rafferty), *even an opera (*Cruel Tears*). "Great Big
Boffs They Are" appeared in a 1977 anthology of his short stories
entitled* Everybody Gets Something Here, *published by Macmillan of Canada.*

THE CHEV gives out just as we're taking the bypass around
this Moose Jaw place, and we have to pull over at a service station.
The guy comes out and whips our gas cap off like a real pro before
we can tell him what's happening. "Fillerup?" he says.

Danny says, "You suit yourself, man. But I can't pay for it—I can't
even afford to get the windows wiped." Danny is cool. He comes up
with lines like that out of the blue.

But we get the guy to take a look, and he says it's no wonder she
quit on us, because we blew out the head gasket. I ask him how

much, and he says, "Oh, it'll cost you—oh, about—twenty bucks, that's counting labor and everything."

"Can't pay it," says Danny. "You couldn't cut her down a bit, eh?" The guy looks at the motor very dubiously for a while and he says he could maybe do it for seventeen, if we're not in a hurry.

Anyway, Danny gets the guy down to fifteen bucks and says we'll be back later. We get a lift off a flashlight-battery salesman who comes along and he takes us into this Moose Jaw dump. It's a real nothing town, mostly used by farmers and imitation cowboys. There are no girls around, so we figure the parents keep them locked up pretty tight. It's a stinking place to lose a head gasket.

"What's up, Dan?" I say when the salesman lets us off. "How are we gonna get the car fixed? We aren't even gonna get as far as Winnipeg."

Danny has a very sarcastic look which he gives me when I ask stupid questions. "Why do you always talk so much?" he says, and walks over to where this guy is leaning against a bank, watching people go past. The guy has this big hat and one of those little string ties with a cow's head holding it together. Maybe he's about forty years old, with a bit of stomach hanging over his cowboy belt. Danny gives him a real hard look.

"Hey," he says. "Where's the pool hall?"

The guy isn't affected by Danny's hard look. He nods down the street. " 'Bout a block and a half."

Danny looks up at a streetlight and snaps his fingers. "Yeah, man, yeah," he says. "What street?"

The cowboy looks sort of surprised and he says, "Main Street—this street here." So Danny and me look around and sure enough, this street is the only one around with any action on it.

"You from out of town, eh?" says the guy, thinking he is pretty sharp. Danny can't resist swelling up and telling him we come from Vancouver. But the cowboy just looks a little disappointed, like he was expecting Russians or somebody, so we saunter off down to the pool hall, which we find in a basement underneath a beauty shop.

The place is a lot like any other pool hall, except the ceilings are pretty low, and the tables are the old style with those fat, round legs. Not many people are around because it's the middle of the week and only about eleven o'clock in the morning. While old Danny is looking around and getting friendly with the counterman, I see this guy watching a game over at the back. This is one of three games going in the whole hall.

I go over to Danny and give him a nudge to look at this yokel, who's wearing one of those old Elvis Presley shirts, just perfect for riding around in an old Ford convertible and letting the sun flash off the silver threads and dazzle chicks on the sidewalk. Over top of the shirt, he has a white sport jacket with little black flecks in it. You probably seen them around. What gets me is this outfit is brand-*new*.

Both Danny and me are pretty good at sizing guys up, just by looking at them. Ever since we were little kids, we had this game, where we guess what a guy is by what he looks like. After a while you can guess pretty close. So we both see right away that this guy, who's maybe seventeen and still out to lunch, is trying to make it with the pool hall boys by hanging around in these flashy clothes that are about twenty years out of style.

Now a guy like Danny, you can tell right away he's a sharpster, even before you hear him talk. Back home, he's always the first to start wearing the latest style. Shirts, shoes, anything; you just *look* at him, and you know Danny is sharp. Me, I usually wear pretty well what he wears, but not as good. He doesn't like it when I do.

Anyway, Danny walks over and stands beside the farm boy like he's watching the game, too. I mess around with one of the pinball machines for a while. Pretty soon, him and the guy go over to an empty table and take some cues down. I ease over and sit down to watch the action.

"Buck a game, okay?" says Danny to the guy. He figures the guy must have some money, with his new clothes and all, so he opens low to get him started.

"That's quite a lot," says the guy, but stands his cue up for first shots anyway. Danny's is longer, so he breaks, and makes a *rotten* break. The guy looks a little startled to see all those open balls, but he recovers and sinks a red and a blue and another red. Danny misses his first shot, and the guy sinks another red. The whole game goes on like this and Danny takes a horrible beating. He throws a dollar bill on the table when the game is over, and the guy asks, like he can't believe what's happening, if Danny wants to play *another game*.

After Danny lets the guy start winning the second game, he says to him, "You must play a lot of snooker," and he winks at me. I keep my mouth shut.

"Oh, the odd game. When I'm downtown, I usually drop in for one or two. You know."

Danny whistles like he can't believe it. "They gotta have some real sharp cues in this town," he says.

"Oh, yeah! And there's dozens of guys better than me," says the guy, whose name, it turns out, is Alex. "We had a big tournament here last week for fifty bucks. I was out in the first round."

"You oughta get up a busload of guys and send them out to Vancouver," says Danny, lining up a shot and missing another red. "They'd clean up."

"Really?" says Alex.

"Really," says Danny. I go over to get a Coke. When I come back, Danny has lost the second game, and Alex is all embarrassed about winning. But he asks Danny if he'd like to play again. Danny mumbles something about blowing all his money, but finally he says okay and wins the third game by a close score. Then he loses the next four games, until he is down a total of five bucks. After hemming and hawing around for a while, he says, "Look Alex, I gotta try and win some money back. I need it bad. How about playing five bucks a game and give me a chance to win her back?"

"No," says Alex.

"No? What the hell do you mean—*no?*"

"Well, I don't wancha to lose any more money, and you *will* if you play anymore. I'm better than you. Don't you see that?"

Danny looks around at me. I just shrug and look innocent.

"Aw, cummon, Alex," he says. "Just for a buck, then, like before."

"Nope. I don't think you should lose any more money. A guy should quit when he loses so bad."

"Look, you stupid clod," says Danny. "I can beat you with one arm in a sling. Just gimme the chance, eh?" He is hollering and waving his pool cue in the poor guy's face. "Just gimme the chance!"

"No use trying to get me riled, Danny. I'm not gonna play any more snooker. Five bucks is enough for me to win in one afternoon."

I see Danny is *really* getting mad now, like he might punch the guy out, so I step in and give him a smoke. "Maybe you better quit," I say. "We gotta get going pretty soon anyway." I give him a look that says I don't think it's any use trying to suck the guy in. Even *I* can see that Alex just isn't greedy enough.

"Okay," says Danny, and we start to go out. I like that about him—if he keeps his temper down, he can usually think pretty cool. But Alex isn't finished yet.

"Where you guys goin'?" he says. We just look at him. "Maybe I could buy yuz a milk shake or something, if you're not in a hurry." We are still looking at the guy. "I mean, I never won so much money before in a snooker game—I don't hardly know what to do with it."

"Okay," says Danny after a minute. "Okay," I say, kind of surprised that Danny accepts. So Alex takes us across the street to this cheesy-looking restaurant called the King George Café. It's one of these old places with the big fans turning on the ceiling and wooden booths. Obviously this is where Alex hangs out, because he nods to the guy on the cash register and leads us to one of the booths at the back.

"Chocolate or vanilla?" asks Alex, when we sit down.

"Strawberry," says Danny.

"They don't have no strawberry, just chocolate and vanilla." Alex is apologetic as hell, until Danny says, "All right for crissakes—gimme vanilla." I nod, meaning that's okay for me too, and Alex goes up front to put in the order.

"Five bills!" says Danny, and he looks pretty miserable.

"Maybe we can roll him," I suggest, thinking Danny might want me to say it first. "He isn't going to play any more snooker."

Danny gives me his sarcastic look, but I know he's thought about it, too. "Fat chance," he says. "I know these guys. Built like plow horses. Think like 'em too. We're lucky to get a goddamn milk shake."

"Too bad it's not a beer," I say.

"Hah! Wait'll he offers to show us the sights of town."

"The shakes'll be here in a minute," Alex announces when he comes back. Nobody says nothing for so long it starts to get uncomfortable. "Did you fellahs say you were from Vancouver?" Silence. "Are you on holidays?"

"Yeah," says Danny. "Holidays."

"Well Moose Jaw's a nice place to visit, I guess. You seen the Wild Animal Park yet?"

"Just goin' through."

"Our car died just out of town," I add.

"Gee, that's too bad," says Alex. "Where you going?"

"Toronto," says Danny.

Alex nods his head a few times and everybody shuts up till it gets painful again. Alex clears his throat. "Maybe you'd like to see the Wild Animal Park," he says.

Danny mumbles something about stinking animals, but I say, "Come on, Dan. The car won't be ready for a while yet. Let's have a look." He gives me his hard look but doesn't say anything. Finally after a while, he says, "Okay, where's your wheels, then?" and we get up.

Alex takes us past the sad little guy at the cash register. "I'm buying my friends' milk shakes," he says.

His car is parked around the corner, and sure enough it's a '51 Ford. While we are driving out to the zoo, Alex tells us all about what we are driving past. Like there is the new high school and they just made this street into four lanes last summer and it's a big improvement for the town. He shows us the biggest seed-cleaning mill in the whole jesus province and where the meat-packing plant used to be before it burned down three years ago.

So we get to this zoo, and they got pretty much the same animals as in Stanley Park, except a lot grubbier and not as many. There's a couple of beat-up lions and a swarm of monkeys and two fat old black bears that lick popcorn out of people's hands. About the only interesting thing they got is a bunch of buffaloes, running around loose—tame as the pigeons in Victory Square. Great big boffs they are, with big fuzzy heads and bare asses. Alex says they were made like this so they could walk headfirst into a prairie blizzard and not get cold. Just go charging head-on into everything. This is the first time I ever seen buffaloes, and I get a huge bang out of them. But Danny is still mad about losing his money and going out to the zoo and everything, and he gets pretty annoyed when I keep talking them up.

"If they're so goddamn terrific," he says, "how come they all got killed off?" I don't know, but this leaves me thinking.

Alex, he buys us all a hot dog. He even offers to drive us out to the station to get the Chev, because Danny is in such a sweat to get moving. "What's wrong with your car?" he asks, while we're driving along. I see Danny is cleaning his fingernails very carefully with a toothpick, so I lean up from the backseat and tell Alex about the head gasket.

"Gee, that's too bad," says Alex. "How much'll it cost?"

"Fifteen stinking dollars," says Danny, who decides to speak up after all. "Our last fifteen dollars." He throws his toothpick out the window.

"But then how'll you get to Toronto?"

Danny turns to him and says real slow. "We are going to stop in the next stinking town and play pool until we earn some stinking money. Okay?"

"Oh," says Alex. Nobody says nothing else until we get to the service station. The car is fixed and sitting out on the lot, ready to roll.

"Uuhhh," says Alex, and we look at him. "I'll lend you fifteen bucks to pay for the car, if you like."

Danny's eyes bulge out like grapes, and I guess mine are almost the same. "Cut it out!" he hollers. "Just lay off, you dumb yokel!"

All three of us sit there, looking back and forth at each other.

"You can pay it back when you get to Toronto," Alex says, offering some bills. Danny grabs the money and goes striding over to pay the pump man. I get out of the car when Danny looks around to see if I'm coming.

"See ya," I say.

"See ya," says Alex. He sits there watching while we jump into the Chev. Danny starts her up, and then we see Alex about halfway over to our car, hollering something. Danny rolls his window down.

"Why don't you drop in when you're finished?" Alex yells.

"Finished? Finished *what?*"

"Finished your holidays!"

"Oh, yeah—holiday," says Danny. "Sure." He floors the Chev and leaves rubber all over the lot.

"Stupid bastard," he says. I just sit there and look around to see old Alex standing beside his beat-up Ford, waving so-long at us while we tear off down the highway.

"What a sucker," says Danny, after a few miles. I don't say anything, just watch the prairie roll past.

"Look," he says, after a while. "If they're so goddamn great, just tell me how come they all died off, and they only live in zoos? Just explain *that* to me, smart guy!"

I still don't have the answer, but I think about it all the way to Brandon. Danny always asks sharp questions like that.

1983

· ·

REMEMBER YOUNG CECIL

BY *James Kelman*

Young Cecil is good, the best snooker player in Glasgow, maybe the best Glasgow has ever seen. How will he do against one of the top English professionals? A match is arranged, the locals put their bets on the hometown favorite, the balls are broken, and . . .

James Kelman has been highly praised for his depictions of working-class life and speech in Scotland. "Remember Young Cecil" is taken from Not While the Giro, *published in 1983 by Polygon Press of Edinburgh. His second collection of short stories was the Kafkaesque* Greyhound for Breakfast *(1987). Novels include* The Busconductor Hines *(1984),* A Chancer *(1985), and* A Disaffection *(1989).*

In 1994, Kelman won the United Kingdom's most prestigious literary award, the Booker Prize, for his novel How Late It Was, How Late. *The choice shocked England's book world because the novel is written in the language of the street, with plenty of profanity, rather than in the classical style of an Oxford Don. Kelman viewed the furor as a clear case of cultural bias.*

Y OUNG CECIL is medium sized and retired. For years he has been undisputed champion of our hall. Nowadays that is not saying much. This pitch has fallen from grace lately. John Moir who runs the place has started letting some of the punters rent a table

Friday and Saturday nights to play Pontoons, and as an old head pointed out the other day: that is it for any place, never mind Porter's.

In Young Cecil's day it had one of the best reputations in Glasgow. Not for its decoration or the rest of it. But for all-round ability Porter's regulars took some beating. Back in these days we won the "City" eight years running with Young Cecil Number 1 and Wee Danny backing up at Number 2. You could have picked any four from ten to make up the rest of the team. Between the two of them they took the lot three years running; snooker singles and doubles, and billiards the same. You never saw that done very often.

To let you know just how good we were, John Moir's big brother Tam could not even get into the team except if we were short though John Moir would look at you as if you were daft if you said it out loud. He used to make out Tam, Young Cecil, and Wee Danny were the big three. Nonsense. One or two of us had to put a stop to that. We would have done it a hell of a lot sooner if Wee Danny was still living because Young Cecil has a habit of not talking. All he does is smile. And that not very often either. I have seen Frankie Sweeney's boy come all the way down here just to say hello; and what does Young Cecil do but give him a nod and at the most a how's it going without even a name nor nothing. But that was always his way and Frankie Sweeney's boy still drops in once or twice yet. The big noises remember Cecil. And some of the young ones. Tam!—never mind John Moir—Young Cecil could have gave Tam forty and potting only yellows still won looking round. How far.

Nowadays he can hardly be annoyed even saying hello. But he was never ignorant. Always the same.

I mind the first time we clapped eyes on him. Years ago it was. In those days he used to play up at the YM, but we knew about him. A hall's regulars kind of keep themselves to themselves and yet we had still heard of this young fellow that could handle a stick. And with a first name like Cecil nobody needed to know what his last one was. Wee Danny was the Number 1 at the time. It is not so good as all that being Number 1 'cause you have got to hand out big starts otherwise you are lucky to get playing, never mind for a few bob—though there are always the one or two who do not bother about losing a couple of bob just so long as they get a game with you.

Wee Danny was about twenty-seven or thirty in those days but no more than that. Well, this afternoon we were hanging around. None of us had a coin—at least not for playing with. During the week it was. One or two of us were knocking them about on Table 3, which has always been the table in Porter's. Even John Moir would not dream of letting anyone mess about on that one. There were maybe three other tables in use at the time but it was only mugs playing. Most of us were just chatting or studying form and sometimes one would carry a line up to Micky at the top of the street. And then the door opened and in comes this young fellow. He walks up and stands beside us for a wee while. Then: Anybody fancy a game? he says.

We all looks at one another but at Wee Danny in particular and then we bursts out laughing. None of you want a game then? he says.

Old Porter himself was running the place in those days. He was just leaning his elbows on the counter in his wee cubbyhole and sucking on that falling-to-bits pipe of his. But he was all eyes in case of bother.

For a couple of bob? says the young fellow.

Well we all stopped laughing right away. I do not think Wee Danny had been laughing at all; he was just sitting up on the ledge dangling his feet. It went quiet for a minute then Hector Parker steps forward and says that he would give the young fellow a game. Hector was playing 4 stick at that time and hitting not a bad ball. But the young fellow just looks him up and down. Hector was a big fat kind of fellow. No, says the young yin. And he looks round at the rest of us. But before he can open his mouth Wee Danny is off the ledge and smartly across.

You Young Cecil from the YM?

Aye, says the young fellow.

Well, I'm Danny Thompson. How much you wanting to play for?

Fiver.

Very good. Wee Danny turns and shouts: William . . .

Old Porter ducks beneath the counter right away and comes up with Danny's jar. He used to keep his money in a jam jar in those days. And he had a good few quid in there at times. Right enough sometimes he had nothing.

Young Cecil took out two singles, a half-quid, and made the rest up with a pile of smash. He stuck it on the shade above Table 3 and Wee Danny done the same with his fiver. Old Porter went over to where the mugs were playing and told them to get a move on. One or two of us were a bit put out with Wee Danny because usually when there was a game on we could get into it ourselves for a couple of bob. Sometimes with the other fellow's cronies, but if there was none of them, Wee Danny maybe just covered the bet and let us make up the rest. Once or twice I have seen him skinned and having to play a money game for us. And when he won we would chip in to give him a wage. Sometimes he liked the yellow stuff too much. When he got a right turn off he might go and you would be lucky to see him before he had bevied it all in; his money right enough. But he had to look to us a few times, a good few times—so you might have thought: Okay I'll take three quid and let the lads get a bet with the deuce that's left . . .

But no. You were never too sure where you stood with the wee man. I have seen him giving some poor bastard a right sherricking for nothing any of us knew about. Aye, more than once. Not everybody liked him.

Meanwhile we were all settled along the ledge. Old Porter and Hector were applying the brush and the stone; Wee Danny was fiddling about with his cue. But Young Cecil just hung around looking at the photos and the shield and that, that Old Porter had on full view on the wall behind his counter. When the table was finally finished Old Porter began grumbling under his breath and goes over to the mugs who had still not ended their game. He tells them to fuck off and take up bools or something and locks the door after them. Back into his cubbyhole he went for his chair so he could have a sitdown to watch the game.

Hector was marking the board. He chips the coin. Young Cecil calls it and breaks without a word. Well, maybe he was a bit nervous, I do not know; but he made a right mess of it. His cue ball hit the blue after disturbing a good few reds out the pack on its way back up the table. Nobody could give the wee man a chance like that and expect him to stand back admiring the scenery. In he steps and bump bump bump—a break of fifty-six. One of the best he had ever had.

It was two out of three they were playing. Some of us were looking daggers at Danny, not every day you could get into a fiver bet. He broke for the next and left a good safety. But the young fellow had got over whatever it was, and his safety was always good. It was close but he took it. A rare game. Then he broke for the decider and this time it was no contest. I have seen him play as well but I do not remember him playing better all things considered. And he was barely turned twenty at the time. He went right to town and Wee Danny wound up chucking it on the colors, and you never saw that very often.

Out came the jam jar and he says: Same again, son?

Double or clear if you like, says Young Cecil.

Well Wee Danny never had the full tenner in his jar so he gives us the nod and in we dived to Old Porter for a couple of bob till broo day because to tell the truth we thought it was a bit of a flash in the pan. And even yet when I think about it, you cannot blame us. These young fellows come and go. Even now. They do not change. Still think they are wide. Soon as they can pot a ball they are ready to hand out JD himself three blacks of a start. Throw their money at you. Usually we were there to take it, and we never had to call on Wee Danny much either. So how were we supposed to know it was going to be any different this time?

Hector racked them. Young Cecil won the toss again. He broke and this time left the cue ball nudging the green's arse. Perfect. Then on it was a procession. And he was not just a potter like most of these young ones. Course at the time it was his main thing just like the rest but the real difference was that Young Cecil never missed the easy pot. Never. He could take a chance like anybody else. But you never saw him miss the easy pot.

One or two of us had thought it might not be a flash in the pan but had still fancied Wee Danny to do the business because whatever else he was he was a money player. Some fellows are world beaters till there is a bet bigger than the price of renting the table then that is them—all fingers and thumbs and miscueing all over the shop. I have seen it many a time. And after Young Cecil had messed his break in that first frame we had seen Wee Danny do the fifty-six so we knew he was on form. Also, the old heads reckoned on the young fellow cracking up with the tenner bet plus the fact that the rest of us were into it as well. Because Wee Danny could pot a ball with a headcase at his back all ready to set about his skull with a hatchet if he missed. Nothing could put the wee man off his game.

But he had met his match that day.

And he did not ask for another double or clear either. In fact a while after the event I heard he never even fancied himself for the second match—just felt he had to play it for some reason.

After that Young Cecil moved into Porter's, and ever since it has been home. Him and Wee Danny got on well enough but they were never close friends or anything like that. Outside they ran around in different crowds. There was an age gap between them right enough. That might have had something to do with it. And Cecil never went in for the bevy the way the wee man did. In some ways he was more into the game as well. He could work up an interest even when there was no money attached whereas Wee Danny was the other way.

Of course after Young Cecil met his he could hardly be bothered playing the game at all.

But that happened a while later—when we were having the long run in the "City." Cleaning up everywhere we were. And one or two of us were making a nice few bob on the side. Once Cecil arrived Wee Danny had moved down to Number 2 stick, and within a year or so people started hearing about Young Cecil. But even then Wee Danny was making a good few bob more than him because when he was skinned the wee man used to run about different pitches and sometimes one or two of us went along with him and picked up a couple of bob here and there. Aye, and a few times he landed us in bother because in some of these places it made no difference. Wee Danny was Wee Danny. In fact it usually made things worse once they found out. He was hell of a lucky not to get a right good hiding a couple of times. Him and Young Cecil never played each other again for serious money. Although sometimes they had an exhibition for maybe a nicker or so, to make it look good for the mugs. But they both knew who the 1 stick was and it never changed. That might have been another reason for them not being close friends or anything like that.

Around then Young Cecil started playing in a private club up the town where Wee Danny had played once or twice but not very often. This was McGinley's place. The big money used to change hands there. Frankie Sweeney was on his way up then and hung about the place with the Frenchman and one or two others. Young Cecil made his mark right away and a wee bit of a change came over him. But this was for the best as far as we were concerned because up till then he was just too quiet. Would not push himself or that. Then all of a sudden we did not have to tell him he was Young Cecil. He knew it himself. Not that he went about shouting it out because he never did that at any time. Not like some of them you see nicking about all gallus and sticking the chest out at you. Young Cecil was never like that and come to think about it neither was Wee Danny—though he always knew he was Wee Danny right enough. But now when Young Cecil talked to the one or two he did speak to, it was him did the talking and we did not have to tell him.

Then I mind fine we were all sitting around having a couple of pints in the Crown and there at the other end of the bar was our 1 and 2 sticks. Now they had often had a drink together in the past but normally it was always in among other company. Never like this—by themselves right through till closing time. Something happened. Whenever Young Cecil went up to McGinley's after that Wee Danny would be with him, as if he was partners or something. And they started winning a few quid. So did Sweeney and the Frenchman; they won a hell of a lot more. They were on to Young Cecil from the start.

Once or twice a couple of us got let into the club as well. McGinley's place was not like a hall. It was the basement of an office building up near George Square and it was a fair-sized pitch though there was only the one table. It was set aside in a room by itself with plenty of seats round about it, some of them built up so that everybody could see. The other room was a big one and had a wee bar and a place for snacks and that, with some card tables dotted about; and there was a big table for Chemmy. None of your Pontoons up there. I heard talk about a speaker wired up for commentaries and betting shows and that from the tracks, but I never saw it myself. Right enough I was never there during the day. The snooker room was kept shut all the time except if they were playing or somebody was in cleaning the place. They kept it well.

McGinley and them used to bring players through from Edinburgh and one or two up from England to play exhibitions and sometimes they would set up a big match and the money changing hands was something to see. Young Cecil told us there was a couple of Glasgow fellows down there hardly anybody had heard about who could really handle a stick. It was a right eye-opener for him because up till then he had only heard about people like Joe Hutchinson and Simpson and one or two others who went in for the "Scottish" regular, yet down in McGinley's there was two fellows playing who could hand out a start to the likes of Simpson. Any day of the week. It was just that about money players and the rest.

So Young Cecil became a McGinley man and it was not long before he joined Jimmy Brown and Sandy from Dumfries in taking on the big sticks through from Edinburgh and England and that. Then Sweeney and the Frenchman set up a big match with Cecil and Jimmy Brown. And Cecil beat him. Beat him well. A couple of us got let in that night and we picked up a nice wage because Jimmy Brown had been around for a good while and had a fair support. In a way it was the same story as Cecil and Wee Danny, only this time Wee Danny and the rest of Porter's squad had our money down the right way and we were carrying a fair wad for some of us who were not let in. There was a good crowd watching because word travels, but it was not too bad; McGinley was hell of a strict about letting people in—in case too many would put the players off in any way. With just on-lookers sitting on the seats and him and one or two others standing keeping an eye on things, it usually went well and you did not see much funny business though you heard stories about a couple of people who had tried it on at one time or another. But if you ask me, any man who tried to pull a stroke down McGinley's place was needing his head examined.

Well, Young Cecil wound up the man in Glasgow they all had to beat, and it was a major upset when anybody did. Sometimes when the likes of Hutchinson came through we saw a fair battle but when the big money was being laid it was never on him if he was meeting Young Cecil. Trouble was you could hardly get a bet on Cecil 'less he was handing out starts. And then it was never easy to find a punter, and even when you did find one there was liable to be upsets because of the handicapping.

But it was good at that time. Porter's was always buzzing 'cause Young Cecil still played 1 stick for us with Wee Danny backing him up at Number 2. It was rare walking into an away game knowing everybody was waiting for Young Cecil and Porter's to arrive and the bevy used to flow. They were good days and one or two of us could have afforded to let our broo money lie over a week if we had wanted though none of us ever did. Obviously. Down in McGinley's we were seeing some rare tussles; Young Cecil was not always involved but since he was Number 1 more often than not he was in there some-where at the windup.

It went well for a hell of a long while.

Then word went the rounds that McGinley and Sweeney were bringing up Cuddihy. He was known as the County Durham at that time. Well, nobody could wait for the day. It was not often you got the chance to see Cuddihy in action and when you did it was worth going a long way to see. He liked a punt and you want to see some of the bets he used to make at times—on individual shots and the rest of it. He might be about to attempt a long hard pot and then just before he lets fly he stands back from the table and cries: Okay. Who'll lay me six to four to a couple of quid?

And sometimes a mug would maybe lay him thirty quid to twenty. That is right, that was his style. A bit gallus but he was pure class. And he could take a drink. To be honest, even us in Porter's did not fancy Young Cecil for this one—and that includes Wee Danny. They said the County Durham was second only to the JD fellow though I never heard of them meeting seriously together. But I do not go along with them that said the JD fellow would have turned out second best if they had. But we will never know.

They were saying it would be the best game ever seen in Glasgow and that is something. All the daft rumors about it being staged at a football ground were going the rounds. That was nonsense. McGinley was a shrewdie and if he wanted he could have put it on at the Kelvin Hall or something, but the game took place in his club and as far as everybody was concerned that was the way it should be even though most of us from Porter's could not get in to see it at the death.

When the night finally arrived it was like an Old Firm game on New Year's Day. More people were in the card room than actually let in to see the game and in a way it was not right, for some of the ones left out were McGinley regulars and they had been turned away to let in people we had never clapped eyes on before. And some of us were not even let in to the place at all. Right enough a few of us had never been inside McGinley's before, just went to Porter's and thought that would do. So they could not grumble. But the one or two of us who would have been down McGinley's every night of the week if they had let us were classed as I do not know what and not let over the doorstep. That was definitely not fair. Even Wee Danny was lucky to get watching as he told us afterward. He was carrying our money. And there was some size of a wad there.

Everybody who ever set foot in Porter's was on to Young Cecil that night. And some from down our way who had never set foot in a snooker hall in their lives were on to him as well, and you cannot blame them. The pawnshops ran riot. Everything hockable was hocked. We all went daft. But there was no panic about not finding a punter because everybody knew that Cuddihy would back himself right down to his last penny. A hell of a man. Aye, and he was worth a good few quid too. Wee Danny told us that just before the marker tossed the coin Cuddihy stepped back and shouts: Anybody still wanting a bet now's the time!

And there were still takers at that minute.

All right. We all knew how good County Durham was; but it made no difference because everybody thought he had made a right bloomer. Like Young Cecil said to us when the news broke a week before the contest: Nobody, he says, can give me that sort of start. I mean it. Not even JD himself.

And we believed him. We agreed with him. It was impossible. No man alive could give Young Cecil thirty of a start in each of a five-frame match. It was nonsense. Wee Danny was the same.

Off of thirty I'd play him for everything I've got. I'd lay my weans on it. No danger, he says: Young Cecil'll sort him out proper. No danger!

And this was the way of it as far as the rest of us were concerned. Right enough on the day you got a few who bet the County Durham. Maybe they had seen him play and that, or heard about him and the rest of it. But reputations were made to be broke and apart from that few, Cuddihy, and his mates, everybody else was on to Young Cecil. And they thought they were stonewall certainties.

How wrong we all were.

But what can you say? Young Cecil played well. After the event he said he couldn't have played better. Just that the County Durham was in a different class. His exact words. What a turnup for the books. Cuddihy won the first two frames then Young Cecil got his chance in the next but Cuddihy came again and took the fourth for the best of five.

Easy. Easy easy.

What can you do? Wee Danny told us the Frenchman had called Cecil a good handicapper and nothing else.

Well, that was that and a hell of a lot of long faces were going about our side of the river—Porter's was like a cemetery for ages after it. Some of the old heads say it's been going downhill ever since. I do not know. Young Cecil was the best we ever had. Old Porter said there was none better in his day either. So, what do you do? Sweeney told Young Cecil it was no good comparing himself with the likes of Cuddihy but you could see it did not matter.

Young Cecil changed overnight. He got married just before the game anyway and so what with that and the rest of it he dropped out of things. He went on playing 1 stick for us for a while and still had the odd game down McGinley's once or twice. But slowly and surely he just stopped and then somebody spoke for him in Fairfield's and he wound up getting a start in there as a docker or something. But after he retired he started coming in again. Usually he plays billiards nowadays with the one or two of us that are still going about.

Mind you he is still awful good.

ONE POCKET

BY *Don Carpenter*

It's a pleasure to put yourself in the hands of a writer who knows what he's talking about—not always the case when pool is the subject. Don Carpenter (see also his story "The Crossroader" on page 155) devoted much of his youth to the game and played pool, three-cushion billiards, and snooker in many parts of the West and South. In the following piece, which is more memoir than fiction, he describes with an insider's voice what it's like to get hot in a "game for people better than kings."

"One Pocket" is part of a much longer work of the same name that appeared in The Class of '49 and Two Stories, *published in 1985 by North Point Press. My thanks to the author for permission to reprint only those sections relating to the game.*

Y O U C A N G E T H O T playing pool. Shooting over your head, shooting the eyes out of them balls. The other players will tell you that you aren't that good and you aren't, but the balls fall into the pockets anyway and the cue ball acts like you had it on a leash. This is the best of it. You don't have to work for anything, you don't even have to size up the next shot. You've put in your time and paid your dues and now here it is, mastery of the art. Nine in the side. *Thop.* Six cross-corner. *Thop.* Four off the twelve inna side. Click *thop.* Game! *Rack!* Next!

It can happen to anybody but it's best when you've worked for it and know what it is, not blind luck, but exactly what everybody in the pool halls say it is, especially when it's happening to somebody else:

Unconscious!

"He's un*con*scious!" is what they say. They roll their eyes, chalk their cues, rattle their change hopelessly, and sit down to wait, because they know they're not just playing the other player but also whatever force has taken over inside. I don't recall ever seeing two unconscious players head-to-head and I wonder if it ever happens. It would be something to see and something to talk about.

You can be cold, too. When nothing works, the balls swell up and roll funny, the pockets move slightly east or west, your crotch is hot and your feet are cold and the cue is bent, and the instant you shoot you know you've missed. Nothing drops but the cue ball. You might as well empty your pockets, you ain't going to win *nothing* today.

Buck fever.

Everybody has a theory, but nobody knows.

You'd think you would feel good, extraordinarily good, if you were shooting like a master and all your pool hall buddies were sitting around watching, even better in a strange place surrounded by strangers—you've come into this town like a shot of penicillin, ready to cure *everybody,* and here you are, the best, and totally unconscious. It should feel great. After all, when you're lousy and can't hit a bull in the ass with a bass fiddle, you feel *rotten;* why shouldn't you feel like a king when you shoot like one? I don't know. It's a mystery.

It seems strange to me that learning how to knock little mud balls into a pocket is less a mechanical process than a spiritual one, but there you are.

I want to tell about a time I got hot, and what it felt like.

It was in Mobile, Alabama, on my first visit. I was stationed for several months in Mobile, just before the end of the fighting in Korea. I was transferred from Keesler AFB in Biloxi, Mississippi (*B'luxi Mississippi*), only about sixty miles west and I was disappointed. I had hoped to be sent back to California, or short of that, anyplace out of the heat and that terrible southern humidity. The humidity was so bad down there on the Gulf Coast that nearly every day around eleven A.M. it would rise to one hundred percent and rain. This would cool things off for ten minutes or so, and then back to the smothering mirage. I hated it.

I got into a cab off Bienville Square, the driver a heavyset guy with a nice thick red cliché of a neck bulging up out of his Hawaiian shirt, and since it was only about two in the afternoon and I didn't want to end the trip before it started, I leaned back, lit a Pall Mall, and airily asked:

"Where's the best pool hall in town?"

I remember the way the guy turned around to look at me. I don't look like the kind of fellow who would want to know this information. He probably would have expected me to ask the location of the library, or the university extension center, or the local chapter of the Audubon society.

"Pool hall?"

"Yeah," I said.

"What's your game?"

So he was a player himself. *What's your game?* I suppose if I had said, "Oh, I just want to knock them around for a while, maybe play some Stars and Stripes, rotation, you know," he would have dropped me at the YMCA, overcharged me, and let it go at that.

It wasn't that I was intimidated by the driver. When I went into a strange town in those days I usually tried to find the best pool hall. That would be the place where I could sit down, relax, eat a decent hamburger, have a place to piss and make phone calls, without being thought of particularly as a stranger. There are no strangers in pool halls, only potential victims. And in most sensible towns, the local Brahmins won't hit on you unless they can see you play. If you take a table by yourself and shoot a few balls, you will slowly gather a certain amount of attention. And after a while, somebody will come over and watch you, and after a few minutes of this, you'll be hit on. (I hadn't yet been to New York City, where just walking into some of the joints around Forty-second Street they hit on you like moray eels even if you've just come in to make a phone call.)

"What's your best game?" That's how they usually put it, variations for localism to one side. What's your best game? Some of the funny ones, like my friend Dick the Motorman from Portland and San Francisco, would say, "What's your road game?"—not so subtly hinting that you are so good at your game you take it on the road, winning fame and fortune in all the little crossroads towns.

When the cabdriver asked me what my game was, I could have said I played a little nine ball, which would have tipped him off that I was at least that far in; I could have said, airily, "I play all games"; but sometimes somebody will ask you a question which takes you by surprise, and without thinking, you reply with a truth you didn't know was in you:

"One pocket," I said. I'm sure that until that moment and even beyond into the future, I didn't know that my game really was one pocket.

We must have been at a stop sign, because I can still remember the cabbie turning his head and looking back at me, his eyes and ears again suffering a mismatch of information. I *did not look* like a fellow who would even know that the game of one pocket existed.

"*One* pocket?"

"Why, do you play?"

"Yeah, I play pool, but I don't play no one pocket . . ."

His retreat popped me open like a cheap suitcase.

"Yeah, I play one pocket, straight pool, bank pool, cribbage, golf, nine ball, six ball, snooker, three rail . . ."

One thing to make clear right away: I didn't think that coming from a big city like Portland was going to give me any advantage over the local talent—the bragging just came out of my mouth like the rest of the air, spit, and effluvia, part of my normal respiration cycle. I was still a teenage punk when I learned the primal fact of pool— that every crossroads hamlet has its sharks and hustlers—Walnut Creek, California, Klamath Falls, Oregon—you name it, you can run into people who have never been past the city limits and don't know how good they are, old duffers who can run sixty pink balls in a row and think everybody can if they'd only try . . .

I didn't know what to expect in this Mobile, Alabama, pool hall except the hope that I would not be as bored and sick with anxiety here in Mobile as I had been in Biloxi, where they played only ro- tation and eight ball in the service clubs, and on the two beer-smelly tables in the little bar under the Erle Hotel the hustle was so obvious as to be practically audible, guys with cast-iron Hollywood haircuts and tailor-made Hawaiian shirts, guys who have chalked up so many times and washed up so seldom that they have a dark blue spray of tattoo between the fingers of their forward hand, guys who have memorized the lumps on the table and the nicks in the balls and who would follow you out into the steamy Gulf night and beat your skull in to take back the sixty cents you might have lucked into. I did not play pool in Biloxi.

ONE POCKET is the master's game. To win at one pocket you have to combine the talents of straight pool, snooker, and three-rail billiards. For long bleak stretches of time you must exercise your mean qualities, your parsimony, your niggling anal tightness; your touch has to be light, your emotions calm, your brain unsizzled by thoughts. You can't get in tune with the balls if your heart's exploding with hope of glamour, you can't make the cue ball execute if you're thinking about the row of onlookers, and there's no way to heaven through the countinghouse. You got to be impeccable, or the other fellow will go through you like a dose of salts.

Each player has a corner pocket, and to win, all you have to do is have eight of the fifteen balls fall into your pocket. That's it. The simplest rules for the best game. Naturally, that is not the essence of the game. The essence is *safety*. Ninety percent of your shots are not to sink a ball in your pocket, but to put the cue ball where your opponent won't have a shot. To snooker him. To make it tough on him, so that when he shoots, you will be left in the clear. Naturally, his hope and dream is the same. A one pocket game can go on for hours. You can go twenty minutes without shooting a gopher. You can get up to seven and scratch back down to two and still win the game. A run of three balls into your home pocket can arouse the crowd to moans and twitters, your opponent thumping his cue in unconscious praise; a safety so tight, so rotten, so calculated to mess up your opponent's life and scatter balls in front of your own home pocket can bring players over from other tables just to see the predicament and make side bets.

You could play one game all afternoon for two dollars and the sharpies make hundreds off you in side bets.

One pocket. The game for people better than kings.

I LOVED TO PLAY one pocket because I knew it was the best, knew it was the only pool game the billiard players respected. But I was never good at it. I was always too impatient. I had one pocket dreams but a rotation nervous system. I kept experimenting with dangerous gopher shots, long banks, intricate combination shots, hopeful massés, my chest full of impatience and awareness of life outside the game. A postal worker named Tommy in Portland used to give me eight to five, meaning I would only have to sink five balls in my home pocket to win, and he beat me consistently 8–2, 8–1, 8–4. These were lessons well paid for, even though I never had the fun of winning. Tommy was teaching me the stroke, the style of the game, the pulse, and collecting a five-dollar bill every twenty minutes or so.

So a one pocket player has to have nerves of kryptonite, be meaner than a wolverine, and play pool like a combination of Willie Mosconi and Uri Geller. I was an asshole to tell that long-ago Alabama cab-driver that one pocket was my game, my *road* game. He could have been taking me to a meeting with Alabama Shorty, the best one pocket player in the world, for all I knew. And then what a consummate idiot I'd be, forking and scratching all over the place in front of that gallery of refugees from Beat Four. If the sweat had not already been running freely it would have begun then, as I sat in the back of that taxicab rolling toward humiliation, exposure, defeat, and censure.

The pool hall was air-conditioned and immediately both the cab-driver and I popped out in quick-running cold sweat. If I had been thinking I would have been glad for the cold air, because it speeds up the action of the balls. A humid cloth slows them down, and so far my experience in the Deep South had been with mystically slow, nightmarish pool games, with grooves, bumps, and wobbles all part of the prognosis. Now I had stepped as if by magic from the blistering wetness of Mobile into a chilling dark room with here and there the foreshortened emerald light, the clicking, the low murmurous voices of the dark-clothed players of a major poolroom, a poolroom where *pool* was played, where beer bottles and cigarettes and sandwich halves were not left on the rail while Fatso draws a bead on the pay-ball, where people did not feel free to comment on your stroke as you were shooting.

Ah! There were rows of raised benches along the walls, and on the benches, the usual hangers-on, the salesmen, the hustlers, the unemployeds, and unemployables; I had never seen any of them before but I recognized them all.

The deep green felt on the tables was not ripped and sewn, not beer-stained or bloodstained—these tables were *wiped* and *brushed* between games, I could now through the dimness see the rackboy with his short leather apron, the pair of brushes tucked in like pistols, I could see the wall racks of cues, all straight as geometry, the electric cigar lighter on the counter, and the gray-faced clerk at the cash register in a quiet conversation with a fellow leaning on the pinball machine and fingering one of the punchboards. I could see a rack of packaged sandwiches and a jar of pickled eggs. Signs painted a thousand years ago reassured me: NO DRINKING ON THESE PREMISES! NO SWEARING! ABSOLUTELY NO GAMBLING! DO NOT WHISTLE! (The last one, of course, taken very seriously. There is nothing more infuriating than having some dork whistle while you are trying to Pay Attention.)

There was a battered, many-painted door with the word MEN in large white faded letters, but no other door marked WOMEN, and from behind the door marked MEN I could hear the nostalgic sound of some tubercular gentleman clearing his lungs in long drawn-out sobbing honks without any sadness to them—the same guy is hawking his life away in the toilet of every pool hall in America, but it is never sad.

There were windows facing the street but years of dust, dirt, and blue chalk turned black with age cut the blistering daylight to a sweet darkness, and the only illumination in the room came from the one gooseneck lamp over the cash register and the square etched-glass triple fixtures over the pool tables. If no one was playing, of course the table lights would be turned out, so that the place would reduce itself to the cone of light from that one gooseneck lamp over the cash register, but when the taxi driver and I came in, there were a few games in progress—look, a billiard table, with two old men in blue suits and gray hats, click, click, by God they were playing *balkline,* the playing surface crisscrossed with straight honorable blue chalk lines; look, snooker tables, pristine, the balls racked and ready, fifteen reds held in by the dark wood rack, six colored balls on top of the reds, with a couple of chalks and a cue ball, by golly, I moved over to the snooker table, the nearest table to the door, and picked up the cue ball, glowing, that translucent glow of the *Red Dash* cue ball. Red Dash! *Ichi Ban!*

This was a major pool hall.

(The kind of pool hall they don't have anymore in towns like Mobile. Instead they have Billiard Parlors where you can get a milk shake and shoot a game of eight ball with a college girl. There is a big window in front so the police can see that there is NO GAMBLING, NO SPITTING ON THE FLOOR, NO DRUGS THIS MEANS YOU, and the tables are every color but green.)

This was a pool hall, incidentally, where a good deal of one pocket was probably played. I found the Number One table. All major pool halls have a Number One table. It is for the Number One players. It is a pool table, the levelest, springiest, untrickiest table, with a cover of Number One or Number Two billiard cloth, which is as different from the average baize pool tabletop as silk is from polyester. A couple of men were playing a quiet game of straight pool on Number One, keeping score on the wooden buttons strung on wires above the table, and all the idlers were watching this game. Nobody was watching the two old men in blue suits with gray hats playing balkline billiards, and nobody was watching the young man with curly hair who was practicing bank shots all by himself on a pool table in the back of the room.

But everybody looked up when my cabdriver, who got out of the cab and opened the door for me, took his fare and a nice tip, and said, "Hell, I want to see this!" and held open the poolroom door for me as well, gave me a minute to orient myself to the darkness, the cold, the sweat popping out on my skin, and then said with a nice warmth and no hostility whatsoever to the room at large, "Here's a fellow wants to play some one pocket."

Every face turned to look at me.

EVEN AS A PUNK I knew the myth of Alabama Shorty. Alabama Shorty is the best one pocket player in the world. All the old men talked about him. Alabama Shorty is so good that nobody will play him, and he has to resort to tricks and disguises just to get up a game. Alabama Shorty is no hustler—a hustler is a guy who shoots badly to get you in deep and then works you over. Hustlers dupe innocent victims with guile and skill. Alabama Shorty, like all Zen masters, is forced into trickery, but he always plays his best and he never uses guile after the game has begun.

Seeing this gem of a pool hall in the middle of Deep Gulf Alabama, practically nestled under tall oaks trailing Spanish moss, and seeing the upturned faces of everybody in the joint made me think, but only for a flashing silly instant, that this was the home court of ALABAMA SHORTY, and that soon he would come out of the toilet, having for the moment stanched his mortality, like Doc Holliday, to pin me down 8–0. *Blamblamblam! Nobody makes a monkey out of Alabama Shorty! (Cough cough.)*

But no. The figure that drifted out of the toilet was just another old guy with red eyes and spittle on his cheek.

But by then I was chalking up.

The young man in the back of the room, the fellow with the curly hair, striped shirt with the sleeves rolled up, the tan pants, the loafer shoes with the heels walked down to a ragged edge, came up to me and asked in a polite Southern voice, "Would you-all like to play?"

"I don't know . . . maybe . . ."

"One pocket? Fifty cents?"

Well, Fifty *cents*. Five little beers. I could hardly refuse.

I went to the wall racks looking for a nice nineteen-ounce stick with an ivory ferrule. There were half a dozen of them, all straight as a chalk line with lovely cared-for leather button tips. I plucked one from the rack, spied down its straightness, and turned back to find that the Number One table had been evacuated by its players, and the rack man was racking the balls under the supervision of my opponent.

I felt a thrill. It is always thrilling to play on the best table.

A salesman came in the door with his sample case and burst into a torrent of sweat. The man back of the counter said in a low polite voice, "One pocket."

The salesman sat on one of the high seats, stowed his case under his legs, and took out a white handkerchief, slowly wiping his face and sneaking looks over at me.

Who was I? he was probably wondering.

I was very careful to chalk my cue by rubbing the chalk against the leather instead of rolling the stick like a goddamn college boy. In this room, playing this game, I wanted to at least appear to know what I was doing. I could feel no performance pressure, I was in no danger, there wasn't any North-South shit going on, it was simply that a stranger, carrying a sawed-off shotgun, had walked into the saloon and asked after Mr. Wyatt Earp. That was all.

We flipped for break; I lost and broke safe, a good safe break, with the cue ball coming back and almost freezing to the nether rail. Everyone in the room approved of the shot by their silent attention. Inside, I felt empty, the richness of being empty of emotion, ideas, everything. I was not savoring anything because there was nothing to savor. I was not afraid because there was nothing to fear. I was no longer tempted to show off because these people would understand. We in that room were in harmony.

IN ONE POCKET you tickle the balls, you don't slam them around. Indirection is the right direction. My opponent shot a good safe, knocking a ball to the rail after contact, as the rules demand in all pool games from straight pool up, and left the cue ball nestled among the others. A bad lay for me, an easy lay to fuck up. I went off the side rail and into the pack and into the end rail, the cue ball ending up on his side of the pack and against his rail. But one of the object balls dropped down off the pack toward the end rail, leaving him a gopher bank shot that was all the better for him because even if he didn't make it, he would probably leave me safe, and if he did make it, he'd be in a position to make another clean shot at his pocket.

He missed the bank shot by a hair and left me a gopher bank shot.

The cue ball was closer to the rail than the object ball, so that if I went for the bank shot my cue ball would move into the pack, breaking loose other balls on his side of the table. I walked around the table, squatted and squinted, chalked up again, moved back into position, and bent over. The cue felt good in my hand. I shot the bank with high English and good stroke, but not hard, and the object ball hit the rail and straightened out on the way back, as the cue ball elbowed gently through the lower end of the pack and got safely to my opponent's cushion without leaving him a shot. But it didn't matter because I had made the bank, already moving around the table sizing up the lay before the object ball had fallen into my pocket and gurgled down the undercarriage of the table and dropped into the wicker basket.

One egg in the nest.

Now, with a couple of balls loose from the pack I had my choice of a ball close to the end rail that I could go for and pull my cue ball back against his rail for safety, but if I shot the shot too hard my object ball might cross into his territory and the cue ball might move out toward the center of the table and leave him wide open.

Or, I had an object ball nearer the pack that I could cut in and loosen things up. But I wouldn't really know where anything would be after the shot—too many balls loose and running around. I went for the ball nearest the rail—the safer play—sunk it, drew back the cue ball so that I still had the other shot, but with a little better angle on it. I could shoot medium force and draw the cue ball a little and hope that a couple more balls would drop down off the now much looser pack, or I could follow high right English, good stroke, and come up in the middle of the table, with a probable three balls loose and easy.

That was what I did, and the object ball fell into my pocket, but the cue ball hit one of the others and instead of coming back out and giving me a shot, went around the pack and almost fell into his pocket. The pack was tight again, and the only two loose balls were on the other side of the pack, where I couldn't hit them.

Squat. Squint. Scrape scrape.

The pack was tight enough for me to fire the cue ball into it with holding English, driving an object ball into the end rail and back into the pack, leaving him with the problem of getting out of the safety without driving the balls over to my side of the table and eventually making things easier for me, but as I looked at the pack to see where best to hit it for this safety, I saw that if I hit one of the balls on this end sharply on the right-hand side, the force would drive through two other balls frozen together and into a third ball that would then, because of its frozen position, strike another ball and then drop into my pocket. This was an ideal frozen combination, if I had plotted the energy properly, and a stupid gopher shot that would scatter the pack carelessly if I hadn't.

I walked around the table, looking at the lay of the balls from every possible angle, not staring at the combination, just looking at it, while something inside me made up its mind.

It looked good. It looked very good, especially since I could put a little draw on the cue ball and expect it to come back to the rail up near his side pocket. The choice was between a shot that might have been circus antics and might also have been Grade-A pool, and an ordinary conservative down-the-middle safety.

I went for the combination, sighting carefully through my glasses, feeling right down to my fingertips that the shot would work.

I fired.

The object ball freed itself from the pack and drifted into my pocket. The cue ball drew back and came off the rail a few inches below the side pocket. I had one straight in, follow and come up on my own side rail. The ball fell, the position was right. I took off a ball frozen to my side rail and was in position for two more, draw back on the first and the second puts me in the middle of the table with choice of safety or a long green gopher. I gopher, the ball drops and rattles down the trough. I walk around and look into the basket.

Nine balls in the basket. I counted them again.

Six on the table, plus cue ball. I counted *them* again.

I had run out and one over.

I looked around. The faces were white blurs in the darkness. Nobody said anything.

I had run nine balls in one pocket.

I had won the game.

A silver half-dollar gleamed on the rail, where my opponent had left it, I don't know when.

"Rack," he said quietly. He looked at me. "You want to play another?"

"No," I said. I put my cue stick back in the wall rack. I said to the cabdriver, "Let's go."

As I was leaving the poolroom, the door held open for me by the stunned but polite cabdriver, the blast of hot outside air slapping my face, somebody should have called out:

"Say, Mister, just who *are* you?"

Then I could have turned, sweeping every gaze with my glance:

"Je suis Alabama Shorty!"

I NEVER WENT back. I never saw that poolroom again, never looked for it, never regretted it for a moment. You're only Alabama Shorty once, and maybe not that often.

1 9 8 6

....

MASSÉ

BY *Leigh Allison Wilson*

Finally, a woman's point of view, and an amusing and unusual woman at that. Leigh Allison Wilson was born and raised in the mountains of east Tennessee, has been mugged for fifty-two cents, had a cat that ate only best-selling books, and has several times lived near nuclear power plants on fault lines. About her pool game she writes: "I am not by any stretch of the imagination as good as the character in my story. I did win second place once in the women's division of a University of Iowa Tournament, but there were only two other entrants."

When I asked her permission to include "Massé" in this collection, she responded, "I've always wanted to be published in a book titled Great Pool Stories, *even* Mediocre Pool Stories.*"*

Ms. Wilson's first book, From the Bottom Up, *won the Flannery O'Connor Prize for Fiction in 1983. "Massé" was featured in* Harper's *in 1986. For the last ten years she has taught fiction writing at the State University of New York at Oswego.*

THE TRUTH IS it's not much of a city. When I moved in two years ago, all I knew about it was from a chamber of commerce brochure I got free at the courthouse. WELCOME, it said, TO THE BIG CITY IN THE LITTLE VALLEY BY THE LAKE. I had six suitcases in the back of my car and $350 and a good reason for leaving the place I'd left. For a woman like me, that's all people need to know. You start explaining things too much, you start giving heartfelt reasons for this and for that, and then nothing becomes clear and people don't trust you and you start looking at your life from bad angles. I like things clear. But the truth is it's not much of a city, not much of a valley, and you have to drive five miles to get to the lake. These are simple facts.

In the brochure they said the population was twenty thousand, but it is really closer to sixteen or seventeen. One problem is that most of the chamber of commerce live outside town, in big houses on the lake, and so maybe they don't come into the city much, to get the accurate head count. One thing I'm good at is counting. On Sunday nights at the local P & C, the average customer head count is twenty-six; on weekdays it is fifty-four after five o'clock. I can tell you the price of leaded gas at ten different stations, the price of unleaded at seven of them. Anytime you get good at something, it's because of a habit; counting things is just a habit with me. Last week I counted twelve geese heading for Canada in two perfect lines, a perfect V, and twelve is enough to prove that spring is coming. You can sometimes live a good life figuring angles and counting things, if you're in the habit of it.

What I've done for the last two years is, I drive a UPS truck during the day and I play pool at night. I have had some trouble lately, but not because of the UPS or the pool. You might think that these are things that women don't do—drive trucks for a living, that is, and play pool—but I do them, and so you probably just don't know enough women. Take into account enough numbers, anything is possible. Phineas says that the opposite is true, that given enough numbers nothing is possible, but he is a bartender who doesn't like crowds. Very little he says makes any sense. I've been seeing him off and on for the past six months, mostly off.

I met him, as I said, about six months ago, when all the trouble started. It was November, but a clear day, and the wind was gusting to forty miles per hour. I know because I listen to the radio in my truck. Every street I drove down that day had hats in the air, like a parade, from all the wind. This is what you could call an economically depressed town, which means that everybody in it is depressed about money, so I remember that November day's weather in particular. It was the only time I have ever seen anything like a celebration on the streets, all those hats in the air and everybody running after them, their faces as red and distorted as any winning crowd on television. I do not own a television, but all the bars have them. There are thirty-three bars in this city, and only nine have regulation pool tables. This is just a fact of life.

That day I was behind in my deliveries, although mostly I am punctual to a fault. I have a map of the city inlaid like a tattoo in my mind—where the easy right-hand turns are, where the short lights are, where the children play in the streets and thus become obstacles. I had to memorize the map in the chamber of commerce brochure to get the job, but anyone can tell you that maps like that are useless to a good driver. Maps are flat, cities are not. Obstacles are everywhere, but the good driver knows where they are and how to avoid them. Picture the city as a big pool table, right after the break in eight ball. Your opponent's balls surround you, like seven stop signs all over the table. You must deliver the goods in a timely fashion. Knowing the correct angles is everything. The simple truth is I know all the angles in this town. But that day I was behind in my deliveries and Danny, the dispatcher, kept coming over the radio, kidding around.

"You're late, you're late," he said. "Frankly, I'm appalled. Frankly, your ass is in a slingshot." He was in his silly-serious mood, jazzing around with the radio, bored to death with his job. He used to be a big shot on some high school football team in the city, but that was years ago, and although he is still a huge, bruised-looking man, the only big shots in his life now come from bars. He drinks too much is my meaning, but in a town like this that goes without saying.

"It's the wind," I told him, clicking the mike. "It's the wind and about fifty zillion hats. I'm not kidding, there's exactly a hundred fifty hats out here today."

"Ignore 'em," he said. "Run 'em down," he said. His voice came out high and crackly, as though any minute he might burst into weird, witchlike laughter. Radios do this to everybody's voice.

"What's the matter with you?" I asked, but I could tell that he'd already signed off, was already kidding around with another truck, his big body hunched over the radio back at the office, surrounded by boxes and handcarts and no windows anywhere. Danny's life is highly unclear. Once I tried to teach him pool, to show him a few straightforward things about the game. He handled the cue stick the way lips handle a toothpick, all muscle and no control, then he tried a crazy massé shot that was all wrong for the situation and ended up tearing the felt of the table. Finesse and control are the names of the game in pool, but he would have none of it. They kicked him out of the bar. I ran the table twelve straight games after he left and picked up about seventy dollars—a very good night for me.

I made my last delivery at about four o'clock, the wind buffeting the truck every yard of the way. Usually I am punctual, but the fact is the elements are an important factor in any driving job. That day the wind was a factor. For another thing, there is always the customer factor. If your customer is in a hurry, he just grabs a pen or pencil and lets it rip; you get an unclear address and end up wasting precious minutes. My advice is, always use a typewriter. That way there is nothing personal to get in the way of the timely execution of your business. Chaos is no man's friend, clarity is everything.

I parked the truck in the lot at four-thirty, tied up some loose ends inside the office, then went outside to my car. It is a '73 navy Impala with a lot of true grit. Most people picture a good car and they think of bright color or sleek line or some other spiffy feature. This is all wrong. The best part of a good car, what makes it a good car, is its guts: pistons that never miss a beat; a carburetor so finely tuned it is like a genius chemist, mixing air and gasoline as if from beakers; a transmission that works smoothly, the gears meshing like lovers. This Impala has guts; even Phineas says so. I drove home and on the way counted smokestacks, eight of them, all rising above town in the shape of cigars stuck on end. Then something strange happened.

I was driving past the pet shop where I buy fish, only six blocks from my apartment. Up ahead the street was empty as an old Western set except for a few newspapers, seized by the wind, that tented up in the air, then fell and lay flat on the pavement. Along the sidewalks on both sides telephone poles stretched way into a distance I couldn't quite see. Maybe being late that day had me all worked up. I don't know. But I began to imagine bank shots with my car. I began to figure out at exactly what angle I would have to hit a telephone pole in order to bank the car across the street and into the pole on the other side. Then I began to do it with buildings—double banks into doorways, caroms off two fireplugs and into a brick wall, a massé around a parked car and into the plate glass of the corner drugstore. By the time I parked at my apartment, the knuckles of my hands were pale on the wheel.

Overhead, slightly distorted by the windshield, I could see Mrs. McDaniels, my landlady, leaning over the second-floor railing of my apartment building, her eyes magnified by bifocals and staring straight down, it seemed, onto my knuckles. I put my hands in my lap and stared back at her. She is a businesslady, never misses a trick; she calls all of us tenants her "clientele," just as if she were the madam of a whorehouse. The apartment building looks like one of those ten-dollar-a-night motels—two stories with lines of doors opening onto a common walkway that has a wrought-iron railing down the length of it. But Mrs. McDaniels runs a tight ship, no monkey business.

"Have you tried goldfish?" she called down when I got out of the car. "My sister says she has goldfish you couldn't kill with a hammer."

"I think so, I don't know," I called back. My hands were shaking so much I had to put them in the trouser pockets of my uniform, fisting them up in there. When I got up to the second floor, I began it again, this time with Mrs. McDaniels—I figured I'd have to put a lot of left English on my body in order to graze Mrs. McDaniels and whisk her toward the right, into the doorway of my apartment. I brought out a fist with my keys in it.

"You're late," she said, her eyes large and shrewd as a bear's. "Are you drunk or what?"

I quit listing sideways, then jiggled the keys. "No," I told her. "Just a dizzy spell. It's from sitting down all day. All the blood goes to my butt or something."

"Goldfish," she said, sniffing the air around me until, apparently satisfied, she moved to the side so I could get to my door. "Well?" she asked, and she asked it again, "Well?" For a moment I thought Mrs. McDaniels wanted to shake my hand, then I noticed the Baggie of water between her fingers. In it two goldfish held themselves as rigid and motionless as dead things. And they might as well have been, because I knew right then that they were doomed.

"I don't know," I told her, opening the door with one arm so that she could go inside ahead of me. "I think I tried goldfish first thing."

Once inside the room Mrs. McDaniels began to war with herself. She prides herself on being someone who is easygoing and friendly with her tenants, but when she gets inside your apartment, she can't help herself. Those eyes behind the glasses glaze over with suspicion, search for holes in the plaster, gashes in the parquet. My apartment is one large room, with a kitchenette and a bathroom off it, a couch, a card table, three chairs, a bed, a dresser, and a fish tank. She went directly over to the couch, studying my new poster of Minnesota Fats.

"You're fixing the place up," she said suspiciously.

"I used the special glue, Mrs. McDaniels. It doesn't peel the paint."

"Oh!" she cried. "I don't mind at all, not at all. Not *me*." I could see that good humor and business were tearing Mrs. McDaniels apart, but finally business won out and she pulled a top corner of the poster away from the wall. It came away cleanly, just as the advertisement for the glue had predicted, though after that the corner bent over and didn't stay stuck anymore. "Silly me," she cried gaily. She was in high spirits now. "I really like that poster."

For a year and a half I had lived in the apartment without anything on the walls. Every time Mrs. McDaniels came inside, she'd say, "You live like a transient, just like a transient." And I always said, "I like things neat." And I did. But this Minnesota Fats poster caught my eye. In it Fats is crouched over the cue ball, looking into the side pocket, which is where the camera is. You don't see the side pocket, you just see Fats looking squint-eyed at you, looking at you as if he knew a pretty good trick or two. And he does. The poster cost me two-fifty but was worth every penny.

"I think I tried goldfish about a year ago," I told her. "They didn't last."

"You never know," she said. "I think these guys are winners." She held up the Baggie and studied the fish for flaws. I did not bother to look at them; I knew. They were already as good as dead.

When I first moved in, the fish tank was the only piece of furniture in the room, if you can call a fish tank furniture. The tenant before me had skipped out on his rent but had left the tank as a kind of palliative gesture. Inside there was even a fish, still alive, roaming from one end of the tank to the other. It was rat-colored, about three inches long, with yellow freckles all over its sides—an ugly, sour-looking fish. I called it The Rockfish. After a month or so, I got to thinking maybe it was lonely, maybe loneliness had made it go ugly and sour, and so I went down to the pet store for some companions to put into the tank. The guy there gave me two angelfish—two pert, brightly colored fish that he said got along famously with each other and with just about anybody else. I put them in with The Rockfish and waited for something to happen. The next day I thought to look in the tank, but there was no sign of the angelfish, not a trace, just

The Rockfish patrolling all the corners. After that I tried every kind of fish in the pet store—guppies, gobies, glassfish, neons, swordtails, even a catfish bigger than The Rockfish. They all just vanished, as if the tank had pockets. Mrs. McDaniels became obsessed when I told her about it. From then on nothing would do but that we find a fish good enough to go the distance in the tank. We didn't know whether The Rockfish was a male or a female or some sort of neuter, but we tried everything again: hes, shes, its, they all disappeared. Soon I wished I had never told Mrs. McDaniels anything about it, because I could tell she was beginning to associate me with the fish. She started dropping hints about what a man could do for a woman around the house, about how a woman like me could use a good man to straighten out her life. I just told her I already had all the angles figured, thank you, and that a good man wasn't hard to find if you were looking for one, which I wasn't.

"Listen," said Mrs. McDaniels, shaking the Baggie. "My sister says these guys don't know the meaning of death. They're right from her own tank. She should know."

"She should," I said, "but frankly, Mrs. McDaniels, I think they're dead meat."

"When are you settling down?" she asked absently. She was bent over the tank, flicking the glass in front of The Rockfish, her glasses pressed right up against it. I wondered then, because it seemed strange, whether Mrs. McDaniels's eyes, magnified by the glasses and the glass of the tank, whether her eyes might look huge as billiard balls to The Rockfish. No mistake, it had to be a strange sight from that angle. "Here's hoping," she said. Then she dumped the goldfish in. They floated for a few seconds, eye to eye with The Rockfish, but then they seemed to glance at each other and, before you could blink, the both of them shot down the length of the tank and huddled behind a piece of pink coral, sucking the glass in the corner for all they were worth.

"They know," I said. "One look and they knew."

"Look at the bright side," she said. "Nothing's happened yet."

"Not yet. But nothing ever happens when you're looking. It waits till you're at work or shopping or daydreaming or something—that's when it all happens."

"A big girl like you," she said, giving me the once-over. "Ought to be married is what you ought to be."

"Thanks for the fish, Mrs. McDaniels." I showed her to the door.

"Listen. Keep me posted. My sister says they're tough buggers, says they can eat nails."

"I'll keep you posted," I said, then I shut the door. For some reason, I began to snicker like crazy as soon as Mrs. McDaniels left. I went over to the tank, snickering, but The Rockfish only hung in the middle, sedate and ugly as sin. The two goldfish were still sucking away in the corner. I had to lie down on the bed to keep from snickering. For a few minutes I thought maybe I was having a heart attack. There were these pins and needles in my arms and legs, this pain in my chest, but then it all went away after a while. I lay like a stick on the bed, trying to get some sleep, counting my breaths to relax a little. Maybe being late had me worked up. Usually I got through work at two in the afternoon, home by two-thirty, but that day I was all off. I couldn't relax and I kept thinking about how I couldn't, which of course just made things worse and aggravated me and gave me the feeling I was in a fix for good. I got to thinking, then, that my life was going to take a turn for the bad, that somehow I would be off balance and out of step for the rest of whatever was coming. Across the room I could see the unclear, rat-colored shape of The Rockfish swimming the length of the tank, banking off the far walls, then swimming back again at the same latitude, back and forth, patrolling. And I wondered, to keep from snickering, to ward off the heart attack, I wondered if it knew I was watching. Did it know I kept count of things going on in the tank? Did it know I had all its angles figured, its habits memorized? Did it think I'd almost masséd my car around a fireplug and into a telephone pole? Did it think I was a friend?

I SLEPT LIKE A dead man, because I didn't wake up until around ten-thirty that night, my neck twisted at an odd, painful angle. The only light in the room came from the phosphorescent green glow of the fish tank. Mrs. McDaniels must have switched the tank light on earlier, because I almost never did. It gave me the creeps, as if the tank were the window onto some obscene green world where the tiniest ripple had profound ramifications, the kind of world you always suspect might happen to you suddenly, like Kingdom Come, if you lost all your habits. You lose your habits, and then you can kiss everything you've gotten good at good-bye.

I got out of bed, but things were still off somehow; the feeling of things gone wrong was like a fur on my tongue. Usually I got home at two-thirty, ate something, then slept until about ten o'clock, when business at the pool tables got going good. But that day I'd overslept and was late to begin with, and I knew as if I'd been through it before—which I hadn't—that trouble was just beginning. All I did was grab my keys and I was out of the apartment, almost sprinting to my car. Outside the wind grabbed hold, but I tucked my chin against it until I was inside the car, gripping the wheel and breathing hard. I figured by hurrying I could get a jump on whatever might come next, though when trouble comes, mistake number one is hurrying. I knew that, but I hurried just the same.

On the way to the bar I kept my mind on driving, no funny business. There are nine bars in this town with regulation pool tables, and I always go to a different one each night, until I have to start over again. That night I was due for a bar called The Office, which is a nice enough place if you can stand seeing typewriters and other office equipment hanging on the walls. Oddly enough, it is a favorite hangout for secretaries during cocktail hours. They seem to like the idea of getting drunk surrounded by the paraphernalia of their daily lives. At night, though, the clientele switches over to factory workers and middle-level management types—supervisors, foremen—and you can pick up a nice piece of change. All the way to The Office I kept myself rigid as a fence post. Only one thing happened. I was passing the button factory, a big yellow building with two smokestacks that went at it all the time, burning bad buttons maybe. It struck me, as I passed, that those smokestacks looked a lot like pool cues aimed right for the sky—that's all I thought, which was strange, but nothing to knock you off balance. Nothing like banking your car off buildings. I'd even begun to think I could relax a little by the time I got to the bar.

Because The Office is situated among gas stations and retail stores, it gave off the only light on the block except for occasional street lamps. The plate glass in front glowed yellow like a small sunset surrounded by nothing at all and out in the middle of nowhere, the kind of sunset people plan dream vacations around, and a sure recipe for disappointment. For a moment I thought better of the whole thing, almost turned around and went home, but the fact of the matter was, I knew that if I did all was lost, because once you gave in you kept on giving in. A habit is as easily lost and forgotten as hope for a better shake in things. So I went on into the bar.

As soon as I got inside I thought it would be all right. The two tables were busy, mostly guys in blue work shirts rolled up to the elbows, holding the cues like shotguns. It was promising because anyone in town recognized the blue work shirts. They came from the nuclear power plant up on the lake, the one that might or might not ever get built, which meant they had money and didn't much mind throwing it away on a fifty-fifty possibility. I had played a foreman from the power plant once, a year before, and during the course of the game he explained that even though the job was dangerous half the time, the money they got was the real health hazard. "More of our men die from drunk driving," he said, "than from touching the wrong wire," and he said it in a proud, fisty sort of way. He was an electrical engineer from east Tennessee, where he said anything that happened had to happen big or else nobody noticed it from one valley to the next. I took him for twenty dollars, then he got unfriendly. But that's the way with those guys: They see a woman playing pool and they automatically assume a fifty-fifty chance, usually more. Then they get unfriendly when they see you've got a good habit. They just don't know enough women. Numbers count.

In The Office, to get to the pool tables you have to finesse your way through about twenty tables full of people who have had too much to drink. Cigarettes, flitting through the air on the tail end of a good story, are obstacles, and so are wayward elbows and legs. One sure sign that you're drunk is if you're in somebody's way. But I got through that part. I made a beeline for Bernie, who was chalking his cue at the second table, the good table, the one with a roll you could figure.

"You are tardy," he said in his formal way, still chalking his cue. Sometime during his life, Bernie was a schoolteacher: astronomy. On certain nights he'd take you outside and point out the constellations, his old nicotine-stained fingers pointing toward the stars. He knew his stuff. And he knew pool, too, except for a tendency to grow passionate at the least provocation, a tendency that combined with old age and Jack Daniel's was ruining his game. Given a population of sixteen or seventeen thousand, Bernie was the only rival I had in town. But we never played together, sometimes never saw each other for weeks; we just appreciated the habits we'd both gotten into.

"You are tardy," he repeated, giving me a dark look. "And the stars are out tonight." He meant that people were spending money like nobody's business.

"I think it's the wind," I told him. "I think there's something funny in the wind."

"Ha!" Bernie cried. He put down the chalk and picked up his cigarette, puffing on it. Then, in a cloud of smoke, he wheeled around to the table, brought up his cue, and nailed the eight ball on a bank into the side pocket, easy as you please. It threw his opponent all off. His opponent had on a blue work shirt that was either too small for him on purpose or else was the biggest size they had: His muscles showed through the material as though he were wearing no shirt at all. On the table only one ball was left, sitting right in front of a corner pocket, and by the look on the guy's face you could tell he'd figured he had the old man on the run, the game sewn up. What he didn't know was that Bernie's opponents in eight ball always had only one ball left on the table. But the guy was a good sport and paid his ten dollars without muscling around or banging his cue on the floor. Sometimes with your big guys chaos is their only response to losing. It is just a fact of life.

"That is that," Bernie said, putting the ten in his wallet. "The table is all yours."

"Where you going?" Bernie always stayed at the tables until about midnight, and if he was around, I just watched and took pointers, waiting for him to get tired and go home before I got busy. Usually I took over where he left off. "It's only eleven," I said, "and you say the stars are out."

"I have a granddaughter coming in on the midnight train." He made a face that meant he was tickled pink, the corners of his mouth stretched and stained with a half million cigarettes. "All pink and yellow, like a little doll. She can point out Venus on the horizon with her eyes shut. A beautiful girl. You should meet her."

"Maybe I will."

"Seven years old and she knows the difference between Arcturus and Taurus. For Christmas last year, do you know what she told her mother she wanted? Guess what she wanted."

"A pool cue," I said, which was exactly what I would have asked for.

"No, you are insane. A telescope! She said she wanted to get close to the sky, close enough to touch it. She's no bigger than a flea and she asks for a telescope!" Bernie slapped his palms together, then sidled closer. "Between us, she is a genius, has to be. My granddaughter, a genius."

"You must be proud of her," I said. All of a sudden I wanted Bernie out of the bar. His very breath smelled like trouble. Then I noticed his shot glass of Jack Daniel's was missing from the stool he usually kept it on; he was sober as a judge. I wanted Bernie gone.

"Oh, she is going places, I can feel it. I can *feel* it!" He slapped his palms together again, bouncing on his feet a little, then he swung toward the men in the work shirts and opened his arms enough to include me in the sweep of them. "Gentlemen, I leave you with this young lady as my proxy. Do not be fooled by her gender." He looked at me appraisingly. "Do not be fooled by the uniform. She can handle herself."

"Thanks, Bernie," I said, but I didn't look at him then, and I didn't look at him when he left. Instead I looked at all the guys in blue work shirts. At first they each one had an expression of irritation and rebellion: they didn't like the idea of me usurping command of the table just because the winner knew me. And I didn't blame them, except that the next expression on each of their faces was a familiar one.

"All right, George, you're up," one of them said. "Take her and then let's us get serious," he said, which was exactly what I had expected from their expressions. I could read these guys like a brochure. Any other night I would have grinned and aw-shucked around, leading them on a little bit. I might have even offered to wait my turn, humbling myself to the point of idiocy, until they said, "No, you go on, honey," gallantry making idiots of them, too. That night, though, something was wrong with me. For one thing, the whole day had been all wrong. For another, seeing Bernie sober and giddy as a billy goat really threw me. I hadn't known he had a granddaughter or a daughter or even a wife. I'd never seen him sober. Something about it all set me going again. I imagined flinging myself headlong into the knot of blue work shirts, sending them all flying to the far corners of The Office, like a good break.

"OK, little lady," said the one named George, winking and grinning to his friends. "Let's see how you deliver." He could not contain himself. "Did you hear that? Did you hear what I just said? I said, I asked her, 'Let's see how you deliver.'"

They all snorted, stamping their cues on the end of their boots, and I regretted not changing out of my uniform. It was a bad sign because I'd never worn it to the bars before, just one result of hurrying trouble. You never knew when somebody might take a wild hair and try to mess up your job, somebody with a poor attitude toward losing and a bad disposition and a need for spreading chaos. I felt dizzy for a minute, as though I'd been submerged in water and couldn't make the transition.

"Winners break," George said. Now he was all business, ready to get the game over with so he could play with his friends. He strutted around, flexing his work shirt. Most nights, when I had the break, I would try to sink a couple, then leave the cue ball in a safe position, ducking my chin and smirking shamefacedly, as though I'd miscalculated. The point is, never let the guys waiting in line see that your game in no way depends on luck; it scares them if you do, shrinks their pockets like a cold shower, so to speak. But that night I was crazy, must have been. George went into an elaborate explanation of how he had to go to the bathroom but would be back before his turn, how I'd never even know he was gone. I said, "Five bucks." He rolled his eyes comically, performing for his friends, then said it was all right by him. "You're the boss, Chuck," he said. I don't know what got into me. Before George was out of sight, I broke and sank two stripes. Then I hammered in the rest of them, taking maybe three seconds between each shot. By the time old George could zip up his pants, I'd cleared the table.

"Fucking-A," said one of George's friends.

"Whoa," another one said. "Holy whoa."

It was a dream, that whole game was a dream. I had read somewhere that a sure sign of madness was when life took on a dreamlike quality, when you started manipulating what you saw as easily as you manipulate dreams. Those pins and needles came back into my feet, prickly as icicles. George came back, too. I figured the night was over. They would all get pissed off and quit playing and begin to attend to their beers. But—surprise—they ate it up, practically started a brawl over who was up next. It wasn't anything you could have predicted. I guess it pumped them up with adrenaline, or else with a kind of competitive meanness, because for the rest of the night they banged the balls with a vengeance. They were none too polite, and that's a fact. Whatever happened during those games happened in a dream. A wad of five-dollar bills began to show through the back pocket of my uniform trousers. The guys in blue work shirts were like a buzzing of hornets around me, their faces getting drunker and redder every hour.

Near closing time, around two in the morning, George came back for a last game. I'd been watching him play on the other table, and even with the handicap of a dozen beers he could run five or six balls at a time, which is not embarrassing for bar pool. But there was real hatred on George's face, sitting there like a signpost. All those beers had loosened his features until his eyebrows met in a single, straight-edged line, the kind of eyebrows the Devil would have if he had eyebrows. Some men just can't get drunk without getting evil, too. I suggested we call it a day, but George would have none of it. He swaggered around, foulmouthed, until I said all right just to shut him up.

"Fucking dyke," he said, loud enough for me to hear. I kept racking the balls. He was the one who was supposed to rack them, but now I didn't trust him to rack them tightly.

"I said," he said, a little louder, "fucking *dyke* in a uniform." He was drunk—and I should have known better—though, as I've said, that day was the beginning of trouble. One rule of pool is never get emotional. You get emotional and first thing you know, your angles are off, your game is a highly unclear business.

"Asshole," I told him. "Fucking *asshole* in a uniform." My hands shook so much I gripped my cue as if it were George's neck. I am not a grisly or violent person, but there you go.

"Just play, for God's sake," said one of his friends. They were all grouped around the table, their faces as alike and featureless as the balls in front of them. I imagined that their eyes were the tips of cues, blue, sharp, nothing you wanted pointed in your direction.

"Radiation mutant," I said. "Rockfish." Then I broke. Sure enough, emotion had its effect. None of the balls fell.

"Fifty bucks, you pervert," George said, rippling those eyebrows at me. "No, make it a hundred." All that beer was working up some weird, purplish coloration into his cheeks.

They say that during important moments time goes by more slowly, elongates somehow just when you need it most. It is a false-hood. Time goes slowly when you're utterly miserable, or when you might be about to die, and both are situations any sane person would want to go by quickly. When you really need it, time isn't there for you. I wanted to study the table for a while, get myself under control and ready. I wanted to go outside and have somebody point out the constellations, show me the difference between Taurus and Arcturus. I wanted somebody to give me a fish that didn't die in the tank. I wanted somebody, anybody, to tell me that I was living a good life, that my habits were excellent, that I was going places.

"This is all she wrote, Chuck," George said, leaning over the table like a surgeon. It looked grim, not because the spread was all in George's favor—which was true—but because I had gotten emotional. Nothing was clear anymore, not the angles, not the spin, nothing. My cue stick might just as well have been a smokestack.

"Shit!" George cried, and he slammed a beefy hand against his beefy thigh.

He'd run the table except for the eight ball, leaving me with some tricky shots—stop signs all over the table. By now everyone in The Office stood around the table, watching, belching, not saying a word. I thought about what Minnesota Fats would do, how Fats would handle the situation, but all I saw was that corner of the poster, unstuck and curled ominously over Fats's head. I wondered what would happen if I picked up each of my balls and placed them gently in the pockets, like eggs into Easter baskets. Crazy, I must have been crazy.

The first couple of shots were easy, then it got harder. I banked one ball the length of the table, a miraculous shot, though it left the cue ball in an iffy position. I made the next one anyway. After each shot I had to heft the stick in my hand, get the feel of it all over again, as if I were in George's league, an amateur on a hot streak. Finally the game came down to one shot. I had one ball left, tucked about an inch and a half up the rail from the corner pocket, an easy kiss except that the eight ball rested directly in the line of the shot. There was no way I could bank the cue ball and make it.

"All she wrote," George said, "all she by God *wrote!*"

I hefted my cue stick for a massé, the only thing left to do.

"Oh, no," cried George. "No you don't. You might get away with that shit in lesbo pool, but not here. You're not doing it here. No, sir. No way."

"Who says?" I asked him, standing up from the table. I was sweating a lot, I could feel it on my ribs. "Anything goes is my feeling."

"Bar rules." George appealed to his friends. "Right? No massé in bar rules. Right? Am I right?"

"Phineas!" somebody called. "Phineas! No massé on the tables, right?"

Phineas came out around the bar, rubbing his hands on an apron that covered him from the neck to the knees. He had short, black, curly hair and wore round wire-rimmed glasses, the kind of glasses that make people look liberal and intelligent somehow. He looked clean and trim in his white apron, surrounded by all those sweaty blue work shirts. For a minute he just stood there, rubbing his hands, sizing up the table.

"What's the stake?" he asked philosophically.

"Hundred," George said. He was practically screaming.

Phineas puckered his mouth.

"Well," he said, drawing the sound out. Maybe he was buying time. Maybe he was leading them on. Or maybe he was a bartender who didn't like crowds and didn't like crowds asking for his opinion—which is exactly what he is. "Anything goes," he said. "Anything goes for a hundred bucks is my opinion."

"I'll remember this," George said, snarling, his purple face shaded to green. "You prick, I'll remember this."

"Fine," said Phineas, almost jovially. He folded his arms across that white apron and looked at me. He might have winked, but more likely he was just squinting, sizing me up.

"Massé on the ten into the corner," I said stiffly, formally, the way Bernie would have done. Anybody will tell you, a massé is ridiculous. You have no real cue ball control, no real control period. You have to bring your stick into an almost vertical position, then come down solidly on one side of the cue ball, which then—if you do it right—arcs around the obstacle ball and heads for the place you have in mind. It is an emotional shot, no control, mostly luck. And anytime you get yourself into the position of taking an emotional shot, all is pretty much lost. I hefted the cue stick again, hiked it up like an Apache spearing fish. Then I let it rip. The cue ball arced beautifully, went around the eight ball with a lot of backspin, then did just what it was supposed to do—kissed the ten on the rail. The trouble was, it didn't kiss the ten hard enough. The ball whimpered along the rail about an inch, then stopped short of the pocket. A breath would have knocked it in, but apparently nobody was breathing.

"That's all she wrote," I told Phineas. He just smiled, looking liberal and intelligent behind his glasses.

THE UPSHOT WAS, George won the game. I'd left the cue ball in a perfect position for making the eight in the side pocket. Any idiot could have made that shot, and George was no idiot, just a drunken jerk. He even got friendly when I paid him his money, wanted to take me home, his breath hot and sour as old beer. But then Phineas stepped in, cool as you please, and said that *he* was going home with me. Between the two there was no choice: I told Phineas to meet me out front at my car. "A '73 navy Impala," I told him. It was not that unusual, even though the day had me off balance. I'd had a couple of guys over to my apartment before, after the bars closed, the kind of thing where in the morning you find yourself clenching the pillows, hoping they don't use your toothbrush or something. Even if I did see those guys again, their faces would mean no more to me than the faces of former opponents in a pool game.

The wind had died, nothing moved when I went out to the car. On the way to my apartment Phineas told me about how he hated crowds, how there was nothing possible with those kinds of numbers. I told him numbers counted, but he didn't argue the point. Then he told me how nice my car was. "True grit," I said. "Nothing spiffy, just good guts." He put his hand on my thigh. We rode like that for a long time. When we passed the button factory, I told him about the smokestacks looking like pool cues. Then, for some reason, I told him about driving my car into telephone poles, banking it off buildings.

"You shouldn't get all out of control over a game," he said. After that I didn't tell him anything else, pretended I was concentrating on his hand against my thigh.

Inside my apartment I didn't turn on the lights. The green glow of the fish tank let me see all I wanted to see, maybe more. Phineas, of course, went right for the tank, which was what everybody did when they came into my apartment.

"How come you only have two fish?" he wanted to know.

"That one there, with the yellow freckles. It kills everything I put in there. Wait and see. In the morning that other one won't be there. It's a shark," I said.

"No kidding," he said, peering in at The Rockfish. "Really? A shark?"

"No. It's just an it. A killer it."

Phineas straightened up. "What's your name?"

"Janice," I said.

"At least in this town it's Janice," I said, revealing myself a little, although I wasn't about to go into heartfelt reasons for this and that. It didn't matter because then he kissed me, hard, standing there in front of the fish tank. In a minute or so, he broke away.

"You can play your ass off in pool, Janice," he said. He began to unbutton his shirt. It was flannel, which matched his glasses somehow; the apron he'd left back at the bar. I took off the trousers of my uniform, then he kissed me again, his hands down low.

"You look real nice," he said. "Out of uniform, as it were." He laughed, and I laughed, too, in a strange kind of way.

After that I was on the couch with him on top of me. He got busy. I put my hands on his back, but he did all the work. The whole time I was thinking, my head to one side, staring into the fish tank. I was thinking that maybe I would leave town. Maybe I would pack up my car and move and get around my trouble that way. I could leave the fish tank, skip out on the rent, just like the guy before me had done. Let The Rockfish chew its own gristle, I thought, let Mrs. McDaniels drop hints to somebody else. The Rockfish was patrolling the tank, whipping beside the lone goldfish like terror on the move, and the goldfish sucked madly on the glass in the corner, behind the pink coral, wriggling whenever The Rockfish swept by. It struck me as the saddest thing I'd ever seen. Then I began it again, with Phineas this time. I imagined he was performing a massé on me, several massés, coming down hard on one side and then the other, one emotional shot after another, only I wasn't going anywhere. I must have snorted, because Phineas worked harder all of a sudden.

"Feel it?" he said, or asked, whispering, and I could tell that he'd come to a crucial moment. "Can you feel it?" And I said, "Yes," I said, "Yes, yes, I can feel it," but I couldn't. I shifted slightly to make things easier, but I couldn't feel a thing, not a thing—nothing.

1 9 8 6

···

MOTHER AND FATHER

BY *Jonathan Baumbach*

Never are the billiard gods crueler—or funnier—than when they allow students to beat teachers, which is what happens in this story, one of my favorites. For another delicious example of pomposity punctured, see the 1914 story by A. A. Milne on page 46. "Mother and Father" was first published in the Iowa Review *and reprinted in the 1987 anthology* The Life and Times of Major Fiction.

Jonathan Baumbach received a Ph.D. from Stanford in 1961 and later founded an organization of writers called The Fiction Collective. His tenth book, the novel Seven Wives, *was published in 1994. His short stories have appeared in* Esquire, Partisan Review, O'Henry Prize Stories, *and* Best American Short Stories.

Baumbach lives in Brooklyn and has a pool table in his basement.

T HE GAME IS POOL, sometimes called eight ball. My father and mother play the game each night before going to bed. I am there as observer, too young to account my age. My father likes to break and my mother, who is new to pool, tends to give the old man his head. It is her habit to admire his every gesture, his hesitations, false starts, benign mischances. Sometimes when he chalks his cue in his unassuming way, she can't help but emit a crow of pleasure at the secret grace of the gesture. Her praise makes him irritable, tends to

255

throw him off his game. "I don't know what's wrong with me," he says when he scratches on the break. "What a stupid thing to do."

My mother allows that there must have been a distracting noise from outside and offers him the occasion to replay the opening hit.

"You usually break so beautifully," she adds. "I can spend whole days just watching you make the break."

"Well, you won't have another chance of watching it today," my father says. "I take full responsibility for my misplays. My failure is already part of the recorded past."

"I don't blame you for saying that," my mother says. "By the way, have you seen my stick? I like, as you know, the little one."

My father hands her his cue, which she accepts for an unhappy moment, then returns. "This is nicer, but I really prefer the one I'm used to."

She goes to the back wall and checks out the four remaining cues, discarding each in turn. "One of them must be yours," my father says, chewing on his impatience. "That's all we have."

Unconvinced, my mother selects the second smallest of the four remaining ones, which is visibly warped and has a worn tip.

"That one's no good," my father says, trying to take it from her. Their struggle produces inertia.

"You never let me use the one I want," my mother says. My father reads the cracks in the ceiling as antidote to that remark.

It is my mother's practice to address the first ball she fixes on and then decide in the ensuing moment that it is not for her. At that point she will ask my father if there is a better shot available, something more in keeping with her limited skill.

Putting symbol ahead of fact, my father denies that there is a shot on the table easier than the one my mother has fixed on. That said, the issue cleared, he manages with undisguised irritation to find her something better.

"I don't know," my mother says, moving between her alternatives, squinting over each as if to estimate its degree of difficulty. "They both look equally hard."

"The one I chose is easier," he insists.

"If you say so," says his skeptical opponent, rushing her shot. She mishits the cue ball, sending it in an alternate direction, accidentally nipping the five ball into a side pocket. Elation comes and goes.

"Was that the ball you were shooting?" my father asks.

The question flusters her temporarily. "I don't remember," she says. "Was that the one you recommended?"

My father chalks his cue to occupy an angry heart. "You can have the ball," he says. "All acts include their intentions."

My mother does not want any favors, reclaims the five from the ball drop, and with the best will in the world is unable to find a place on the table to give it rest.

"I want you to have it," my father says.

"You're too good to me," my mother replies, stuffing the ball in her apron pocket. With a flourish of determination, she drops the two in a side pocket and leaves herself in the worst possible position for a following shot.

"What do I do now, Max?" she asks.

The question does not elicit an answer, perhaps does not expect one. My mother studies the table as if the geometric language of the balls were an indecipherable code. If she doesn't take her shot in the next moment, my father will break down and tell her all.

My mother chooses the most impossible shot of several improbable alternatives, reordering the table, and leaving my father without a shot to call his own.

His chronic irritation rises to the occasion. After circling the table a few times, he narrowly misses a bank shot on the ten the laws of physics had denied him in advance.

My mother claps her hands politely, fingers to palm. "That was almost wonderful," she says.

"It's the story of my life," says my father.

As the game goes on, attrition works its will. Father moves ahead three balls to two, his first advantage of the match. My mother rises to the occasion at her next turn when, her intent elsewhere, she drops two of the solid balls with a single shot.

"I told you I was better off shooting my way," she says.

My mother's way, let it be said, is notable for having the cue move tremulously from side to side as it approaches the cue ball, coming at it from all sides. My father has advised her to tighten the groove between her fingers, but my mother's success, accidental or not, is dependent on her own method.

My mother mishits the one ball into a corner pocket and assumes a five to three advantage.

My father chalks his cue to excess while my mother calculates her next play. As the game progresses, her pace becomes correspondingly deliberate. My father, a man of no patience in the best of seasons, appears on the verge of urging her to get whatever it is over and done.

"I have such trouble choosing my shots," she says in anticipation of his complaint. "Won't you help me just a little bit, Max."

"You're killing me, Helen," he says. "Why should I be complicit in my own defeat." He informs her that the four ball might be gently kissed into a corner pocket.

"The four?" My mother charts the distance with a glance. The ball idles in the foyer of a corner pocket at the far end of the table. "Max, you could make that shot, but I couldn't. Is there anything closer?"

My father says nothing to this, apparently aware that her complaint is obligatory, and hums an idle tune to himself to pass the time.

Sighing at his generosity, she lines up the shot with her character-istic astigmatic perception. (The wobble of her stick, like the blowing of a wind, tends to compensate for the inaccuracy of her aim.)

The cue ball, at my mother's touch, skips across the green in the general direction of its intent, kissing the four ball in such a way as to deny it sanctuary, the white ball visiting the pocket in its place.

"That's what you call a scratch, isn't it?" she asks. My father makes an affirmative noise in his throat. "I knew all along the shot was too long for me."

"You were proven right," my father says.

My mother has difficulty deciding what ball of hers to return, her fondness for them equal and indiscriminate. "Is the one all right," she asks, "or must it be the last one I made?"

"Any one," says the authority.

While my mother procrastinates, my father charts the sequence of his remaining three shots, chalking his cue idly.

My mother returns the five, offering an elaborate rationalization for a decision that might have gone several different ways.

Concentrating on getting suitable position for the second of his three shots, or perhaps deflected by the pressures of irritation, my father misses a routine play on the fourteen, which had been lolling just to the right of a side pocket.

My mother is outraged at fate on my father's behalf. "You de-served to make it," she says. "If there was any justice, the ball would have fallen for you."

"Justice wasn't wanting," says her adversary. "Merely skill."

"Well, I thought it was a difficult shot," says my mother, "and that you did beautifully with it." That issue out of the way, she proceeds (who can say how?) to run her next two balls and barely miss a third, leaving her with one solid (the resurrected five) and the eight ball to carry off victory.

Up until this point, my father has not taken her quite seriously as an adversary. It has begun to dawn on him that there is more art in Mother's game than accident, or that she is a mistress of benign fortune. He adjusts himself in imperceptible ways to whatever knowledge he is willing to own. Losing is too important to him to accept without a struggle.

Father is responsible for the stripes, the balls from nine through fifteen, the higher denominations, while my mother's province is the solids (balls one through seven). The eight ball, which gives the contest its name, is the final reckoning.

My father has a reasonable shot at the nine ball, which resides on the rail some six inches from a corner pocket. To make the shot he must hit ball and cushion simultaneously. Though margin for error is small, the shot is unambiguous. My mother leans over his shoulder as he calculates his play, a student of father's expertise.

"I can't shoot when you sit on my shoulder," he reminds her.

"Try," she says, teasing. "I bet you can do it if you try." My father makes the shot without looking back, then makes another. Anger inspires him.

My mother oohs and ahhs, creating a din of admiration. "Some days you just don't seem to know how to miss," she says.

"It happens that you're winning this game," he says.

"That's because I don't play to win," says my mother. "Winning and losing are the same to me."

"That's a lot of shit if I may say so," says my father, rushing his shot, cue ball following the twelve into a corner pocket. He mutters a mild oath, waving an arm as if knocking flies away.

"You ought to be pleased that you made the ball in the first place, and not always focus on the bad side of things."

"I didn't put enough backspin on the cue ball," he says, returning the twelve to the designated spot. "It was a failure of concentration."

My mother misses her next four attempts at the five ball, misses them badly, insisting with each failure that she plays the game merely for the pleasure of it. My father, who plays without pleasure, manages to dispose of the two remaining stripes and has only the eight ball to put away to claim victory. The sudden collapse of my mother's small skill troubles him. He suspects her of intentionally letting him win and is disposed, before taking what could be his final shot, to inform her of his suspicion.

The charge doesn't surprise my mother and she denies it categorically without conviction.

My father misses a middling difficult bank shot on the eight.

My mother sinks her cue ball in the corner and is obliged to return another of her solids to the table.

"You didn't need to do that," my father says.

"I'm doing the best I can," my mother protests. "I told you I don't care about winning."

The eight ball, my father's final quarry, awaits him in front of the far right corner pocket. There is much green between cue ball and eight, but the shot is less troubling to him than what he takes to be his wife's patronizing play. He hangs up his cue and sits down on a high stool, his arms folded in front of him.

"Aren't you taking your turn?" my mother asks.

"I'm retiring from the fray," says my father. "If I wanted to play solitaire, I wouldn't have engaged an opponent."

"Anyway, you've won the game," she says, offering the hand of a graceful loser.

My father gets off the stool and retrieves his stick. "This is the last time I'm playing with you," he says, "the absolutely last time."

This news ruffles my mother's feathers, though not so my father would notice. She says it's all the same to her whether they play or not, the game childish in her view, puerile, callow, infantile, a primitive pastime.

My father scratches on the eight ball, losing the game.

My mother refuses to claim victory, insists that my father really won, offering him the temptation of a replay. He almost accedes to her offer, rejecting it with visible pain.

When my mother walks off with her unclaimed victory—"You lost, I didn't win," she insists—my father racks the balls for another round.

I watch him from a high stool in the back of the room, his only spectator.

He walks around the table once before chalking his cue, businesslike in his aspect, characteristically harried. Father always looks as if he's trying to remember something he's supposed to do and for-gotten.

The white ball explodes off his cue, bears down on the triangulated pack with uncompromising violence, dispersing the balls every which way, banging them about from end to side, three perhaps four balls escaping the table into waiting pockets. In five succeeding turns, six more balls retire from the table, my father announcing their desti-nation before each shot.

Finally, a ball refuses to do as it's told, and my father, who had been moving about the table in a hurry, disappears into the bathroom for some private reckoning. I grow to doubt his return.

He misses twice again before he cleans the table, sinking his final ball by banging it into a corner pocket with self-conscious flourish.

He hangs up his cue, puts out the lamp over the arena, takes one last look over his shoulder, and leaves, some misplaced notes from a song on his tongue.

I remain behind on the higher of the high stools, deserted and forgotten, too small to climb down without aid, a first and final witness.

···

LONG GREEN

BY *Miles Wilson*

*Having trouble with your game lately? Could it have something
to do with getting laid off at work? If so, you'll sympathize with
the player in this vignette.*

*"Long Green," which I wish were longer, was part of a collection
of Miles Wilson's stories titled* Line of Fall, *published by the University of Iowa Press in 1989. The book won the John Simmons
Short Fiction Award, presented annually by the Iowa Writers
Workshop. His fiction and poetry have appeared in many academic
quarterlies.*

On hearing that "Long Green" was going to appear in Great
Pool Stories, *Miles Wilson wrote, "This anthology is as close to
greatness as I'll ever come at pool."*

O N FRIDAY NIGHTS I pick up the sitter, a tight little piece
who thinks I look like Jack Nicholson, drop off Marlene and whatever
friend she's talking to this week at the movies, and take it easy in the
Chev out to Mel's. I used to wind out the last block of State and
take the little hump in the bridge at sixty-five, but the Chev needs
new shocks and besides I can't afford any tickets right now.

At Mel's I do a quick count of how many Fords and Chevys there
are in the lot, including trucks. It's a little habit I got into and keep
up even though it doesn't exactly mean anything. If there was more

Fords, I used to figure I was in for a good night. A man drives a Ford, you know his hands are going to be so greasy and banged up from working on it all the time he can't have much feel for a cue. These days, though, even Chevys fall apart.

Walking up to the side door, I always have to think about which way it opens. It's funny how little things like that get away from you. When I get inside I say hello around, grab Karen, who pretends she doesn't like it, and put my quarter on the table. Eight years ago, when I was back from the Army, I liked to watch how the regulars looked at each other when my quarter went down. But I don't pay attention to that kind of stuff anymore.

I generally have a couple of beers before I shoot, to sort of loosen up and give me a chance to check out the competition. The place is OK, but it hasn't been itself since Ron bought out Mel a couple of years back. The really good sticks don't come here now because Ron won't let you play for more than five, but some of the kids shoot an interesting game. When my quarter starts coming up, I notice lately how I get sticky—not in the palms, but between my fingers. I was talking to Phil the other day at the union hall and he said I should see a doctor because his sister-in-law sweated like that when she started dying of cancer.

But I use plenty of talc and that smooths the action out. Anyway it's the stick that's important. I got to get one of my own pretty soon; nothing fancy, just something I can count on. The company's supposed to be making some deal with the Japs that would crank up the line again. Phil said we're sure to get called back; maybe even suck up some of that sweet overtime. When we do, I figure I owe myself something.

Anyhow, Ron won't throw out a cue till it's busted, and he gets away with it because the kids don't even bother to check for warp or a bad tip. Most of them put so much juice on the ball it doesn't matter anyway. I've got to admit they're lucky, though. Luck will beat experience without luck oftener than you'd think, and I've been in kind of a slump lately.

I think it started when I blew a couple of five-dollar games to some jerk that didn't know which end to spot the balls on. After that I guess I started pressing. I took too long lining up shots, talked too much when I missed, and started thinking about the long green every time I had to go all the way down the table to pick up a ball. I use to be a sweet position player. I could make a razor cut and still set up just about anywhere on the table I wanted. But lately the ball isn't alive coming off the tip and the corner pockets feel like bumpers instead of funnels. I used to be surprised when I missed.

There are a couple of things that bother me most, though. One is that the regulars don't like to shoot me. It isn't that I don't pay up and there's nothing funny about me but they just don't. Maybe they think I'll rub off on them or something. For a while there they rode me when my game was off. Now they sort of act almost like they hope I'll beat them. I don't know, but all it'll take is one good night and they'll be making up lies to explain where their folding money went. Right now I mostly get games with guys who only hang around a couple nights.

But the other thing is worse. It is really bad. Back just recently I used to wind up for the fast kids with the hot sticks. I'd let them cock around the table for a while and then . . . it was sweet. Now when I come up against one I get a sick little rush like I just twisted my ankle, and the kids fool around—try double banks, play the jukebox, hustle tit. Nobody watches me shoot anymore.

I know I haven't lost the touch; once you got the touch you can't ever really lose it unless you get blind or crippled up or old or something. I never was much for banks, but I can still cut with anybody. It's the straight-in shots that give me trouble. Maybe it's confidence, I don't know. It used to be all one thing, all together—the smoke, the game, the music, everything. Now there's me, the stick, the pocket, and two balls. And it doesn't fit together anymore.

Ron wishes I'd drink somewhere else but he's too cheap to say so. He's afraid I'll get tired of losing and start some trouble. If I wanted to I could tell him he don't have to worry. Pool is different than being laid off. Pool takes nerve and talent, and getting stuff out of the way so you can get back in the game is just as close as the next rack.

I read lately where Cale Yarborough won the Firecracker Four Hundred, and he said the trick was to just step in there and do what you knew you could do. I thought maybe I'd call him up about that, but Marlene used the sports page to wipe up where the dog pissed and anyway I don't think it said where he was going next.

1989

....

EXIT

BY *Andrew Vachss*

"Exit," only 850 words long, would serve nicely as the climax of a much longer work. When you finish it, you'll wonder about what led up to such a high-tension, pressure-cooker game of straight pool. Why was Gene late? Why do both Gene and Irish hate Monroe? Discuss.

Andrew Vachss is a full-time attorney in New York City who confines his practice to cases concerning the physical and emotional abuse of children. He is the author of eight novels, including Shella, Sacrifice, *and the recently released* Down in the Zero. *The short-short story following first appeared in 1989 in an anthology called* New Crimes #1. *It also appears in* Born Bad, *a 1994 collection of Vachss's stories.*

THE BLACK Corvette glided into a waiting spot behind the smog-gray windowless building. Gene turned off the ignition. Sat listening to the quiet. He took a rectangular leather case from the compartment behind the seats, climbed out, flicking the door closed behind him. He didn't lock the car.

Gene walked slowly through the rat-maze corridors. The door at the end was unmarked, a heavyset man in an army jacket watched him approach, eyes never leaving Gene's hands.

"I want to see Monroe."

"Sorry, kid. He's backing a game now."

"I'm the one."

The heavyset man's eyes shifted to Gene's face. "He's been waiting over an hour for you."

Gene walked past the guard into a long narrow room. One green felt pool table under a string of hanging lights. Men on benches lining the walls. He could see the sign on the far wall—the large arrow indicating that *EXIT* was just beyond Monroe. They were all there: Irish, nervously stroking balls around the green felt surface, waiting. And Monroe. A grossly corpulent thing, parasite-surrounded. Boneless. Only his eyes betraying life. They glittered greedily from deep within the fleshy rolls of his face. His eight hundred dollar black suit fluttered against his body like it didn't want to touch his flesh. His thin hair was flat-black, enameled patent leather plastered onto a low forehead with a veneer of sweat. His large head rested on the puddle of his neck. His hands were mounds of doughy pink flesh at the tips of his short arms. His smile was a scar and the fear aura coming off him was jailhouse-sharp.

"You were almost too late, kid."

"I'm here now."

"I'll let it go, Gene. You don't get a cut this time." The watchers grinned, taking their cue. "Three large when you win," Monroe said.

They advanced to the low clean table. Gene ran his hand gently over the tightly woven surface, feeling the calm come into him the way it always did. He opened his leather case, assembled his cue.

Irish won the lag. Gene carefully roughened the tip of his cue, applied the blue chalk. Stepped to the table, holding the white cue ball in his left hand, bouncing it softly, waiting.

"Don't even think about losing." Monroe's voice, strangely thin.

Gene broke perfectly, leaving nothing. Irish walked once around the table, seeing what wasn't there. He played safe. The room was still.

"Seven ball in the corner."

Gene broke with that shot and quickly ran off the remaining balls. He watched Monroe's face gleaming wetly in the dimness as the balls were racked. He slammed the break ball home, shattering the rack. And he sent the rest of the balls into pockets gaping their eagerness to serve him. The brightly colored balls were his: he nursed some along the rail, sliced others laser thin, finessed combinations. Brought them home.

Irish watched for a while. Then he sat down and looked at the floor. Lit a cigarette.

The room darkened. Gene smiled and missed his next shot. Irish sprang to the table. He worked slowly and too carefully for a long time. When he was finished, he was twelve balls ahead with twenty-five to go. But it was Gene's turn.

And Gene smiled again, deep into Monroe's face. Watched the man neatly place a cigarette into the precise center of his mouth, waving away a weasel-in-attendance who leaped to light it for him. And missed again . . . by a wider margin.

Irish blasted the balls off the table, waited impatiently for the rack. He smelled the pressure and didn't want to lose the wave. Irish broke correctly, ran the remaining balls, and finished the game. *EXIT* was glowing in the background. As the last ball went down, he turned:

"You owe me money, Monroe."

His voice trembled. One of Monroe's men put money in his hand. The fat man spoke, soft and cold: "Would you like to play again?"

"No, I won't play again. I must of been crazy. You would of gone through with it. Yes. You fat, dirty, evil sonofabitch . . ."

One of the calmly waiting men hit him sharply under the heart. Others stepped forward to drag him from the room.

"Let him keep the money," Monroe told them.

Gene turned to gaze silently at the fat man. Almost home . . .

"You going to kill me, Monroe?"

"No, Gene. I don't want to kill you."

"Then I'm leaving."

A man grabbed Gene from each side and walked him toward the fat man's chair.

"You won't do anything like that. Ever again."

Monroe ground the hungry tip of his bright red cigarette deep into the boy's face, directly beneath the eye. Just before he lost consciousness, Gene remembered that Monroe didn't smoke.

He awoke in a grassy plain, facedown. He started to rise and the earth stuck to his torn face.

His screams were triumph.

....

ONE UP

BY *Robert Abel*

Pool and poker players, black and white, come to life and walk off the page in this vivid slice of life by Robert Abel. The story appeared in a collection of the author's short stories called Ghost Traps, *published by the University of Georgia Press in 1991.*

Robert Abel has taught English and creative writing at many colleges and universities, most recently at Trinity College in Hartford, Connecticut. Other collections of his stories are Skin and Bones *(1979) and* Full-Tilt Boogie *(1989), which won a Flannery O'Connor Award for Short Fiction. His novels are* Freedom Dues *(1980) and* The Progress of Fire *(1985).*

THE FAT MAN had graceful hands and he held his cards in an almost effete way, or as if he thought them valuable, full of secrets, and he studied them as another might study cuneiform, runic characters, cabalistics, and somehow his eyes never lost the curious attention, never displayed certainty or doubt. Neither was the Fat Man one who displayed the coarser kinds of gambling dynamics, taunts, jibes, distractions, teasing. He played simply, as if no two hands were alike and each had to be rediscovered.

Of course he was a dangerous player. If usually conservative, he would also take risks. His presence in a game gave Roosevelt several feelings at once: that it would be a serious game, demanding constant attention and calculated betting; that if the Fat Man lent a certain ease to the table, was almost a comforting figure, then the Fat Man was also deception itself, for the truth of the matter was that he remained unknown. Some people called him Browny. Some people called him Fats. He had no past, and yet it was rumored that, with those delicate, manicured hands of his, he had killed. Perhaps there was another creature inside that composed and attentive facade, but Roosevelt saw no outward sign of it.

The Fat Man dressed like a gambler, like a street sharpie, with a snap-brimmed gray hat with a black-and-yellow striped band around its crown; he wore white shirts and thin black ties and a gray-and-white checked sports coat; his black leather shoes always gleamed. Roosevelt had seen him shoot pool, too—where he could hold his own, but which was a game also that obviously did not hold the same fascination for him as poker, which he was addicted to, Rosey thought, in the way of an opium smoker who has plenty of opium and a sure line of supply—like the man in Saigon they had called Moto-wan, or Papa-san Wan.

The Fat Man laid down his cards now with a little flourish, so that the edges snapped on the table. The tips of his fingers remained on the borders of the cards, too, like a Ouija reader's fingers on the moving pointer. "Three ducks," he said. Roosevelt folded his two pair, aces and fives, and tossed them a little hard and recklessly into the discard pile. He had six dollars left. He was on the edge of disaster. In this game, six dollars could be easily overwhelmed. He tossed in his fifty-cent ante and waited for the next round of cards to be dealt. Maybe lightning would strike. He picked up his cards and thumbed them open, but lightning did not strike. When the Fat Man opened the betting for two dollars, floating the bills into the center of the table with a flick of the wrist, Roosevelt left his cards on the table and pushed back his chair.

"You leavin', Rosey?" the Fat Man asked.

"Yeah."

"Better luck next time."

"Screw ya."

"You goin' to play some nine ball?"

"Maybe."

"Don't go away sore," the Fat Man said. "Have a beer on the house."

"Ain't thirsty." Rosey stood behind the chair and watched the game progress. It was a cut-and-dry hand won by Smitty, the chauffeur, whom Roosevelt did not particularly like, with a simple pair of aces. Smitty, his black face gleaming, gloated over the take as if he had won a great deal of money. As far as Roosevelt was concerned, it was a pot wasted. Smitty would do one of two things if he won fifteen or twenty dollars: quit and go drinking or blow it on a bluff that everyone else knew was coming.

In a way, Roosevelt felt sorry for Smitty. He really didn't know what was happening. Everybody knew his game, and yet he still thought he was being slick. He was at the other end of the scale from the Fat Man, and yet somehow just lucky enough to keep coming back for punishment. Nobody discouraged him because he primed the pump, thanks to his job, and also, thanks to his job, had plenty of free time in which to make his contribution. Maybe, Roosevelt had thought, I should take the brother aside and set him straight. And yet he didn't like Smitty and thought he got what he deserved for being such a fool, and never acted on this impulse. Smitty was a grown-up and Rosey let him hang.

Yeah, sure, he thought now, and who is it going out the door broke today?

Rosey drifted down the main street of the neighborhood feeling irritated, as if he had needles under his fingernails. All morning long he had held second-best hands, cards good enough to bet on, but not, by chance, good enough to win. Three times the Fat Man had stung him for about twenty dollars, and the hands Rosey won did not come close to taking up the slack. "Don't gamble if you can't afford to lose," the Fat Man was fond of saying. He said this to everyone who found his way into his daily game. Once he told Rosey, as they sat alone at the table playing gin rummy and waiting for enough men to drift in to start a poker game, "About the only thing I know about you, Rosey, that I would tell you, is that you are not a sucker. I believe we can say with confidence that you are not a sucker." He had chuckled when he said this curious and yet obvious thing.

Or was he pulling my leg? Rosey wondered now. Maybe he sees me the same way I see Smitty. The thought made Rosey momentarily furious. He hated not to understand things, not to know how things worked. He hated to think the Fat Man might have his number.

There was a lot of broken glass in the gutter lately, Rosey observed.

Why the hell can't they clean this goddamned street up? He hated things not being clean. When he showed up at Pointer's Rack and Cue now, the attendant took a brush out from beneath the counter, ambled down to Rosey's table, and brushed up all the crumbled chalk dust and raised the nap on the deep-green felt. He did this even when Rosey joined a game in progress. That was good. Rosey appreciated it and tipped him well. Pool was beautiful when it was perfect, and clean, the balls gleaming in the lights, the felt unmarred by scars or spots of grime, the rails without any ragged edges, fraying, bald patches. An immaculate table and good equipment left you with no excuses. The game was merciless enough, physics incarnate, determinism manifest. So why couldn't they clean up the streets? Why did the garbage men leave so much detritus behind? Didn't people *notice*?

Rosey came into the pool hall jangling, letting his anger bubble up. The attendant broke his attention on a men's magazine long enough to hand Rosey his cue from a rack, which he had to unlock first, on the wall behind him. Rosey turned the magazine around so he could observe the foldout the man had been studying.

"Look here," he said, tapping his finger in the center of the page, "these white women got that sweet thing, too?"

The attendant, who was white, wrinkled his nose and handed Rosey his cue. "That's what it looks like," he said. "But you couldn't prove it by me."

"I ain't surprised." Rosey snatched his cue.

"I'll be down in a minute to brush that table for you."

"Right." Rosey's irritation crescendoed because, along with a couple of the regulars who showed up to play nine ball on their lunch break, today there was the Sailor, hobbling around the table, his crutch against the wall. Good old Sailor leaned his head of black curls over the table and jabbed away, shooting the ball too hard to make good sense, but also rifling the shots in and finding good position.

Rosey could never make up his mind about the Sailor, whether he was just damned lucky or whether he was good and faking clumsiness. The Sailor was, in the way he played pool, like the clerk on the command ship Rosey had been on, who typed with two fingers, but at a monumental pace. Everything the Sailor did was wrong. He didn't concentrate, he shot too hard, he leaned all over the table reaching for shots, tried ridiculous combinations—and yet he always seemed to make money. He made a lot of shots that counted, and he never felt pressure. He played as if he didn't give a damn if he lost everything he owned, and Rosey thought it was probably true, that he didn't care.

His whole crap-filled being spilled out on the table when he played, Rosey thought. A big part of his game was mouth. The Sailor wouldn't shut up and he couldn't stop either a constant dither of insults and challenges that he didn't seem to understand were, for a white boy of his particularly obnoxious stamp, genuinely provocative and dangerous. By some miracle, he had not yet been thrashed in Pointer's, though he had also come in on more than one occasion with bruises under his eyes or scabs on his lips. Maybe he thought being crippled would save him; or maybe—Rosey thought this the likeliest—he wanted to be beaten, to be punished and humiliated. It wouldn't exactly be easy—the Sailor had biceps that swelled the sleeves of the gray T-shirts he perpetually wore, a broad chest, and, Rosey was sure, a thick, bull-like forehead. He could take and give a few punches. Like some punchy fighter, he'd enjoy the process of his own murder if he could meanwhile just get in a few licks of his own.

And the Sailor lied. Rosey hated him most not just because he lied, but for what he lied about. Rosey had seen men maimed and killed in combat. He had seen too much of it. The Sailor had told him, as he told everyone, that he was crippled in Vietnam. But Rosey had a habit of suspicion, and of curiosity, and he had found out the truth, that the Sailor's injuries had resulted from an automobile accident, caused by the Sailor's drunkenness, and which resulted, too, in the deaths of a fifty-seven-year-old mechanic and a sixteen-year-old girl. The mechanic was in the other car; the girl had been in the Sailor's.

Steebs was his real name. And Steebs, in Rosey's book, was a lying, motormouth motherfucker cruising for a concussion. He had done a little time for the accident, two years, and he was not allowed to ever drive again. Rosey figured that the Sailor hadn't paid enough for those deaths and was hell-bent on self-destruction. He pretended to be bitter about his disabilities, about his bad luck and the treatment he got as a veteran, and he pretended to hate the world. But Rosey was one up on him, because Rosey knew what Steebs really hated, that he could never shake it, never with booze, never even with supreme concentration on the billiard balls, not even when someone he angered and provoked obliged him by stunning him into unconsciousness.

Steebs's disease, his cancer, was himself. The only real cures were total. Rosey understood his recklessness, his zeal for insult, and he felt used and nauseated by it. In spite of himself, he loved taking Steebs's money, loved beating him on the tables, and was infuriated when, rare occasion that it was, Steebs came out on top. Do Steebs and everybody a favor and murder the son of a bitch, Rosey thought now.

Rosey filched a piece of chalk from a neighboring table and carefully covered the tip of his cue with the sky-blue dust. The Sailor hobbled around the table, blasting away.

"You want to get in this shit?" he said to Rosey. "Five ball pays a dollar, nine ball pays two."

"Hear my knees knockin'?" Rosey said. "I'm so scared, I might lose a buck or two."

"It's for a good cause," Steebs cackled. With a gentle tap, he knocked the nine ball into the side pocket. "Sorry about that," he said to the two men staining the wall with the heels of their shoes, a young kid named Landry who was supposed to be in school and somebody they called Lefty, a seaman who was only irregularly on the scene. Lefty was a little nuts. He kept opening his eyes as wide as possible, then squeezing them shut, and he wore a manic smile perpetually on his coal-black face.

Rosey wondered if the sea had made him crazy, or if you had to be a little crazy in the first place to want to go to sea. Rosey had found the big boats of the Navy boring as hell to travel on, and he wondered what Lefty's life was like as a freighter rat, grease monkey in overextended engine rooms. The difference between the Sailor, Steebs, and Lefty, the seaman, was vast: Steebs was a screwed-up veteran on a big guilt trip; Lefty was an ocean addict, virtually a hermit, so concentrated in his own crazy self that nothing was very real to him—certainly not the pay he could be throwing away again—except the constant undulation of the sea.

"Your mama ain't callin' you?" Rosey said to Landry, the kid.

"Don't 'mama' me," the kid said.

"You ain't got no money to lose anyway," Rosey said. "Unless you been beatin' old ladies."

"Kiss my ass," Landry said.

"How much you owe this Sailor motherfucker?"

"I don't know."

"You'd better know."

"I don't know. Seven dollars."

The Sailor laughed. "Right now it's ten dollars, kid. I got 'em both last time, five and nine."

"Yeah," the kid said. "We'll see."

"You ain't got no credit here," Rosey said. "You got ten dollars?"

"Hey!" Landry said. "Who are you? FBI? Rockefeller? Mind yo' business."

"I'm going to win the next five games," Rosey said. "You got fifteen dollars more than the ten you already owe?—twenty-five dollars?"

"You know I'm good for it."

"Bullshit," the Sailor said. "If Rosey's getting in, let's settle up now."

"Why you pickin' on me special?" the kid wailed.

"Get serious," Rosey said. "You got the money or don't you? Pay up or I'll have Charlie toss your ass out of here."

The kid threw some bills on the table. "Six dollars," he said. "That's all I got."

"Not enough," the Sailor said.

"It's what I *got.*"

Rosey stabbed his finger into the kid's chest. "I told you about that. I told you before. You can't play if you can't pay."

"He lets me," Landry said. "He said my credit's good, so get off my case."

"Not true," the Sailor said.

Rosey threw four more dollars on the table. "OK, Sailor, you're square. You owe me four," he said to the kid. "But you're through for today." He took the kid by the shoulder and pushed him toward the door. "Let me tell you something," he spat. "The Sailor's dyin' to mix it up with you, man. He'll tell you any shit to get in a row with you. That's his weirdness. Believe me. Don't let him work his weirdness on you."

"I'll kill that sucker," Landry said.

"It's a Bozo game." Rosey let go of the kid now. "You can't let him Bozo you. You have to be cool, you have to be clean, have no debts, ask no favors, ever. Once he gets you sore, he keeps pressing it until you pop. That's his game."

"I'll pay you back," Landry said.

"Do you hear what I'm telling you?"

"Yeah, Rosey, I hear you."

"I don't pay any more of your bills."

"Right."

Landry banged out of the pool hall, and the clerk came down to brush up the felt as Rosey returned to the table.

"Leave some nap on it," the Sailor said. "The table's fast enough."

"You know we don't allow gambling in here, don't you?" The clerk stopped brushing and looked deadpan at the Sailor.

"Don't worry about it," the Sailor said. "If we see any gambling we'll let you know."

"Keep your money off the table. I mean it. There's all kinds of assholes running around here today. I don't want to be shut down again. Do me the favor." He raised a cloud of blue dust as he finished his chore.

"Sure as shit," the Sailor said.

Rosey was breaking his own rule, with only two dollars left, going into a game with the Sailor and Lefty. He was doing exactly what he had told the kid not to do, but he felt so sure, as he racked the balls, so confident today, so angry that he could concentrate hard enough to see his own face reflected in the shine on the balls. He could see right through the balls today. There was no way he could lose. Today, he could talk to the balls, and they would pay attention and do his bidding. He imagined each of the games before they happened. Once he got a break he was going to stay on the table for a long time.

"Pretty enough," Rosey said as he smashed open the rack and saw just an orange blur of the five ball vanishing into the corner pocket. "Pretty enough."

ROSEY LEFT POINTER'S with thirty-five dollars and hustled the three blocks back to the Fat Man's game. He was tired, but he figured his luck was running good now, and he had a settled, savage feeling in his gut after stinging the Sailor so well, well enough to get him bitching and whimpering, Bozoing himself. He had cut Lefty pretty deep, too, but Lefty didn't know any better, and, like the chauffeur, you had to have Lefties in the game to spice it up a little bit, throw in a wild card, build up the pot. Lefties made the world go 'round. Fringe cats, between the money supply and the streets. Hooray for Lefties. Hooray for trickle-down.

The Fat Man was sucking his teeth and studying his cards when Rosey came in. There was a big pot in the center of the table, and a big pile of money in front of the chauffeur, too. The other two players leaned back in their chairs, sipping beer and waiting. One of them nodded to Rosey and said, "Smitty's gone crazy."

"Definitely," the other man said. "Dude's on a *roll*, Jim."

The Fat Man counted out several bills and dropped them into the pot. "I'll just call you, Smitty."

Smitty, laughing so hard the tears rolled out of the corner of his eyes, laid down his cards. "Three aces."

The Fat Man leaned across the table and spread Smitty's cards with the tips of his fingers. "Right, three aces." He dropped his own cards facedown on the table and sat back as Smitty raked in the pot. "Your deal, Wallace," he said.

The man he had spoken to raised his hands in mock surrender and said, "I'm out."

The other player pulled back his chair. "Same goes for me," he said. "Smitty raised hell with me on that last one."

"And I'm steppin' out myself," Smitty said. "Can't play three-handed."

"Don't split now," Rosey protested. "I just got here."

"Time to go," Smitty said. "Time to grab hat." He strangled bills and stuffed them carelessly into the pockets of his tan suede jacket.

"What you got to spend your money on?" Rosey asked.

"Redhead," Smitty laughed. "Lord, what a day! Them cards were so good to me today!"

The Fat Man glanced away when Rosey looked at him. His eyes just sort of disappeared, acknowledging nothing. Maybe there was a trace of disgust in the way he chewed his gum, but then he leaned back in his chair with his hands behind his head, stretching and yawning.

"Don't go away sore," the Fat Man said. "Have a beer on the house."

But nobody stayed. There was a momentary clatter of men on the stairs, and then a smoky silence. The Fat Man yawned again and started to shuffle the cards.

"Damn," Rosey said.

"He pulled one out of his ass, what can I say?" The Fat Man started to deal Rosey a hand. "Gin rummy. Nickel a point."

"No way. I can't play for stakes like that," Rosey said.

The Fat Man continued to deal. "It's OK, Rosey. Your credit's good with me."

Rosey sat down and picked up the cards. He felt a little sick, a little betrayed, found himself hissing at the Fat Man, the unexpected words burning out of his mouth, "What the fuck is it you know about me? Huh? What the fuck is it you think you know?"

The Fat Man chewed his gum like a cud. He fanned his cards. He said nothing.

1992

....

PLAYING FOR MONEY

BY *Theodore Weesner*

Playing pool for money is better than washing cars, or is it? For a melancholy teenager, even winning sometimes feels like losing. The setting of "Playing for Money" isn't named, but it could be Flint, Michigan, where the author grew up . . . back in the days when Buicks were made there and two hours of time on a pool table cost only $1.45.

Theodore Weesner's novels include Winning the City, The True Detective, *and* The Car Thief. *His short stories have been published in the* New Yorker, Atlantic Monthly, *and* Esquire. *The following story is taken from the spring 1992 edition of* American Short Fiction, *published by the University of Texas Press.*

Weesner teaches at Emerson College in Boston.

A S HE WALKS, sideways, past the landlord's Buick Roadmaster in the driveway, a longing comes up in him. The car is big enough to live in, has four portholes ringed with chrome along each side of the hood. Its sidewalls are white as milk and its chrome teeth reflect the blazing sun from all angles. Covered with dust at the moment, too hot to touch, the big Roadmaster's power triggers in him a deepening summer desire to do something, to go somewhere. To be another person.

In time, while his father—who works second shift at Buick

Assembly—continues to sleep, he looks up and sees the landlord back the long, celery green car out to the street and drive away. When Mr. Lewis returns and is lifting a bag of groceries from the front seat, Glenn is waiting in the midday sun and offers to wash the car for a dollar.

"A dollar?" the man says. "Yeah, OK—dollar sounds OK."

Glenn likes washing cars, and a dollar is the going rate. He does not know it at the time—he is fifteen—but what he also likes is doing a perfect job. He washes cars when he can, to pick up spending money, to have time stop adding up on him. When luck is on his side, he gets caught up in doing a perfect job. No spots, no water marks, no film left on the glass inside or out. Doing a perfect job can transport him into dreams that are something of the somewhere where he longs to be.

He also imagines igniting the dusty Buick's powerful engine and driving it, if only thirty feet, into the shade behind the landlord's house. Pail, rags, scrub brush ready, he fixes the landlord's garden hose to a faucet along the foundation and unrolls it to see if it will reach the grass. The hose reaches, just barely, and on the man's small rear porch he taps on the loose screen door.

"Water will help the grass," he says. "Main thing—it'll streak if it's washed right in the sun."

"I'll move it," the man says.

"I can move it—you know."

The man looks right into him. "You're how old?"

"Sixteen—when school starts."

"Yeah, yeah, I'll do it. All I need is some kid run my car in a fucking wall he ain't even got a driver's license."

Glenn and his father live in the garage house at the rear of the landlord's lot. They have lived in one other garage house before this, one with a smelly kerosene heater, and being called "some kid" and having "½" as an address, Glenn knows by now, are a couple of the cards he has been dealt.

SHIRT OFF, BAREFOOT in the grass, he occasionally sends sprays overhead, creating flash-rainbows and cool spatterings on his shoulders and back. The car hisses when he first runs water on it, and he floods the body, to cool it down, before going at it with an old, soaked T-shirt of his own, a panel at a time. At last, the car washed and rinsed, he will wring out the T-shirt repeatedly and pull it like a chamois over areas of dripping metal. He gets into it. Tires, windows, added buffing, and interior will follow. Ashtrays, trunk, and floor mats will follow that. He gets into it; making the car's metal shine is a dream within which he has begun to sail.

Scrub-brushing a tire, leaning into it with both hands, he hears his father say from the driveway, "Looks good, when you gonna do mine?"

Glenn walks over. His father has his lunch bucket under his arm, ready to leave for work. "Whatever he's paying you, it ain't enough," his father says with a faint smile.

"I said a dollar."

"That's what he gives you—well, you'll have a look in the shifty eyes of a cheapskate," his father says.

His father seems sober in spite of his words. At this time of day, on his way to working second shift at Buick Assembly, he wouldn't have been up long enough to have had more than a couple of drinks; as always, though, on even a couple there is something dangerous about him that makes Glenn uncomfortable. He agreed to a dollar and a dollar is OK. He doesn't want his father to knock, smiling, on the landlord's door and invite him out to the driveway.

Money hardly seems to matter anyway. Water sprays from the hose have let him imagine he is at a lake in the country, riding in a boat, diving from a raft into green lake water, and talking to fish rather than talking to himself here in the sweltering, half-deserted city. "I'll ask if I can use the hose and do yours in the morning," he says to his father.

"Well, we'll see—better let me do the asking."

"I could do it before you went to work."

"I'll talk to him myself," his father says. "Right now I have to get a move on. I put a couple cans on the table so you can fix yourself something for supper."

Glenn glances after his father as he returns to the alley and their house, which is not much higher than the car. The pint thermos in his father's lunch bucket, he knows, might carry coffee or Seagram's Seven, or a mix of the two. His father's lunch. There might be an actual pint in there as well, in a paper bag, to be slipped under the driver's seat, into the glove box, the trunk, hidden in a tree near the parking lot. Maybe to be sneaked into the plant, even as it is a violation—if a guard on the gate happens to check—which can get a worker suspended or fired.

Glenn knows most of his father's drinking patterns. At the same time, in spite of the booze, he has gone on with his own life. So he tells himself. He does not dislike his father, rather he loves him, perhaps adores him, as some sons do. Glenn rarely makes friends, though, he'd have to admit, and never brings any of them to the apartments or garage houses where he and his father live. He goes to school, hangs out in town or at the park when school is out for the summer. He gets along OK. So he tells himself.

He is drying a window when he hears his father's Merc start up in the alley. It is like his father to work at GM and drive a V-8 Merc. Glenn looks over. As the car with its evil-eye windows rolls into view, his father gives a toot, as Glenn knew he would. Glenn cannot see into the car, but he waves his hand as if he had seen his father wave. He had not known anything was wrong, then the horn toot called up being alone again, seemed to say that his desire to do a perfect job had been keeping back all morning a childlike impulse to cry.

"LET'S TAKE A LOOK," Mr. Lewis says when Glenn taps on his door and says he is finished.

Glenn follows as they circle the car. Mr. Lewis, he realizes as the man touches places with a finger and looks at it, smells the finger once, is not looking to see what has been done right, but is looking to find things done wrong. Glenn sees how different Mr. Lewis is from his father. When Glenn polishes his father's dress shoes, which he often does on Saturday afternoons as his father drinks and dresses in preparation to go out and prowl, his father holds the shoes to a window for light and exclaims over how new they look. Their agreed-upon price is two bits, but his father never gives him less than a dollar, or two or three, even a five spot when his drinking is that far along.

"OK, not bad," Mr. Lewis says, pausing, removing his wallet. "Wha'd we say, a buck?"

"That's right," Glenn says, surprised at the question.

Mr. Lewis crouches to glance at his reflection in a window of the car. Removing a dollar from his wallet, he extends it, folding it on the way—to make it look like two, Glenn thinks.

"Don't forget to clean up this mess," the short man says, waving a hand at the ground as he walks away.

"Don't worry," Glenn says, although not quite defiantly.

He makes a decision to roll the hose undrained, even though he knows better. He carries it ends up to the landlord's porch, to let the water seep out where the man will have to step over the puddle and, in the process, Glenn knows, will have something to say about the kid who lives in the garage house back on the alley. His father was right; he'd seen into the eyes of something—a cheapskate for sure, he thinks—and it occurs to him that praise is as good at times as having a dollar in your pocket.

Well, up his ass with a ten-foot pole, Glenn says to himself, returning along the driveway. Take your fat-ass Buick and stick it up your fat ass next to your brains, he imagines saying to the man, smiling to himself at last and thinking he is feeling better.

THERE IS SOMETHING sexy in the cooler canyons between buildings downtown, where pigeons peck and an amount of litter lies about. Glenn looks forward to that downtown feeling—especially when he has some money in his pocket—although today is just another summer day and he has no more idea now than he did earlier of what it is he is looking for. He counted his money on the walk down—sixty cents and the dollar—and wonders, as his father sometimes remarks, if it is burning a hole in his pocket. Downtown can be a magnet, although he rarely has the kind of dough he'd really like to have. Some days he feels a desire to go to the park and shoot practice shots again, to resurrect his basketball dream, while other days he feels the desire that is stirring in him now, to be here in the midst of twenty-four-hour movie theaters, of glass bricks and amber lights of forbidden cocktail lounges, even of ice cubes in iced-tea glasses in luncheonettes where middle-aged women sit at small tables and hold high their skinny cigarettes.

At Playland, there in the skids of lower downtown, there are games to play, one especially, a glass case wherein for a dime a mechanical woman with pointed, black-nippled breasts and a headband like Wonder Woman boxes a mechanical man who wears tights and an old-fashioned black handlebar mustache. Playland itself is run by a seventy-year-old blond whose lipstick defines lips she seems never to have possessed and a man, her husband, who has a single gold tooth, threads of hair over his bare skull, and a never-ending scowl. Playland sells sneezing powder, trick matches, make-believe dog dung, playing cards of pinups, and offers coin games that are vaguely dirty. The problem Glenn has with Playland is the feeling of being seen entering or leaving. He enjoys himself when he is inside, feels excited in a way, but he knows kids whose parents will not allow them to go near the place, knows churchified kids who claim the decision not to enter is entirely their own.

In lower downtown he might also park on a stool at one of the half dozen Coney Islands, have a hot dog smothered with chopped onions and chili sauce, and watch the world go by out on the sidewalk. Or, on the bridge, tracing the warm caramel smell in the warm summer air, he might buy a box of KarmelKorn. And a bottle of root beer. Or two bottles of root beer—tall, dark Hire's, which has become his drink—one with the Coney and one with the KarmelKorn, even though it would take all his money and he would be broke again.

Or—even if he is not yet old enough—he might shoot pool at one of two pool halls in lower downtown. He could buy cigarettes, move around with one in his lips, and shoot imaginary games for money—straight pool, nine ball, eight ball—games in which he makes believe he doesn't miss even when he does, games, another of his secret dreams, in which he wins that commodity which always promises to make things OK, a wad of actual folding money. Or, he might walk uptown a few blocks to another pool hall—a subterranean cavern where various gangsters, hoodlums, and high-school boys hang out—and see if he might run into someone he knows.

Glenn has circled the green tables often lately, and his shot with a cue is coming into its own. Several weeks ago, on a Saturday night, his father, dressed in a sharkskin suit and a little juiced to be sure, spent an hour with him at AllSports and showed him some technical things—an appropriate way to use his eye, how to relax the hand guiding the cue, a lighter touch—and it was a breakthrough for Glenn. Almost at once his game was twice, three times as good as it had been. Times followed when he might run six, eight, ten balls, and ever more rarely did he have to make believe a missed shot belonged to the imaginary person whose clock and wallet he was steadily cleaning.

His father told him, too, of a legendary pool hustler out of Jefferson City, Lefty Withers, who had once made a living in towns along the Missouri River. The man's secret, even when he was well-known, his father told him, was that he made it look like he had been lucky to squeak out a win. People would think the next time they'd get him, then he'd squeak out another win. He'd let them come close, his father said, and they'd keep coming back like suckers along life's midway who thought luck had something to do with things.

It was a new world of talk with his father—who treated him just about like an adult—and Glenn told his father in turn of a couple pool shooters who worked the pool halls in their own city. One was a colored man, Henry Little, who hung out at Capital Recreation, the underground world further uptown. Henry Little had great, long fingers, Glenn told his father, black on one side, pink on the other, and what he did was hang around the pool hall and challenge businessmen who stopped in at lunchtime and thought they were pretty good.

"Short games, I bet," his father said right away.

"Well, yeah," Glenn said. "Usually pretty short."

"You see—sounds like he puts on a show," his father said. "That's not the way to do it. Might impress you kids, but he probably makes about six bits and the game's over."

"He always wins, though," Glenn said.

"That ain't hustling," his father said. "That's more like whoring."

Not quite knowing what his father meant by whoring, Glenn tucked it away. "Guy who's really the best shot of all plays at T. J. Halligan's," he said. "Name's Sandy Solomon and he only shoots straight pool. I don't know if they play for money or not."

"Oh, they play for money," his father said. "I know who Sandy Solomon is—I've seen Sandy Solomon shoot a few games around Chevy Corners."

"You have?" Glenn said, pleased that he and his father had this in common. "I've seen him run forty, fifty balls without missing. The more he makes, the quieter it gets."

"I've seen Sandy Solomon do that," his father said. "There's an upstairs pool hall at Chevy Corners where he plays some of these guys. They play for money, though, you can be sure of that. Sandy Solomon. Bill Kennedy. They got the kind of class they don't try to put on a show like that colored fellow you were talking about."

THERE NOW, at work under the lights, are the long fingers Glenn had described. Standing in shadows to watch, he realizes how much admiration he feels for them nonetheless. Nor are they pink on the inside, as he had said, but beige.

On the thought—the sudden anticipation in fact—of seeing a game for money, maybe even being in one, he'd turned away from lower downtown and headed uptown to The Rec and found this game in progress. Whatever his father meant about whoring, Glenn's thought is that he'd still give anything to have fingers like that. The ring, too, on the little finger of the man's bridge hand—filled with apparent rubies and diamonds—which sparkle under the light.

His father was right about the amount of money, though, for after but one more game the two white men say they've had enough. As Henry Little suggests they shoot a game for time, one of the men tosses a dollar on the table and says, "That oughta cover it," and Glenn has the uncomfortable feeling that even though Henry Little won and doesn't have to pay for time either, something else has taken place.

Glenn steps over, drops coins into a machine, and pulls the knob under Camels. The package and a book of paper matches fall into the trough. He hadn't quite meant to buy cigarettes and does not know why he changed his mind. If he is going to go after his basketball dream in high school in the fall, he knows, he should get off butts altogether.

As he returns to where he was standing, Henry Little is unscrewing his cue stick and placing it in its case. He has checked in the box of balls, to conclude time on the table, and slipped on a stained, blue pinstriped suitcoat he always wears, and as Glenn stands and smokes a cigarette, he sees the truth of something else his father said about Henry Little: Sandy Solomon—and the other white men who shoot straight pool at T. J. Halligan's—they all dress like they're schoolteachers or bankers. Nobody passing them on the street would guess that one or another of them might be that most admirable of creatures, a wolf in sheep's clothing.

Still, he thinks, it's hard not to admire the great, long fingers of Henry Little, who is just then coming his way. Henry Little winks.

"How's it going?" Glenn says.

"Got a smoke?"

"Sure," Glenn says, pleased to give a Camel to the celebrated man. Pack in hand, trying to jump one up, he has at last to pull it loose with his fingers. Striking a paper match, he cups it for Henry Little to catch a spark.

"Cain't make fifty cent round here no more," Henry Little says, taking a sizable drag, standing there with Glenn and looking over the rows of tables, nearly all of which remain dark on this warm summer day.

"Everybody knows you."

"S'pose," the man says. "Wanna shoot a game?"

"Me? You think I was born yesterday?"

"Shoot, you ain't so bad. I seen you play; you goan be a stick one a these days."

"Don't have enough to shoot for money," Glenn says, thinking Henry Little might play for the fun of it.

"Make some scratch, you know, you got the scratch you need to make some scratch. Get the other guy to pay time. Always shoot a game for time, y'know."

Glenn exhales, tries to think of something else to say. He feels self-conscious standing with a man who is both celebrated and colored. "Yeah," he says, too loudly.

"Ain't even old enough to be in this place, is you?" Henry Little says.

"Almost," Glenn says, nodding toward the white-haired man, Jake, at the counter. "He never says nothing."

"You how old?"

"Fifteen."

Henry Little pops with wonderful laughter. "Shoot, man—see you around," he says. "Thanks for the butt."

Glenn feels good in the wake of talking and laughing with Henry Little. He almost feels like somebody. In feeling almost like somebody, however, it occurs to him that he often feels like nobody. What is he doing here anyway, he wonders, besides dreaming of himself as this person and that person? Winning this and winning that? Where his father works they produce Buicks; he produces dreams. What good are you, he wonders, if all that comes off the assembly line in your head are dreams of winning money?

He circles to the section of the underground world that contains the billiard and oversize snooker tables. Henry Little, talking to the shoe-shine guy, T-Man, pistol-points a forefinger in passing, as if they had not just been talking. Glenn feels again, for the moment, that he is known to others, and it is almost a good feeling.

Next to T-Man's two-seater shoe-shine platform a doorway leads into the pool hall's underground lunch counter, where Glenn pulls up on a stool and orders a bottle of Hire's. To the left of the counter a hardly recognizable hallway leads to a door marked "Private." It is a card room, off-limits except to members, and the men who pass on their way to the secretive interior are middle-aged and older, although a few may be in their thirties, and none ever shoots pool or is colored. They come underground from the marble-floored Capital Arcade, an interior mall of marble walls and small fancy shops, cross between the rows of pool tables, enter the lunch counter, and disappear behind the marked door.

In time, one or another of them comes out and walks away. Richer or poorer, who knows? Their faces say nothing. Upstairs they move along the arcade, slip outside through the row of brass-handled doors, pass under the marquee of the Capital Theater, the city's largest and most plush, and reenter pedestrian traffic along the sidewalk, lighting a cigarette probably, looking not a little, any one of them, like Wendell Corey or George Raft, or Little Caesar or Rick Blaine. Many are Assyrian, Syrian, Lebanese, Greek, some are Jews—all seem to be gangsters—and few if any are factory workers although eighty percent of those who work in the city work, it is said, for General Motors. None are like Glenn's father, who migrated north a couple of decades earlier to find work in the burgeoning auto industry. None are hillbillies.

Sitting at the counter, Glenn sees Abadeen Leo Abadeen pass on his way to the card room. Maybe forty, Abadeen Leo Abadeen once lived up the street from where Glenn and his father lived. One thing he has is money, everyone says, and he is famous for driving a white Cadillac convertible, wearing silk suits—rumor has it that he runs a prostitution ring made up of white girls from Central High School—and is seen at night, by Glenn among others, driving by on downtown streets with one or another bleached blond at his side. Another story has it that when shouts came from half a dozen high-school football players standing on a corner, Abadeen Leo Abadeen pulled over and parked, turned off the Cadillac's lights and motor, stood up from a flashy blond sitting in the car, removed his suit coat, walked back and took on all six, was the last one standing, and, returning to the car, took his time wiping his hands with a handkerchief and slipping on his suit coat before sliding in beside the blond and driving away.

"One thing about Syrian guys is they always have folding money and they know how to treat women," is a line repeated often in the pool hall. "They get the best-looking women, and none of them would ever think of talking back or messing around or they'd get their teeth knocked in."

"Maybe they got something there, I don't know," Glenn's father remarked with a smile once when Glenn mentioned the Syrians. "You stay away from those guys, though," he said. "Those are tough guys and I'll bet every one of them's got an ace in the hole that'd catch you off guard and put you right on your ass when you least expect it."

Glenn does not fear for himself but fears, oddly, for his father—as in a bad dream—although his father has no relationships with such men. His father has his edge, though, his pride, a swagger in his drinking and in his muscles and curly hair, his V-8 Merc, three-piece suits, and chasing around. That certain danger in things he says. His father came home once with a black eye, another time with a swollen, broken lip, and Glenn has a fear of him responding to some insult and turning to take on the Syrians, having little idea himself how money talks or how brutal they are and that they own the city.

THE NINE BALL GAME seems to start accidentally. Glenn is near the pinball machines again when a boy he knows only slightly comes along and bums a cigarette. Denny Leach is the boy's name, and most of what Glenn knows of him is that he is eighteen and is called The Leach. He is someone to talk to, and they stand looking over the empty tables, puffing Glenn's cigarettes. As if the person were Willie Pep or Roger Bernard, Glenn remarks that he saw Abadeen Leo Abadeen go into the card room.

"Owns part of the Tigers," Denny Leach says.

"Detroit Tigers?"

"Not in his name, in someone else's. Part of them."

"What's he own, a catcher's mitt?"

"Joke, asshole. Those guys hear you joke like that they find you floating in the fucking river your throat cut ear to ear, man, I kid you not."

Glenn thinks to joke about this, too, but lets it go.

In another moment two boys pass before them carrying a box of balls, and a light goes on over Table 5, reaching out to contain the field of brushed green felt. The boys are brothers and Glenn knows them slightly, although they go to one of the city's parochial schools. Jim and Richie Carr. The younger, Richie, is Glenn's age; Jim, lifting the balls two at a time, placing them like eggs on the table, is a year or two older.

"Let's get into that game," The Leach says. "Come on, we'll win a couple bucks."

Glenn follows; they approach tableside where Jim and Richie Carr are rolling cue sticks, checking heft and tips. All fifteen balls are in the wooden rack.

"How about some nine ball?" The Leach says.

"Get lost, Leach, you never got any money," Jim Carr says.

"Where you been lately, Carr?" The Leach says in turn. "Haven't seen you around."

"I been around."

"You still carry old ladies' groceries at Hamady's?"

"Least I work; more'n anybody'll ever say about you."

"Afraid to shoot nine ball? We'll split the time."

"Not afraid to shoot nine ball with you, dipshit, don't worry about that."

"Let's do it then, nickel-dime—put your money where your mouth is."

"You, too, Whalen, you wanna play?" Jim Carr says.

"Sure," Glenn says. "For a while."

"We were just gonna shoot eight ball for fun," Jim Carr says. "You got money, Leach, or not?"

"I got money," The Leach says.

"Let's see it."

"Let's see yours, what're you talking about? Don't give me that shit!"

"You got money, Whalen? Neither you or Richie is old enough to be in this place, and I bet you both got the same amount of cash in your pocket, which is about fifteen cents."

"I got money," Glenn says.

"OK—couple games is all. Pay up after each game! OK? I'll pay for Richie. Split the time four ways. It's OK, Richie," Jim Carr adds to his brother. "We'll take some bucks from these dinks, game won't cost us nothing."

"Double on the nine," The Leach says.

"Goddamn right," Jim Carr says. "Double on the nine."

"Double on the five, too," The Leach says.

"Your funeral, asshole," Jim Carr says.

The Leach and Glenn select cues and, with the Carrs, lagging the cue ball one cushion lengthwise, mark the table with moist fingertips to determine the order of shooting. The last to lag, Glenn, on a sudden thought, strokes the ball slightly hard, so he will shoot last. Maybe they'll screw up ahead of him in the first game, he thinks, or maybe they'll leave him the nine and the break for the next game. The break in nine ball, his father has told him, is money in the bank.

"I'm paying for Richie," Jim Carr says as he chalks to break.

"Jesus, man, didn't you just say that?" The Leach says.

"But he doesn't have to pay me," Jim Carr says.

"Jesus, break will you, shut the fuck up!"

"Split the time four ways."

"I can't believe this shit—break will you!"

As something in the exchange is funny to the brothers, so is it funny to Glenn. He notes a comfort the two have in being brothers. They do not equal two people but three somehow, and it doesn't seem that either of them would know the feeling that he knows of coming and going by himself.

On Jim Carr's short, piston stroke, the cue ball slams into the diamond formation, the balls scatter, and the game is under way. No follow-through, Glenn notes, and finds himself taken with a competitive urge he has not felt, shooting pool, before. Has to do with time he's been giving to dream games, he thinks. Let them bicker; he'll slip up on them, take their dough, and leave them in the dust.

TO HIS AMAZEMENT, the first game goes as he had anticipated, although he fails to seize the full opportunity. By the time his turn comes—Jim Carr has pocketed the five—only the eight and nine are left, but the nine is a cherry on an end pocket. Taking a slice of the eight, he strokes the cue ball gently, and kissing the eight the ivory ball rolls along to put away the nine on a tap and return off the cushion. The nine spotted, however, blocks his line to the eight, and Jim Carr ends up sinking both and winning the break for the next game.

"We're even," Jim Carr says to Glenn. "Leach, you owe me twenty cents."

"You owe me for your brother," Glenn says.

"Right, I owe twenty cents for Richie," Jim Carr says. "We still made money; come on, Leach, pay up, you fuck-stick asshole."

The Leach pays up, twenty cents each to Glenn and Jim Carr. To Glenn, handing him two dimes, he says, "I get down, man, cover my time, OK?"

"Don't have that much money," Glenn says.

"Jesus, man, I'm talking twenty cents."

"You already out of money, Leach?" Jim Carr says. "What a creep you are. Jesus, man, go walk in front of a bus."

"Don't call me a creep, creep! Your break, man. Your rack, Whalen, and don't make it too tight."

After but one more game, fifteen cents to Jim Carr on a double five and the straight five, and a dime to Glenn on the nine, The Leach is a nickel short paying up.

"You're ahead, loan me a half," he says to Glenn.

"Any of that crap and we're out," Jim Carr says.

"What crap? What do you mean? You talk like a donkey, you know that."

"You owe for time, Leach."

"Up your ass, man. What do I owe, a nickel? You pay it—you make all that money lugging old ladies' groceries. I'm out—fuck all of you. Whalen, give me a goddamn cigarette."

Glenn gives him a cigarette, does not know how not to. He adds, though, "That's it," as he lights one for himself and holds the match for The Leach.

"Yeah, yeah," the older boy says, exhaling a cloud of smoke as he walks away.

"Still wanna play?" Jim Carr says.

"Sure," Glenn says, thinking he has the break coming and, fifty cents or so ahead, has little to lose, at least for a while.

Richie, who has said even less so far than Glenn, racks the balls, lifts away the rack. Glenn chalks up. Taking into account what his father told him about following through, he creams the formation and two balls go down, one of them the nine. The double credit on the biggest money ball goes through him like a shot; he calculated, executed, is already up forty cents for the game. He continues, and before he finishes his turn, adds the five; by the time the game is over, he adds the nine straight and has the break coming yet again.

"Seventy cents," he says to Jim Carr.

"Thirty-five each," Jim Carr says.

Glenn only makes an expression to this, as Jim Carr is giving him the coins. "You're better'n you used to be," Jim Carr adds. "You been living down here?"

Glenn does not say. "Your rack, Richie," he says.

"Don't tell my brother what to do," Jim Carr says.

"His rack," Glenn says. "You tell him."

"Don't ever tell my brother what to do."

Glenn says nothing to this, but hair on his neck tingles. Thinking he will miscue if he puts his anger into his shot, he strokes lightly and, in a lesser clattering, nothing falls.

"Nice break," Jim Carr says.

He's working at pissing me off, Glenn tells himself. For even as it is obvious, he has never been the object of such a tactic in a game where anything like money was at stake.

Still, when the game is over, although Richie has made the five, the younger brother's only money ball so far, Glenn ends up sinking two nines and collects fifty-five cents and another break.

"Wanna quit?" he says to Jim Carr, not meaning it.

"Hell no, I don't wanna quit. I'm gonna win our money back. Your break."

Chalking to break, Glenn feels remote amusement, but also a touch of fear. He asked the boy if he wanted to quit to make him angry, and it worked with surprising ease. He splatters the balls then, and before his turn is over, he's up sixty cents and both money balls remain alive. For the first time in the game he feels he cannot lose. He is simply better, and when you're better, you're better. If he doesn't choke, he can't lose. The present game over, he adds a dollar ten to his winnings, a greenback this time and a dime. He's won nickels and dimes before; this time, for the first time in his life—he can feel it—he's going to win some bucks.

As they continue, Jim Carr grows increasingly angry, while Glenn keeps focusing with added concentration, stroking ever easier, running two, three, four balls on each turn, racking up money balls at a rate of four or five of his to one or two of theirs. It comes home to Glenn that each shot he makes causes Jim Carr to tighten even more. He can't lose, he knows—not this time out—even if winning seems a distance yet away.

"Richie, hang it up," Jim Carr says in time. "I'll take on the pool-room bum myself and get our money back."

Rather than being angered by the remark, Glenn feels sorry for Jim Carr, sees that he is making a fool of himself in front of his brother. Glenn takes a risk then, makes an offer he knows he shouldn't.

"Let's all hang it up," he says. "I'll pay time from what I'm ahead."

"No fucking way," Jim Carr says. "You owe me a chance to win our money back. And I'll pay our fucking time."

Glenn was going to walk to the counter to sprinkle talcum powder on his hand, but decides not to. He chalks his cue by standing it on the floor. "Rack'em," he says. "My break."

"Quarter-half," Jim Carr says.

Glenn stands there. He notices that Richie, who stands watching, appears frightened. It's getting out of hand, Glenn thinks, isn't at all what any of them expected. When he walked over with The Leach, rather than enemy to the two brothers, Glenn imagined himself as friend. "OK," he says. "Quarter-half."

Glenn's game only improves. He experiences added calm. Outside his ears there seems but a blur of sound. Within, between eyes and mind, a few simple gears seem to function with ease. There are the balls. Each time he sees a possible shot or two. Decisions are easy. He calculates, chalks, leans in. So much English, so much draw, so much cut or topspin. His bridge is steady, his stick hand relaxed. He strokes. Click, clack. One ball rolls left, another angles right. *Plop.* Position is everything, and more often than not position is his. There's no way he can lose. He's going to destroy Jim Carr.

He chalks, circles, calculates. Outside his ears is a blur of sound, laughter, remote games. He looks down the cue, hefts the handle in two or three fingers, strokes. Click, clack. *Plop!* He is doing it. He is hot. He is playing for money and winning big.

As another game ends, Jim Carr owes him two and a quarter. Short paying up, he turns to his brother. "Give me a quarter."

"You know I don't have any money."

Glenn stands there.

"I have my check from Hamady's," Jim Carr says. "I'm good for it."

"Let's just quit, Jimmy," his brother says.

"Shut up!" Jim Carr says. To Glenn, he adds, "Well?"

"Dad's gonna *kill* you," Richie says from the side.

"I said shut up!" Jim Carr says. Removing his wallet, he heads to the counter.

Glenn glances at Richie and to the boy his age makes an expression of sympathy or understanding. With the vaguest of sneers, however, the boy utters, "Screw you," and Glenn's heart drops, it seems, to his waist.

"Half-dollar," Jim Carr says, returning.

"Nah," Glenn says.

"You won't give me a chance to win my money back?"

"I'm not playing double or nothing."

"Prick."

"You owe me a quarter for the last game."

"Add it to this game; I didn't get any change."

Glenn feels another risk coming up in him, and all at once he says, "Dollar–two dollar," not knowing why he says it except that he remains stung over being called a prick.

The turnaround seems to confuse the other boy. "OK," he says. "OK! Dollar–two dollar! Fuckinay, man! Dollar–two dollar!"

"Rack 'em—my break," Glenn says. "You owe me a quarter."

"I know what the fuck I owe you."

Sighting down his stick, Glenn realizes that he is ready to attempt to slam the cue ball so hard the balls will explode, and in the midst of his emotion he knows this is wrong. He can see the ivory ball airborne, hitting a wall. Back off, he thinks, and he stands upright, steps away, rechalks, studies the cue tip. Leaning back in, he looks down the stick, goes with a softer break, sees the five ball leave the pack, roll to the left side pocket and drop cleanly, the only ball to do so.

Spotting the five, calculating his next shot, he says, "Two and a quarter."

The two brothers stand in the shadows in silence. Glenn shoots again, drops the one ball, chalks, studies, knows that nothing is going to change. "You can't beat me," he says.

No remark is forthcoming from the shadows.

Nothing changes. Glenn collects over three dollars for each of the next two games, and after another game, when Jim Carr owes him close to four dollars, the boy throws two bills and a nickel on the table and says, "I'm cleaned out."

Glenn's right pants pocket is stuffed with coins and wadded greenbacks. He has won big, he knows that. He doesn't know how much, nor does he know what to do here in the face of the other boy being out of money. But he knows he has won big.

"Let's go, Richie," Jim Carr says. Looking at Glenn, he adds, "I'll have to owe for time but I'm not paying that asshole Leach's time. Richie, come on, goddamnit!" As Jim Carr walks off, his brother moves to trail behind him.

Glenn stands alone. He has to take up the two dollar bills and the nickel from the green felt, and he has to take care of the table, although it is not checked out in his name. He has never won big before, and the feeling within him now, to his surprise, is closer to disappointment than satisfaction.

He feels unclean picking up the nickel. Why is it, he wonders, that his pride seems shaky and Jim Carr's pride seemed OK?

Forget it, he tells himself as he boxes the balls. Forget it. When you win, you win. You don't lose when you win. He carries the box over and pays the time. They played over two hours, and he doesn't mind paying time. A dollar forty-five. He pays by extracting bills and coins from his stuffed pocket and turns to walk to the piss-and-disinfectant-smelling bathroom to wash his hands.

THE CITY remains warm even though the sun is near the horizon. Glenn crosses the street where there is little traffic—relieved to be out in the air—and walks in the direction of lower downtown. It's dinnertime and only a scattering of people and cars are around. Stores have closed; middle-aged men stand at curbs, not to cross but to watch pass whatever it is that might pass on a summer evening. City air. It's downtown at an hour that he likes, and he thinks as he walks that he is shaking off whatever it is that has gotten under his skin.

You won big, he tells himself.

At the U.S. Coney Island, he sits on a stool near the windows and orders a Hire's. Two other solitary customers are in the place, and when bottle and glass are before him he begins to remove his winnings almost secretly from his pocket. He presses grimy bills, stacks coins, counts to himself. Fifteen. Twenty. Twenty-five. Twenty-six, twenty-seven. Odd change. Factoring in the time and what he started with—no, he bought cigarettes and a root beer—he calculates that he won over twenty-eight dollars. Nearly thirty if Jim Carr had paid up, he thinks. He won big. He had, for sure, although he is trying still to call forth the feeling the money is supposed to give him. Why does he feel like he lost?

He leans along the counter to a jukebox console, thinking to play something that will move his mind elsewhere. He drops in a quarter and pushes letters and numbers. Often when he plays a jukebox he conceals his true selections in the midst of others, as if to conceal from some waitress a revelation of himself and his secret dreams.

Staring ahead, he waits. He hears a record turn into place within the mother ship against the wall. He doesn't look that way; he looks to the street and wonders if the first song will be a decoy or the real thing.

From on high there comes a hum and Marty Robbins begins to sing for the three customers sitting apart in the summer evening's lull, looking wherever they are looking:

> *A white sport coat . . .*
> *And a pink carnation. . . .*

Glenn keeps looking through the window to the street. The sun is below the horizon, and he sits hearing the music, looking away, and can see that he is on the wrong side of something, maybe of everything. This is what he can see.

Looking for a dream to get started, he thinks. That's what he's doing. Looking for a dream to get started, to have somewhere nice to go.

Further reading

Readers who want to know more about the grand old game will enjoy the following books:

Hustlers, Beats, and Others, by Ned Polsky, Aldine Publishing Co., 1967, 220 pages. Polsky, who was a professor of sociology at the State University of New York at Stony Brook when he wrote this insightful study of pool hustling as an occupation, now operates a book service in Manhattan called Biography House. The book recently slipped out of print but is readily available in libraries.

William Hendricks' History of Billiards, self-published in 1974, 58 pages, available for $15 from the author at P.O. Box 1, Roxana, Illinois, 62084. Not a feast for the eye, but an impressive, pathbreaking look at the game's long history with much fascinating detail, especially from European sources. The book is often relied on and cited by later writers (including Robert Byrne).

Pool, by Mike Shamos, Mallard Press, 1991, 130 pages, $25. An attractive, large-format, well-illustrated look at the history, art, equipment, and technique of cue games, written in a breezy yet authoritative style. Shamos is curator of the Billiard Archive in Pittsburgh, Pennsylvania, one of the largest collections of billiardiana in the world, all of it indexed and accessible by computer.

The Illustrated Encyclopedia of Billiards, by Mike Shamos, Lyons and Burford, 1993, 310 pages, $35. A valuable, easy-to-use reference full of wit, erudition, and surprises, with 200 illustrations and 2,000 alphabetized entries.

The Billiard Encyclopedia—An Illustrated History of the Sport, self-published by Victor Stein and Paul Rubino in 1994, 512 pages, $110. One of the most amazing and beautiful books ever published on any subject, the result of six years of obsessive research around the world by the authors and a spare-no-expense approach to printing and binding. There are 760 illustrations, 520 of them in full color. Especially good on early ball games and the development and craft of cue making. This splendid book, cheap at $110, has to be seen to be believed. For information, write to *The Billiard Encyclopedia,* 3801 Hudson Manor Terrace, Riverdale, New York 10463.

Permissions acknowledgments

"The Billiard Table" by James Hall. From *The Western Souvenir, A Christmas and New Year's Gift for 1829*, published in 1829.

Excerpt from *The Captain's Daughter* by Alexander Pushkin. Originally published in Russian in 1834. From *The Captain's Daughter and Other Stories*, translated by T. Keane. Published by Hodder and Stoughton in 1915.

"Recollections of a Billiard Scorer" by Leo Tolstoy. Originally published in Russian in 1855. From *The Russian Proprietor and Other Stories* by Count Lyof N. Tolstoi, translated by Nathan Haskell Dole. Published by Books for Libraries Press in 1887. Reprinted in 1970.

"A Game of Billiards" by Alphonse Daudet. Originally published in French in 1869. From *Monday Tales*, translated by Marian McIntyre. Published by Little, Brown and Company in 1900.

"Fate" by H. H. Munro (Saki). First published in Great Britain in 1904. From *The Toys of Peace and Other Papers* by Saki, published by the Viking Press in 1928.

"A Billiard Lesson" by A. A. Milne. First published in *Punch* (circa 1911). From *Once a Week* by A. A. Milne, published by Dutton in 1925. Reproduced by the permission of Curtis Brown, London, on behalf of the author's estate.

"Beyond the Sunset" by Jesse Hill Ford. First published in the *Atlantic Monthly* (1960). Copyright © 1960 by Jesse Hill Ford. Copyright renewed 1988 by Jesse Hill Ford. Reprinted by permission of Harold Ober Associates Incorporated.

"The Crossroader" by Don Carpenter. From *The Murder of the Frogs and Other Stories* by Don Carpenter, published by Harcourt Brace & World in 1969. Reprinted by permission of the author.

"The Snooker Shark" by William Harrison. First published in the *Saturday Evening Post* (1967). Reprinted by permission of the author.

"Lem the Barber" and "De Oro's Bladder" by Danny McGoorty, as told to Robert Byrne. From *McGoorty, the Story of a Billiard Bum,* published by Lyle Stuart in 1972, Curtis Books in 1973, and Citadel Press in 1984. Copyright © 1972 and 1984 by Robert Byrne. Reprinted by arrangement with Carol Publishing Group.

"The Hungarian Cinch" by Bill Pronzini. From *Arena: Sports,* edited by Ferman and Malzberg. Published by Doubleday in 1976. Reprinted by permission of the author.

"Great Big Boffs They Are" by Ken Mitchell. From *Everybody Gets Something Here* by Ken Mitchell, published by Macmillan of Canada in 1977. Reprinted by permission of the author and Bella Pomer Agency, Toronto.

"Remember Young Cecil" by James Kelman. From *Not While the Giro* by James Kelman, published by Polygon in 1983. Reprinted by permission of Polygon, Edinburgh University Press Ltd.

"One Pocket" by Don Carpenter. From *The Class of '49 and Two Stories* by Don Carpenter, published by North Point Press in 1985. Reprinted by permission of the author.

"Massé" by Leigh Allison Wilson, First published in *Harper's* (1986). Reprinted by permission of the author.

"Mother and Father" by Jonathan Baumbach. First published in the *Iowa Review* (1986). From *The Life and Times of Major Fiction,* published by the Fiction Collective in 1987. Reprinted by permission of the author.

"Long Green" by Miles Wilson. From *Line of Fall* by Miles Wilson, published by the University of Iowa Press in 1989. Copyright © 1989 by Miles Wilson. Reprinted by permission of the University of Iowa Press.

"Exit" by Andrew Vachss. First published in *New Crimes #1* (1989). From *Born Bad* by Andrew Vachss. Copyright © 1994 by Andrew Vachss. Reprinted by permission of Vintage Books, a Division of Random House, Inc.

"One Up" by Robert Abel. From *Ghost Traps* by Robert H. Abel, published by the University of Georgia Press in 1991. Copyright © 1991 by Robert H. Abel. Reprinted by permission of the University of Georgia Press.

"Playing for Money" by Theodore Weesner. From *American Short Fiction* (no. 5, spring 1992), published by the University of Texas Press. Copyright © 1992 by Ted Weesner. Reprinted by permission of Sterling Lord Literistic, Inc.